In the Midst of a Revolution

IN THE MIDST OF A REVOLUTION

DAVID HAWKE

Philadelphia
University of Pennsylvania Press

© 1961 by the Trustees of the University of
Pennsylvania

Published in Great Britain, India, and Pakistan
by the Oxford University Press
London, Bombay, and Karachi

Library of Congress Catalog Card Number: 60-7078

All Rights Reserved

Printed in the United States of America

TO
HELEN
AND
JANE

Acknowledgments

Anyone who has been exposed to the generous way those in the academic world or connected with it give of their time to the serious student must fumble for words when he comes to acknowledge their help. It is difficult to express adequate thanks to such people as Catherine Miller, Lois Given, Raymond Sutcliffe, and Harry Givens for their trips far beyond count into the stacks and manuscript vaults of the Historical Society of Pennsylvania, often to rout out on their own material I might otherwise have missed; to Barbara Rex, Jr., whose interest and enthusiasm helped bolster a sometime sagging spirit; to Leonidas Dodson and Roy Nichols, of the University of Pennsylvania, whose careful readings saved me from many errors of judgment and fact; and to the staffs of the American Philosophical Society, of the Ridgeway Branch of the Library Company, of the Public Archives in Harrisburg, and of various local historical societies in Pennsylvania, who treated every query, every request with unending courtesy. To these people and to others unnamed who in countless ways made the research for this book both an adventure and a continual pleasure, my deepest thanks.

Contents

1 THE ELECTION 13

2 THE CITY 33

3 THE BACKCOUNTRY 59

4 THE COUNTERBALANCE 87

5 AN EPOCHA 111

6 AN ENTERTAINING MANEUVER 129

7 PROTEST AND REMONSTRANCE 139

8 THE ASSEMBLY 151

9 NEW MEN – NEW IDEAS 165

10 THE CONSTITUTION 181

BIBLIOGRAPHICAL NOTE 201

INDEX 217

In the Midst of a Revolution

I THE ELECTION

This is the story of a revolution—one of the few real revolutions in American history. The story centers on a small band of men who successfully overthrew an established government and replaced it with one based on a radically new idea. These men overlooked none of the classic techniques of revolution in their drive for power. They staged expertly organized mass meetings and flooded the land with propaganda. They masked their goals behind patriotic slogans, captured control of party machinery by assiduous attendance at caucus meetings, hoodwinked conservatives that their motives were pure, and branded those who opposed them as traitors. This revolution occurred in Pennsylvania during the spring and summer of 1776. The beginnings of great events are always elusive, but Wednesday, May 1, 1776, which was an election day in Pennsylvania, seems an appropriate place to start the story.

That particular Wednesday dawned clear and cool in Philadelphia, with a fresh wind blowing in from the northeast.[1] No one could have asked for better election-day weather, for both the Moderates and Independents hoped that a large turn-out would help carry their tickets. Still, for William Bradford, Jr.—a young man as warm for independence as anyone in the city—the day began badly. "Notwithstanding my determination to rise early,"

---

[1] Christopher Marshall, Diary, May 1, 1776, Historical Society of Pennsylvania (hereafter HSP). William Duane's edition of the diary, *Passages from the Remembrancer of Christopher Marshall* (Philadelphia, 1839) is an abbreviated version of the original. To avoid confusion, all references will be to the manuscript. Unless otherwise noted, all dates in the annotated material that follows refer to the year 1776.

he wrote in his diary, "I did not get up till seven O'Clock."[2]

Bradford was twenty-one and, except for the one day a week he drilled with his company on the city common out near the Bettering House, the war had not seriously interfered with a full and pleasant life. His prosperous father — publisher of the *Pennsylvania Journal* and proprietor of the city's most popular tavern, the London Coffee House — had supported him since he had graduated from the College of New Jersey.[3] He was now studying law, but not so assiduously that he lacked time to argue politics, drink a mug of sillibub, or play a game of billiards with his cronies. Occasionally he whiled away an afternoon visiting any of several attractive young ladies he knew about the city. These lax habits had lately begun to bother Bradford, and being still young enough to believe that a man could, if he put his mind to it, turn a new leaf in life, he resolved to change his ways. Hereafter each day would be carefully planned and a nightly report written up to see how well the schedule had been adhered to.

Bradford chose to start this "revolution" in his personal life on May 1, a day he expected to be equally momentous for Pennsylvania's future. For on this day, after weeks of bitter campaigning, the freemen of Philadelphia were selecting four men for the Assembly. Seventeen seats were up for election throughout Pennsylvania, but the pivotal contest was in Philadelphia. Here the campaign had been longer and warmer and the issues sharper between the contending parties. The platforms of both had been clear: the Moderates favored reconciliation with and the Independents immediate separation from Great Britain. A landslide victory for the Independents in Philadelphia would probably hand them control of the Assembly and thus the chance to send a pro-

---

[2] William Bradford, Jr., "Memorandum and Register, for the months of May & June, 1776," HSP.

[3] Bradford went to college with and remained a close friend of James Madison, which helps to explain why the best account of his life during the Revolution occurs in Irving Brant, *James Madison, The Virginia Revolutionist* (Indianapolis, 1941).

independent delegation to Congress. A switch in Pennsylvania's stand on this question would work to swing Congress into a favorable mood for independence.

The election, and perhaps the desire to ease gradually into his new regime, had led Bradford to plan a light day for himself. He took time after arriving at his office to read the weekly issue of his father's newspaper, which was just off the press. With what remained of the morning he studied his law books. In the early part of the afternoon he abridged two law cases and repeated from memory "the six last chapters of the first book of Blackstones analysis of the law of england."[4] About two o'clock, still following his schedule, he headed toward the election being held at the State House.

The State House lay on the western outskirts of the city, along Chestnut Street between Fifth and Sixth. Aside from its size, which was imposing for the day, it blended perfectly into the surroundings. It was built of the same light red brick used throughout the city and designed in the clean, plain style that satisfied Quakers "as the least expensive, but also as the most neat and commodious."[5] The King's arms hung over the main entrance through which voters stepped to hand in their ballots, and above the building rose a squat tower "of such miserable architecture, that the Legislature have wisely determined to let it go to decay (the upper part being entirely of wood) that it may hereafter be built upon a new and more elegant construction."[6] The tower housed a large bell and the works for the two clock dials hanging beneath the eaves of the east and west outer walls. (Probably not one in a hundred Philadelphians could have told a visitor that the bell bore a Biblical inscription appropriate for this election. It read: "Proclaim liberty

---

[4] Bradford, Register, May 1.
[5] Harold Donaldson Eberlein and Cortland Van Dyke Hubbard, *Diary of Independence Hall* (Philadelphia, 1948), 37. The quote is from a Remonstrance by Andrew Hamilton.
[6] [Jacob Duché], *Observations on a Variety of Subjects* (Philadelphia, 1774), 12.

throughout all the land unto all the inhabitants thereof.") The Assembly, the Supreme Court, and, since last year, the Continental Congress met here. A tavern conveniently located across the street probably to some degree influenced the conduct of business within the State House. Behind the building a large yard surrounded by a seven-foot brick wall stretched southward to Walnut Street. Here members of Congress often strolled out to smoke and relax from their long, tedious sessions. Today, in deference to the election, Congress had adjourned.[7] The yard was filled only with electors, many of them considerably agitated when Bradford arrived.

Bradford found a throng of Germans "in a ferment," as he put it. The Germans had apparently come in a body to the polls, for many still stumbled with their English and wanted friends handy in case they got confused by the voting procedures. Bradford learned that the cause of the disturbance was "some rash words which had fallen from Mr. Swift's lips relative to them." Now, Joseph Swift was one of Philadelphia's "gentlemen," one of the "respectable" sort, to use the language of the day. He was a wealthy merchant, a member of the city council, on the Board of Managers of the Pennsylvania Hospital, a vestryman of Christ Church.[8] He did not favor independence. He feared the Germans did and this infuriated him, for as strangers to British-American traditions they were obviously ignorant of the virtues of the King's rule. He told them that except for the fact that they were naturalized they had no more right to vote than a Negro or an Indian.[9] (Germans, unlike immigrants from Great Britain, were considered foreigners and had to be naturalized to become citizens of Pennsyl-

---

[7] See Worthington Chauncey Ford, ed., *Journals of the Continental Congress* (34 vols., Washington, 1904–36), IV, 321, April 30 entry.

[8] The *Pennsylvania Gazette,* May 6, lists Swift on the hospital's newly elected board. His name appears among the Christ Church vestrymen in the *Pennsylvania Magazine of History and Biography* (hereafter *PMHB*), 19 (1895), 518–526. *The Minutes of the Common Council of the City of Philadelphia, 1704–1776* (Philadelphia, 1847), 810, has him on the city council for 1776.

[9] Marshall, Diary, May 1.

THE ELECTION 17

vania. This process was not particularly onerous, involving little more than a two-year wait, a resident requirement for all voters, and a two-dollar fee to the lawyer who handled the legal details.)[10] Swift's remarks led the Germans to treat him "very rudely," according to Bradford, and "obliged him to seek protection in [George] Clymer's house."[11] The effect of Swift's outburst, unless promptly repaired, might seriously damage the Moderates' chances in the election. His friends quickly tried to explain away or apologize for his remarks. They, too, were treated equally rudely and also had to seek shelter.

The fracas pleased Bradford. He felt Swift's indiscretions had lost the Moderates votes. The affair had occurred early enough in the day that news of it could be spread through the city by the Independents and perhaps influence the decisions of Germans who had yet to vote. Clearly, the city was in for an exciting election afternoon and evening.

Normally Philadelphia took its elections casually. Apathy generally prevailed and a large turn-out of voters was a rare event. Throughout the recent campaign citizens had been reminded what a shamefully "small proportion of the electors of this city have thought it worth their while to step from their houses to give a vote in some late instances. . . ."[12] A visitor in 1775 who found that in New York "nothing is heard but Politics" was impressed with Philadelphia as a place where "people only minded their business."[13] Still, when feelings were aroused Philadelphia elections could be wild affairs. The one in 1764 had been a memorable event that had kept the city in a turmoil for thirty-six hours. When one side had tried to end the balloting, "the old hands kept it

---

[10] "We have already naturalized near two thousand Germans. Each of whom pays two Dollars . . . ." Edward Burd to his sister, October 5, 1765, in J. Bennett Nolan, ed., *Neddie Burd's Reading Letters* (Reading, Pa., 1927), 24–25.
[11] Bradford, Register, May 1.
[12] *Pennsylvania Evening Post,* April 30.
[13] Philip Padelford, ed., *Colonial Panorama—1775—Dr. Robert Honyman's Journal for March and April* (San Marino, Calif., 1939), 29.

open, as they had a reserve of the aged and lame . . . [who] were called up and brought out in chairs and litters."[14] During a lull in the evening, horsemen were dispatched to Germantown to round up more voters, and through the rest of the night hundreds of electors poured into the State House. Not till three o'clock the next afternoon, when apparently every white male in Philadelphia County had voted, could the polls finally be closed.[15]

All the ingredients of that epochal affair twelve years earlier seemed on hand again in May of 1776. Caesar Rodney of Delaware, using the day of leisure the election had handed Congress to write home, said: "This day is like to produce as warm if not the warmest Election that ever was held in this City."[16]

Philadelphia had had plenty of time to get worked up about the election. Tension began building up back in February when, on the last day of the month, the City's Committee of Inspection and Observation abruptly threatened Pennsylvania with a political revolution. This committee was one in a network that spread throughout Pennsylvania and all the colonies. The committees had been created in 1774 — prompted by the urgings of Congress — to see that the resolves of Congress were properly carried out. The Philadelphia Committee originally consisted of forty-three members; it soon expanded to sixty-six and then — "for the purpose of giving them more weight & influence"[17] — to an even one hundred members. Influence increased with size. Under the guise of executing the resolves of Congress it began to usurp more and more authority, even to the point of interfering in citizens'

---

[14] Charles Pettit to Joseph Reed, November 3, 1774, William B. Reed, *Life and Correspondence of Joseph Reed* (2 vols., Philadelphia, 1847), I, 36.

[15] Cortland F. Bishop, "History of Elections in the American Colonies," *Columbia University Studies in History, Economics, and Public Law*, vol. III (New York, 1893), presents the elaborate statutes governing Pennsylvania elections, but both the 1764 and 1776 elections, to give only two instances, indicate practice seldom jibed with the law.

[16] Caesar Rodney to Thomas Rodney, May 1, G. H. Ryden, ed., *Letters to and from Caesar Rodney, 1756-1784* (Philadelphia, 1933), 74.

[17] Charles Thomson to W. H. Drayton, in Charles J. Stillé, *Life and Times of John Dickinson* (Philadelphia, 1891), 349.

personal affairs and private opinions. By 1776 it regulated or attempted to regulate the price and sale of scarce items, such as salt. It checked ship cargoes for contraband, padlocked shops of merchants who ignored its regulations, publicly reprimanded those it judged disloyal, and imprisoned those it considered traitors. Its resolves, like those of a County Committee with similar duties that one man remembered in later life, were "of more sanctity, then even statuary Law. It was a primary concern, to grow wool. None dar'd to offer Lamb's flesh in Market, in disregard of the resolve." [18]

This aggrandizement of power, seemingly a threat to constituted authority, distressed few of the gentlemen of Philadelphia, for the gentlemen controlled the Commitee's affairs, just as they had been controlling Philadelphia and Pennsylvania politics for generations. They controlled the Committee's affairs, that is, until February 16, 1776. On that day the semi-annual election was held. No public discussions, no hint of the need for great changes preceded the election. It was a typically dull, quiet Philadelphia balloting and probably less than a thousand votes were cast.[19]

When the election results were published, no great upheaval in Committee membership appeared to have occurred. Sixty-eight of the men on the 1775 Committee, or over two-thirds of the old membership, reappeared on the new one.[20] The key men on the old Committee—John Dickinson and Joseph Reed, along with such gentlemen as John Wilcox and John Allen, both members of the city council—were still present. Yet twelve days after the February election the Committee put out a call for a Provincial Convention whose vague purpose would be to take "into consideration the present state of the province."[21] The Assembly, which up to now

---

[18] Philip S. Klein, ed., " Memoirs of a Senator from Pennsylvania: Jonathan Roberts, 1771–1854," *PMHB* 61 (1937), 469.
[19] See Cato's comments on the election, *Pennsylvania Gazette*, March 13. He says fewer than two hundred votes were cast.
[20] All Philadelphia newspapers printed complete lists of Committee members in their first issue after both the August 16, 1775 and February 16, 1776 elections.
[21] *Pennsylvania Evening Post*, March 2.

had worked hand in glove with the Committee, suddenly found itself "thwarted in their measures by a body of men from whom they expected to derive the firmest support." [22]

The full story of the events and men behind the Committee's new personality will come later. It is enough now to say that the change both surprised and shocked the gentlemen of the city. When word of the convention decision leaked out, one gentleman in the city wrote: "Tim. Matlack & a number of other violent wrongheaded people of the inferior Class have been the chief Promoters of this wild Scheme; and it was opposed by the few *Gentlemen* belonging to the Committee—but they were outvoted by a great Majority." [23]

This convention scheme aimed, it would seem, at one thing: to force Pennsylvania to accept the idea of independence. ("The Scheme of the Convention was principally to get Andrew Allen and a few other good Men removed from Congress. They have stood forth and dared to expose the designs of the Cunning Men of the East [New England], and if they continue Members of Congress will prevent this province from falling into their favourite plan of Independency.") [24] The men behind the scheme had petitioned the Assembly earlier to change the instructions of Pennsylvania's delegates in Congress so they might vote for independence if the question came up. The Assembly had refused. A subtler tack was taken. The sentiment for independence was assumed to be strongest in the back counties of Pennsylvania. These counties, along with the city of Philadelphia, were notoriously under-represented in the Assembly. The three eastern counties of Bucks, Philadelphia, and Chester had long controlled Pennsylvania politics. Complaints about this turned up occasionally and even moderate-minded men in these counties felt the situation was unfair. But at no time did

---

[22] Charles Thomson to W. H. Drayton, Stillé, *Dickinson,* 349.
[23] Joseph Shippen, Jr., to Edward Shippen, February 29, Shippen Papers, vol. 12, HSP.
[24] Edward Shippen to Jasper Yeates, March 11, Shippen Papers, vol. 7, HSP.

THE ELECTION

an outraged populace try to improve their political position. Pennsylvanians did not care that much about politics. Still, the discrimination existed and the Independents decided to use it to further their schemes. They sounded out the Assembly about revising the representation along fairer lines. The hope was that once the city and back counties got their share of seats the Independents would be able to manipulate the Assembly. But again the Assembly balked. This second rebuff had led to the call for the Convention.

Once the Committee's decision had spread through the city it stirred up a great noise, at least among the "thinking People." [25] These people, according to one report, said "that when they elected a Committee it was for a particular purpose but by no Means as a Legislature in the Room of the Assembly. If they had imagined that to be the Case, there would have been 10 times the Number of Electors." [26]

Public pressure may have influenced the Committee to back down. A more decisive reason would seem to have been the Assembly's willingness to compromise. Dickinson and Reed, members of both bodies, worked out the acceptable proposal and on March 8 the Assembly reluctantly agreed to enlarge its membership by seventeen seats — four to go to the city, the remaining thirteen to the back counties. The eastern counties, understandably, received nothing. As with most workable compromises, this one satisfied both sides. It stopped the "Mouths of those violent Republicans belonging to the Committee. . . ." [27] They were appeased because they were convinced that the people would, of course, fill all seventeen seats with men who shared their views on independence. It pleased the Assembly partly because a long-known wrong had been righted, but mainly because it fended off, for a time at least, the most serious threat to its existence the legislature had

---

[25] Jasper Yeates to James Burd, March 7, Shippen Papers, vol. 7, HSP.
[26] Edward Burd to James Burd, March 15, Shippen Papers, vol 7, HSP.
[27] Joseph Shippen to Edward Shippen, March 12, *ibid.*

faced. The question of amending Pennsylvania's instructions to its delegates in Congress had been by-passed. That decision was left up to the men the people would send to the enlarged Assembly.

The Committee sent out a circular letter to all the county committees explaining why it was rescinding the call for a convention. "As the present unequal representation is the ground of every other complaint," it stated, "the Committee had this principally in view." When the Assembly amended its stand on the matter, the letter continued, further need for a convention ended.[28] Overconfidence had here led the Committee into a tactical mistake. What if the people failed to give the Independents control of the Assembly? The Assembly had generously gratified the Committee's greatest wish. The Committee admitted this and thus left itself with no sound excuse for complaint, regardless of the Assembly's future action.

The Assembly designated May 1 for the election. The date had hardly been fixed when a Moderate party, standing for reconciliation, and an Independent party took shape. The Moderates, sensing they were for the first time on the defense, began to campaign at once. Many wrote letters to like-minded friends in Lancaster, York, Carlisle, and other parts of the backcountry, urging them to run for one of the open seats in their counties.[29] But their main efforts centered on Philadelphia. They now realized, belatedly, that to lose control of Philadelphia meant to lose control of Pennsylvania.

The Reverend Doctor William Smith, a Church of England divine and provost of the College of Philadelphia, became the Moderates' chief publicist. He was a man of many parts. Benjamin Rush, who disliked him, admitted he "possessed genius, taste, and learning." He swore and drank like a frontiersman and preached, some said, like an angel, capable at times of leaving his congrega-

---

[28] For the complete letter see the *Pennsylvania Evening Post,* March 9.
[29] See, for example, Edward Shippen to Jasper Yeates, March 11, Shippen Papers, vol. 7, HSP.

tion awash with tears. Years earlier he had sold himself and his ideas on education—less Greek and Latin, more emphasis on practical subjects—to Benjamin Franklin, who drew him to Philadelphia to head up the College. The city became a livelier place with his arrival. Contention traveled wherever he did, for Dr. Smith's explosive temper and contempt for people provoked disputes with unhappy ease. "It was a favorite maxim with him," Dr. Rush said, "that to gain mankind it was necessary not to respect them." [30] The gentlemen of the city could have ignored a man of lesser talents. Dr. Smith was too able to ignore and so the gentlemen used him without, necessarily, accepting him.

As Cato, Dr. Smith squared off at the Independents in a series of newspaper articles, the first one appearing on March 13, only five days after the Assembly had agreed to compromise. In the opening piece he unmasked the Committee's contention that calling a convention would serve to give rule to all the people of the colony and not just the privileged few in the eastern counties. If the convention did meet, he wrote, "and could succeed in assuming the powers of government, they must all at length be vested, for the sake of execution, in the hands of a *few men*, who consider themselves as leaders in the city of Philadelphia; and the province in general have but little to say in the matter." [31]

From this point Dr. Smith moved to broader ground—the merits of reconciliation. He approached the issue by two routes. He began by unfolding the first full-scale, intelligent attack made on *Common Sense*, concentrating particularly on Paine's theories of government.[32] This, in turn, led him into extended praise for the glories

---

[30] George W. Corner, ed., *The Autobiography of Benjamin Rush—His "Travels Through Life," together with his Commonplace Book for 1789-1813* (Princeton, 1948), 263, 264.
[31] *Pennsylvania Gazette,* March 13.
[32] It is curious how long the Moderates delayed answering *Common Sense.* Joseph Shippen notes this in a letter on February 29: "No Answer has yet been published to the pamphlet called 'Common Sense,' except a short one contained in Hall's paper of this Week, which I think is a good one. I herewith inclose you a small pamphlet entitled '*The Sentiments of a Foreigner*'

of Pennsylvania's government. He made clear that so far as he could see the Independents had coupled the idea of independence with a political revolution. To vote for them ran the risk of sanctioning an overturn in Pennsylvania's constitution. None of the moderate-minded men among the Independents, such as Benjamin Rush, who would soon moan loudly about the passing of the Assembly, attempted to rebut this side of Dr. Smith's argument.

Cato provoked the ablest penmen among the Independents into vitriolic replies. First came James Cannon, writing under the name Cassandra. His scurrilous attack suggests that Cannon's position on Dr. Smith's faculty at the College influenced his judgment. When Cannon had exhausted his supply of invective, he settled down to answering Dr. Smith's criticisms of the Committee. The substance of his reply was that the Committee represented the people more truly than the Assembly.[33] The Forester, whom the city promptly and correctly took to be Tom Paine, understandably concentrated on replying to Cato's attack on *Common Sense*. Meanwhile, the newspapers up and down the coast were reprinting the controversy as it unfolded in the Philadelphia papers. By mid-April a good part of America had been alerted to the election battle going on in Philadelphia.

While the battle of words raged in the papers both parties worked on drawing up a ticket with the widest voter appeal. The Moderates held many private meetings, eventually coming up with a ticket that must have shocked even the Independents in the direct, bold way it faced a challenge.[34] The one man above all others—aside from Dr. Smith—the Independents would gladly have seen shipped to hell was Andrew Allen. The name Allen alone was

---

(against Independancy) in my opinion a sensible performance; it is an Extract from the Works of Abbe Reynell, a Frenchman." (Shippen Papers, vol. 12, HSP). *Plain Truth*, published later, was a curiously inept job. Dr. Smith was the first to give an intelligent, cogent rebuttal.

[33] *Pennsylvania Gazette*, March 20.
[34] Marshall, Diary, April 21.

THE ELECTION

anathema to them, for old William Allen, the family patriarch and the colony's Chief Justice of the Supreme Court, had dominated Pennsylvania politics for a generation and his sons were continuing what was on its way to becoming a family tradition. Andrew Allen, the oldest son, seemed ready to outdo his father. He was Recorder for the city council, a member of the provincial council, the King's attorney general for Pennsylvania, and, worst of all in the eyes of the Independents, had been chosen by the Assembly, though not a member of that body, to serve as a delegate in Congress. He personified Philadelphia aristocracy and the rule of the elite in Pennsylvania affairs. The Moderates selected Andrew Allen to head their ticket.

If republican tastes were on the rise in Philadelphia, the Moderates' ticket conceded little to the fashion. The next man on their ballot was Thomas Willing, close to being the richest man in Philadelphia, a justice on the Supreme Court, and, by marriage, a member of the Penn family. He, too, had been appointed by the Assembly as a delegate to Congress and ranked with the Independents only a notch below Andrew Allen. The third man nominated was Samuel Howell, a wealthy merchant of Quaker background. (He had been disowned from meeting in 1762 for "disunity," a vague term that can account for a variety of sins, major or minor.)[35] Howell was a member of the city council, a post available only to the city's elite. Finally, the Moderates chose Alexander Wilcox, another wealthy merchant and also a member of the city council.

The Independents were in anguish over their ticket at least a week longer than the Moderates. A sub-committee of the Committee of Inspection and Observation conferred nearly a fortnight on the decision. It discussed likely candidates with the Committee of

---

[35] For the record of Howell's disownment see William Wade Hinshaw and Thomas Worth Marshall, *Encyclopedia of American Quaker Genealogy* (6 vols., Ann Arbor, Mich., 1936–1950), II, 556.

Privates[36] — an informal organization of enlisted men in the voluntary military Associations scattered throughout the province — and with the Patriotic Society, which had been created in 1772 for the purpose of organizing the workingman's vote.[37] The Independents searched hard for candidates with the widest appeal to the voters. Private discussions among Tom Paine, James Cannon, Timothy Matlack, Christopher Marshall, and a few others of the inner council went on nightly for a week.[38] Finally, with election day only a few days away, a ticket was settled on.[39] George Clymer, a prosperous thirty-seven-year-old merchant, headed it up. Colonel Daniel Roberdeau, a large, jovial merchant who was considered to be the most popular man in the city since the people always chose him to chairman their public meetings, seemed a certain winner. Owen Biddle, who had put aside his Quaker convictions to join the Independents, was an obvious counter-balance to Howell's appeal to the Society of Friends members who were drifting away from pacifism. Frederick Kuhl, another merchant and of German descent, seems to have been chosen to attract the German vote.

The Independents settled on their ticket on April 25 but decided it should be "kept as a Secret from the Public till after our next meeting on next 2d day night . . . ." — that is, April 29.[40] Why the delay? One reason seems to be that the Moderates had still not officially announced their ticket. As late as election day morning George Read of Delaware did not know for certain the "fixed candidates" of either side. He wrote: "One side talk of Thomas Willing, Andrew Allen, Alexander Wilcox, and Samuel Howell, against Independency; the other, Daniel Roberdeau, George

---

[36] For the formation of the Committee of Privates see *Pennsylvania Evening Post,* September 19 and 28, 1775.
[37] *Pennsylvania Gazette,* August 19, 1772, quoted in Arthur Meir Schlesinger, *The Colonial Merchants and the American Revolution 1763–1776* (New York, 1918), 280.
[38] Marshall, Diary, April 18 and 25.
[39] *Ibid.,* April 25.
[40] *Ibid.,* April 25.

THE ELECTION   27

Clymer, Mark Kuhl, and a fourth I don't recollect [Owen Biddle]." [41] Delayed announcements of candidates were the rule rather than exception of eighteenth-century Pennsylvania elections. The reasoning of the day apparently went this way: the campaign must appeal to men's minds, emphasizing principles and issues involved, and personalities must not muddy the waters. But the eighteenth-century politician, no less shrewd than his modern counterpart, trusted reason only so far, to judge by the care he gave to selecting the men on his ticket. Both sides in the May election no doubt were being purposely vague about their slate in order to feel out public sentiment. If the people showed strong feeling against any candidate, a last-minute substitution could be made without much difficulty. The politicians on both sides were leaving nothing to chance.

The Moderates may have tarried with an announcement of their ticket, but not with their campaigning. Even gentle John Dickinson, though not running for office, joined in the tedious job of knocking on doors, shaking hands with the voters, and making the Moderates' position clear to anyone willing to listen. An Independent—Tom Paine, one suspects—gave backhanded praise to these tactics. He admired how they brought the aristocratic gentlemen down to the level of the humble. "How many poor men, common men, and mechanics have been made happy within this fortnight by a shake of the hand, a pleasing smile and a little familiar chat with gentlemen. . . . This year their humility is amazing; for they have stooped to the drudgery of going from house to house to circulate election lyes about division of property. . . . Do you think ever Mr. J—— —— would ever speak to you,

---

[41] George Read to his wife, May 1, William Thompson Read, *Life and Correspondence of George Read* (Philadelphia, 1870), 157. After listing the supposed candidates of both sides, Read adds this intriguing line: "but it is thought other persons would be put up." Does he refer to both tickets or only to the Independents'? And what candidates had the people expected? Was the public surprised by the boldness of the Moderate ticket and the mildness of the Independents?

if it were not for the May election? Be freemen then, and you will be companions for gentlemen annually." [42]

The Independents lost their light touch as the campaign advanced. The class approach — gentleman against common man — came more and more to the front. Two days before the election one who called himself Elector came forth with the most novel suggestion of the campaign. He advised that all men in the armed forces, regardless of age, length of residence in Pennsylvania, or the amount of property they owned, deserved the vote.[43] He was quickly reminded "that a great number of the associators in this city are minors and apprentices, a great number of them new men lately arrived among us, who know not the happy form of the government of Pennsylvania. . . ."[44] Elector's radical proposal may have seriously hurt the Independents' chances, for the public was reminded by another that his "*novel system* . . . may teach us what we are to expect, should we suffer men, professing such principles, to get the direction of our affairs."[45] Once again, no moderate man among the Independents attempted to separate the Elector's rash demands from the drive for independence.

The Moderates' election-eve statement asked the electors not to turn the government over to "violent men." It promised to seek "*peace upon honorable terms.*" It said that the Moderate candidates were not irrevocably committed to reconciliation: "If the fatal necessity should evidently arise, which will justify new declarations, and a change of measures, *such men* will never dissent from the general voice of their constituents."[46]

---

[42] *Pennsylvania Evening Post,* April 27.
[43] Elector, *Pennsylvania Packet,* April 29. I suspect Elector is Dr. Thomas Young, late of Albany, Boston, and Newport. Civis points out that Elector is not well acquainted with Pennsylvania politics, and the accusation is not denied in later articles. Young was a warm friend of the Connecticut settlement in Pennsylvania's Wyoming Valley; among the things Elector dislikes about the Assembly is that it plans to "frame new expeditions to Wioming" (*Pennsylvania Gazette,* May 15).
[44] Civis, *Pennsylvania Gazette,* May 1.
[45] *Pennsylvania Evening Post,* April 30.
[46] *Ibid.,* April 30.

THE ELECTION

The Independents answered this with a handbill addressed "To the TORIES." The electors were reminded once again that Willing was one of the King's judges and Allen the King's attorney general; and that those on the Moderate ticket had "grown rich from *nothing at all* and *engrossed* every Thing to ourselves, would now most willingly *keep* every Thing to ourselves."[47]

The Independents continued campaigning right into election day. Christopher Marshall was on the go almost from sunup, though the polls did not open till ten o'clock. He attended a strategy meeting at William Thorn's schoolhouse, then traveled down to the drawbridge on the south side of town—probably to pass out broadsides or otherwise influence voters headed for the State House—then up to the scene of the election. He loitered around the State House till one o'clock. He went to lunch at his son's house, having invited Tom Paine to accompany him. After lunch Marshall, Paine, and Cannon spent the afternoon at the State House. All three were on hand when Joseph Swift burst forth at the Germans.

At five o'clock Marshall went with James Cannon to drink coffee at Cannon's home, after which both returned to their posts at the State House. Shortly past six o'clock Sheriff Dewees, with no advance warning, closed the polls. He said they would stay closed till nine o'clock the next morning. "This alarmed the People," Marshall reported, "who immediately resented it, flew to the Sheriff & to the Doors & obliged him again to open the Doors & continue the Pole. . . ."[48]

The Independents interpreted the Sheriff's action as a Moderate subterfuge to prevent the workingman, who was not free to vote until the evening, from casting his ballot. Bradford once again exulted in the turn of affairs. He was convinced that thanks to

---

[47] Broadside Collection (1776), Item 43, HSP.
[48] Marshall, Diary, May 1. The ten o'clock opening of the polls, standard for Pennsylvania elections, is mentioned in Sheriff Dewees's announcement of the forthcoming election, *Pennsylvania Packet,* April 29.

these two untoward events "the independent party [was] greatly increased by those things which were looked upon as the act of the moderates."[49]

Marshall went home at eight o'clock, ate a quick supper, and hurried back to the State House. He remained till shortly past ten o'clock, then, obviously exhausted, headed home, for the Sheriff had said the polls would close in a half-hour. They did not close till past midnight.[50]

The confidence that Marshall and Bradford took to bed with them that night died with the sunrise. "The first news I heard this morning," Bradford wrote, "was that the Moderate party, or those for a reunion with britain had carried the Election."[51] The final tally was exceedingly close.[52]

Moderates			*Independents*		
Allen	...	923	Clymer	...	923
Howell	...	941	Biddle	...	903
Wilcox	...	921	Roberdeau	...	890
Willing	...	911	Kuhl	...	904

The Moderates had won three of the four Assembly seats. This meant that even if the backcountry vote went solidly for the Independents they would still lack a majority in the Assembly. This meant further that the Moderates could still effectively block any independent-minded moves not only in Pennsylvania but also in Congress. With a good part of the continent aware of what had been going on in Pennsylvania, Moderates everywhere could take cheer and resist more heartily than ever this idea of independence.

For one so enthusiastic for independence William Bradford, Jr., was not especially disheartened by the election results. When he went down to the State House to study the posted results, he saw that Thomas Willing had been defeated. "Being satisfied in this I

---

[49] Bradford, Register, May 1.
[50] *Pennsylvania Gazette*, May 8.
[51] Bradford, Register, May 2.
[52] Marshall, Diary, May 1. Also *Pennsylvania Gazette*, May 8.

went to the office."[53] For Bradford the election had ended; perhaps now he could give more attention to his law books. The people had expressed their opinion and that was that.

If, for all their enthusiasm for independence, affairs had been shaped by young men like William Bradford, Jr., no political revolution would have occurred in Pennsylvania. As it turned out, control of Pennsylvania politics, though for the moment once again in the hands of the gentlemen, was swiftly being taken over by a group of middle-aged tradesmen and small merchants, who, spurred on by a tight little band of zealots, refused to accept the results of the May election as final.

---

[53] Bradford, Register, May 2.

2 THE CITY

On May 2 Marshall, Paine, Young, Matlack, and Cannon gathered at Cannon's home in the evening for a post-mortem analysis of the election.[1] " I think it may be said with Propriety that the Quakers, papists, Church, Allen family, with all the Proprietary party, were never seemingly so happily united as at this election...."[2] Paine complained about "having many of our votes rejected"; about the sheriff shutting up the doors, thus deceiving many that the election was over; that the Independents "had to sustain the loss of those gallant citizens who are now before the walls of Quebec, and other parts of the continent"; and that "a numerous body of Germans, of property, zealous in the cause of freedom, were likewise excluded for non-allegiance." Essentially, however, he agreed with Marshall: the combined power of the "Tory non-conformists," the "testimonizing Quakers," the Roman Catholics, and, especially, the "proprietary dependents" defeated the Independents.[3]

No one condemned the election results as the expression of a privileged minority. Even Elector could not blink the fact that the Moderates' support bulked large. "I aver," he wrote, "there is more opposition to independence in this Province than in all the Continent besides."[4] And even Paine admitted that the provincial law requiring a man to swear or affirm himself worth fifty pounds currency deprived few who really wanted it of the right to vote.

---
[1] Marshall, Diary, May 2.
[2] Ibid., May 1.
[3] The Forester, *Pennsylvania Journal,* May 8.
[4] Elector, *Pennsylvania Gazette,* May 15.

"The only end this answered was, that of tempting men to forswear themselves," he said. "Every man with a chest of tools, a few implements of husbandry, a few spare clothes, a bed and a few household utensils, a few articles for sale in a window, or almost anything else he could call or even think his own, supposed himself within the pale of an oath, and made no hesitation of taking it."[5] Thus, sad to admit, the people, the common people and not the gentlemen alone, had defeated the Independents.

Too much emphasis on the democratic aspects of the election can obscure something more meaningful about the results. The May election above all made clear that as spring merged into summer the people of Philadelphia were suspended in a balance so nearly perfect that a shift of only ten Moderate votes would have given each party one seat and left the remaining two candidates in a dead tie; a shift of eleven votes would have exactly reversed the official result, giving the Independents three seats, the Moderates only one.[6] Philadelphia neither lagged in enthusiasm

---

[5] " A Serious Address to the People of Pennsylvania on the Present Situation of Their Affairs," *Pennsylvania Packet*, December 5, 1778, in Philip S. Foner, ed., *The Complete Writings of Thomas Paine* (2 vols., New York, 1945), II, 287–88. I make no attempt to argue just how democratic Philadelphia was in 1776. I do not, for instance, go along with Professor Robert Brown's view that democracy flourished in colonial America. There is more to democracy than the right to vote, or even in using that right. Democracy is an attitude and in 1776 — in Pennsylvania, at least, where the people again and again re-elected the elite to office — voters clearly rejected the democratic attitude. Nonetheless, Paine's remarks suggest that the property qualification was not so restrictive as has been generally believed. Carl and Jessica Bridenbaugh, *Rebels and Gentlemen* (New York, 1942), 13, state that about only one man in fifty could meet the property qualifications for voting. Elisha P. Douglass, *Rebels and Democrats* (Chapel Hill, N.C., 1955), 216, writes: " Of Philadelphia's taxable male population, 90 per cent was disenfranchised by a suffrage qualification of £50 personalty or a fifty-acre freehold." Both books base their views on Albert E. McKinley, *The Suffrage Franchise in the Thirteen English Colonies in America* (Philadelphia, 1905), which assumes, mistakingly I believe, that election procedures always adhered strictly to legal requirements.

[6] This assumes, of course, that the elector voted a straight four-man party ticket. Among many things unknown about the election is how men voted. Did each hand in a ballot for four candidates or did he mark down only

for independence nor embraced the idea of reconciliation with fervor. It simply hung in delicate balance between the two. Why? No simple answer will do. For one thing, those Independents with republican tastes complicated things for the voters. Many electors may have favored independence but recoiled at the Elector's suggestion that the ballot be given to all those in the armed forces. Then, there is the possibility that Philadelphians voted more for men rather than issues. Though the campaign seems to have been based on issues rather than men, neither party ignored the personality factor as an influence on the voter. The voters had eight able and respected men to choose from. When an elector began to ponder his ballot, it may be he forgot about the question of independence and reconciliation and put down the men whose judgment he trusted most to act wisely in confusing times. This could explain Samuel Howell's high vote. His success, at least, did not displease the Independents. Tom Paine, for one, seemed satisfied. "Mr. Samuel Howell, though in their ticket, was never considered by us a proprietary dependent," he wrote.[7] Mr. Howell, in other words, would probably have won regardless of the ticket he ran on.

Paine and other Independents allude several times in their post-mortems of the election to the "Proprietary dependents" as a cause of their defeat. The question of proprietary government as distinct from royal government had been an issue endemic in Pennsylvania politics through the 1760's. During those years the lesser merchants, tradesmen, and artisans of the province, led by Franklin, fought hard to take the government away from the Penn family and hand it over to the king. They believed, with some justice, that they and the colony would prosper more under the less restrictive control of the crown. Their efforts were resisted by the wealthy conservatives of the colony, men who had already prospered sufficiently and

---

one or two men on his slip? And was the election confined to the city proper, bounded by South and Arch Streets, or did it include the suburbs?
[7] The Forester, *Pennsylvania Journal,* May 8.

who usually received special favors and lucrative posts from the Penns or their agents and thus saw little reason to be dissatisfied with things as they were. This issue of proprietary versus royal control had died out by 1776, but the bitterness and deep division it had engendered still flourished. The old factional alignments remained surprisingly intact, except now the issue was reconciliation versus independence. Most of those who had been "Proprietary dependents" in the 1760's now fought the idea of independence. While Mr. Howell opposed independence he was not a member of the entrenched aristocracy that had controlled Pennsylvania politics through most of the eighteenth century, and thus he was somewhat more acceptable to Paine and his friends.

All this — old issues added to the current one, plus the candidates themselves — no doubt influenced voters in varying degrees. The time and the place of the election were also important, but not, in or by themselves. It is the juxtaposition of the two, of Philadelphia's uniqueness coupled with the fact that the election was held when it was, that had the most pervasive effect on the election results. An understanding of Philadelphia's peculiar character and of the effect of events on that character should help much to explain the strangely balanced election results.

Philadelphia in 1776 still sufficiently resembled William Penn's dream of "a greene Country Towne" that when Samuel Oliver, living opposite Mrs. Pusey's brewhouse, advertised among the thirty thousand inhabitants for his lost red-and-white cow, he considered it enough to note that she "had two small hind Teats, and a Star in her Forehead."[8]

The bucolic tone of Mr. Oliver's advertisement disguised the fact that Philadelphia was the largest city in America and the second largest in the British Empire.[9] Cows still roamed about the city commons in 1776, but not much else remained of Penn's vision

---

[8] *Pennsylvania Gazette,* May 15.
[9] It may have been fourth, exceeded by London, Edinburgh, and Dublin, according to the revised judgment of Carl Bridenbaugh, *Cities in Revolt* (New York, 1955), 217n.

of a "greene Country Towne." Penn's gridiron layout had created a city of giant squares, and the plan had been that these would be split up into generous-sized lots surrounded with sufficient light and lawn to prevent the development of squalid tenements. The early settlers, however, promptly sub-divided the lots and cut through the expansive squares with dingy alleyways. Soon the dirt and congestion and noise of a typical English city that Penn had hoped to avoid sprang up. In 1776 the city still hugged the banks of the Delaware River.

Not all of William Penn's hopes for Philadelphia had died. Penn had been a man who blended the ideal and practical to a fine balance, and it would have satisfied him to see that no city in the colonies—nor in England, for that matter—had coped better with the problem of growth. The streets were for the most part paved and flanked by raised brick sidewalks. Lamps lighted the city at night, except when the moon was full, an indication that a Quaker's sense of thrift still controlled the attitudes if not the politics of the city. The walks were shaded with towering elms and Italian poplars and every hundred feet or so stood public water pumps—some five hundred in all scattered throughout the city.[10]

Penn had envisioned Philadelphia as a haven for the oppressed, but also as a prosperous haven. His city had preserved those parts of his dream, too. Lutherans, Jews, Catholics, Moravians, Presbyterians, Quakers, and Church of England men lived here in reasonable harmony and prosperity.[11] The city had a few families of great fortune. The few who could be called impoverished were cared for in the Bettering House—or, as it was often called, House of

---

[10] For details on Philadelphia in this period see the Bridenbaugh volumes *Cities in Revolt* and *Rebels and Gentlemen*.
[11] Facts about colonial Philadelphia are hard to nail down. Take something seemingly so easy as the number of churches in the city. Jacob Duché, who, as a clergyman should know, gives fifteen (*Observations*, 63); *The Journal of Nicholas Cresswell* (London, 1925), notes twenty-one (155); Andrew Burnaby, *Travels Through North America* (New York, 1904), finds thirteen (90); the Bridenbaughs in *Rebels and Gentlemen* (18) settle for eighteen but give no source for their figure.

Employment or Alms House—out near the city commons, where Mr. Oliver had lost his cow. The bulk of Philadelphians lived as comfortably as any people on earth in the eighteenth century.

And yet among the notable things about the city was the fact that almost no one, except the people who lived there, liked the place. A visitor from the South found the city "disgusting from its uniformity and sameness."[12] The brick homes for which the city was famous appeared shabby and cramped to a New England youngster. ". . . I say, give me a wooden one, that I may swing a cat around in. . . ." he wrote home.[13] Complaints were heard of the housewives' custom of washing down their front door stoops and sidewalks on market day mornings, a "lunacy [that] exposes passersby to a danger of breaking their necks."[14]

Occasionally there was some backhanded praise. For one visitor Christ Church "will do pretty well" and the State House "may not be despised."[15] A visiting doctor found the hospital elegant on the outside but overcrowded within and pervaded by "a strong smell of Sores & Nastiness [that] rendered it insupportable even to me, who have been pretty much used to such places." He judged the Bettering House "a very pretty building, large & in a good taste," but complained that "it cost me a half Bit to see through this place."[16] And the city was judged hard on its "Monster of a large strong Prison" on Walnut Street: "if it is necessary, [it] is no Credit . . . to any Province."[17]

Curiously, the things that would have distressed Penn about his city passed unnoticed by most visitors. The hogs that ran wild through the streets evoked no comments, nor did the stench from Dock Creek, a stream that twisted through the heart of the city

---

[12] Jonathan Boucher, *Reminiscences of an American Loyalist* (Boston, 1925), 101.
[13] "Dr. Solomon Drowne," *PMHB* 48 (1924), 238.
[14] Kenneth and Anna M. Roberts, *Moreau de St. Méry's American Journey 1793-1798* (New York, 1947), 262.
[15] "Letters of Dr. Solomon Drowne," *PMHB* 48 (1924), 239.
[16] Padelford, *Dr. Honyman's Journal*, 15-16, 18.
[17] "Dr. Solomon Drowne," *PMHB* 48 (1924), 239.

THE CITY

and was flanked by stables and tanyards that used it for an open sewer.[18] No one mentioned the filth that accumulated in the streets and remained until a heavy rain washed it away,[19] nor the thick clouds of flies that quickly blackened uncovered food, nor the bedbugs, mosquitoes, and roaches that tormented inhabitants through the sweltering summer.

These sights and smells were familiar and tended, if anything, to make visitors feel at home. It was the lack of the familiar in Philadelphia that annoyed most strangers. John Adams of Massachusetts detested Philadelphia, except for those few hours in any week that he could listen to Reverend George Duffield, whose preaching sounded so much like a good New England sermon.[20] Most Virginians disliked Philadelphia. They complained of the small rooms, of the uniformity of the buildings, and called the inhabitants "remarkably grave and reserved; and the women remarkably homely, hard-favoured and sour." Whenever they found something familiar they felt better. The rolling land outside Philadelphia was much like the Virginia tidewater area and so, understandably, they admitted that "The face of the Country & the method of farming . . . delights them."[21]

Philadelphians seemed as strange as their city and thus were judged equally severely. The women rated little praise. Admittedly, a few good-looking ladies flourished among the upper classes, but, went one judgment, "I think there is a greater proportion of

---

[18] Alexander Graydon, *Memoirs of a Life Chiefly Passed in Pennsylvania* (Harrisburg, 1811), 34.

[19] "Our city is more healthy than usual at this season of the year, owing to the frequent rains which have washed the miasmata from our atmosphere and conveyed a large portion of the filth of our streets which exhale from them, into the Delaware." Benjamin Rush to Thomas Jefferson, August 29, 1804, Lyman Butterfield, ed., *Letters of Benjamin Rush* (2 vols., Princeton, 1951), II, 886.

[20] John Adams to his wife, June 11, 1775, Charles Francis Adams, ed., *Familiar Letters of John Adams and His Wife Abigail Adams, During The Revolution* (New York, 1876), 65.

[21] H. D. Farish, ed., *Journal and Letters of Philip Vickers Fithian 1773–1774* (Williamsburg, Va., 1943), 257.

homely ones than I have seen in any place of an equal size, & the old women in general are really ugly, some of them absolutely scare crows."[22] All visitors agreed Philadelphians were not "remarkably courteous and hospitable to strangers."[23] There was a sense of community among Philadelphians, a contentment, a self-satisfaction that enraged some visitors. "Not contented with being not agreeable, they are almost disagreeable," wrote one disgruntled stranger. "The almost universal topic of conversation among them is the superiority of Philadelphia over every other spot of the globe. All their geese are swans."[24]

All their geese *were* swans to Philadelphians. "Don't call me a country girl, Debby Norris," wrote a young lady named Sally Wister from the confinement of a Bucks County farm. "Please observe that I pride myself upon being a Philadelphian, and that a residence of some 20 months has not at all diminished the love I have for that dear place."[25] Sally Wister, whose lively diary dispels the myth that a plain-garbed Quaker girl was necessarily dull and demure, had not been totally bored in the country. She passed the time reading such books as Fielding's *Joseph Andrews* and flirting with soldiers, ("When we were alone our dress and lips were put in order for conquest," she says at one point, and at another, of a handsome army captain, "ain't he pretty, to be sure.")[26] But she missed her city friends and, equally, "the rattling of carriages over the streets — harsh music, tho' preferable to croaking frogs and screeching owls."[27]

Philadelphia was a city — bigger, noiser, richer, and busier than any spot on the continent — and this is what delighted citizens like Sally Wister and distressed strangers. Compared to it all other so-

[22] Padelford, *Dr. Honyman's Journal,* 20.
[23] Burnaby, *Travels,* 96. Burnaby, incidentally, found Philadelphia women "exceedingly handsome and polite" (97).
[24] Boucher, *Reminiscences,* 101.
[25] Albert Cook Myers, ed., *Sally Wister's Journal . . . 1777–1778* (Philadelphia, 1902), 175.
[26] *Ibid.,* 76, 164.
[27] *Ibid.,* 35.

called cities in America were only overgrown villages. Other towns had markets but nothing like the immense colonaded shed of Philadelphia's market, which stretched the length of two city squares down the center of High Street. Other towns were noisy but here, wrote an appalled New England lad, "the thundering Coaches, Chariots, Chaises, Waggons, Drays and the whole Fraternity of Noise almost continually assails our Ears."[28] One of the clichés of the day was to judge things in terms of Philadelphia. "This infant Village," wrote a traveler of backcountry Pennsylvania, "seems *busy & noisy* as a Philadelphia *Ferry-House*."[29]

Everything in Philadelphia seemed outsized. Such was the case, at least, with one visitor just off the boat from Scotland. "When we met several large Lancaster six-horse waggons, just arrived from the country," reported Crèvecoeur, his guide, ". . . he stopped short, and with great difficulty asked us what was the use of these great moving houses, and where those big horses came from." When asked if Scotland had no horses like these, he said: "Oh, no; these huge animals would eat up all the grass of our island."[30]

Philadelphia encompassed several worlds in one. Here a man could amuse himself "looking at some Indians, who were shooting with Bows & Arrows before the state house," and the next moment meet "a man with a blue Scotch bonnet on his head[,] a sight I have not seen a long time & which made me smile."[31] In the space of an hour a man might meet a bearded Amish farmer arguing in German with a shopkeeper, talk to a Jew, visit a Catholic mass, or hear a plainly dressed Quaker asking if "thee is well." He could see being built "as fine Ships here as any part of the World and with as great dispatch."[32] He could find manufactured here "most

---

[28] "Dr. Solomon Drowne," *PMHB* 48 (1924), 237.
[29] R. G. Albion and L. Dodson, eds., *Philip Vickers Fithian Journal 1775–1776* (Princeton, 1934), 39.
[30] Hector St. John de Crèvecoeur, *Letters from an American Farmer* (Everyman edition, London, 1912), 74–75. It seems evident that Crèvecoeur's Scot came from one of the Hebrides rather than from the mainland.
[31] Padelford, *Dr. Honyman's Journal*, 16, 18.

kinds of hard-ware, clocks, watches, locks, guns, flints, glass, stoneware, nails, paper, cordage, cloth, &c, &c."[33] (Invariably any list of things manufactured in Philadelphia ended up with a catch-all "&c.") And, if he wished, he could sink himself unobtrusively in sin, mild or otherwise. One man remembered well "an obscure inn in Race Street" — the city was filled with obscure inns — where as a boy he first tasted strong drink. "Dropping in about dark," he recalls, "we were led by a steep and narrow stair-case to a chamber in the third story. . . . Here we poured down the fiery beverage; and valiant in the novel feeling of intoxication, sallied forth in quest of adventures."[34]

The Philadelphia of 1776 was an anomaly, more like the America that was to be than the America that was. This was the spot Crèvecoeur had in mind when he asked: " What then is the American, this new man?" A mixture of English, Scotch, Irish, French, Dutch, Germans, and Swedes, Crèvecoeur answered, melted down into a new race of man, a "promiscuous breed."[35] Crèvecoeur, more intuitive than observant, anticipated a melting-down process that was still firmly resisted in the Pennsylvania back-country and had hardly begun in Philadelphia. But he hit upon the distinctive feature that set Philadelphia apart from the rest of America. This "strange mixture," as another called it,[36] had made Philadelphia into a city.

The Quakers had set the tone for Philadelphia — or perhaps one should say Penn had set it, for rarely has the personality of one man been more enduring than Penn's in his city of brotherly love — by welcoming all men, asking only that they worship one supreme God. Now, religion meant much to the people of the eighteenth century. Their lives centered in their church. Men

---

[32] *Journal of Nicholas Cresswell,* 156.
[33] Carl Bridenbaugh, ed., " Patrick M'Robert's *A Tour Through Part of the North Province of America* (1774–1775)," *PMHB* 59 (1935), 166.
[34] Graydon, *Memoirs,* 71.
[35] Crèvecoeur, *Letters from an American Farmer,* 43, 41.
[36] *Journal of Nicholas Cresswell,* 265.

repressed in the way they wished to worship were likely to syphon off incredible amounts of energy attempting to relieve the repression. In the free air of Philadelphia those energies could be released for other purposes, usually practical ventures.[37] There was little need for a sustained interest in politics since the government gave the people the one thing they most desired—freedom of worship. This may to some extent explain why Philadelphians were judged by nearly all visitors as "remarkably industrious,"[38] and the city as a place where, even in the midst of war, the people paid little attention to politics but "only minded their business."[39]

Religious freedom attracted a variety of peoples to Philadelphia but it was the strange mixture itself, the interplay between cultures, that raised Philadelphia to the status of city. The basic pattern fixed by the Society of Friends was constantly being reshaped and forced in new directions.[40] The Quakers' affection for neat, simply designed buildings had set the architectural tone of the city; the elegance of Christ Church indicated a change at work on the old pattern. The Quakers had been resisted in politics by the Germans and Scotch-Irish and the conflict in the long run had made the Pennsylvania Assembly more amenable to public opinion than any legislature on the continent. The influx of races had worked subtler changes. The Scotch preference for whiskey over ale had begun a shift in city drinking habits. Even the guttural language of the

[37] The effect of relieved religious tensions on men's activities in America is noted by Henry Bamford Parkes when he says that men here "had increasingly great opportunities for the expression of aggressive energies and the pursuit of ambition. . . . In America the individual's chief source of anxiety was the natural environment rather than his own repressed desires." *The American Experience* (New York, 1955), 70.
[38] *Journal of Nicholas Cresswell*, 265.
[39] Padelford, *Dr. Honyman's Journal*, 29.
[40] On the importance of "cultural interaction" in colonial Pennsylvania's history see Frederick B. Tolles, "The Culture of Early Pennsylvania," *PMHB* 81 (1957), 119–137. Tolles finds the source of Philadelphia's flowering in the richness, the variety, and, "above all, in the creative interaction of the elements in its cultural hinterland" (137). I think that the city-backcountry interaction was less important than that between various groups within the city.

Germans had been contagious; at least one visitor was convinced that it was from the Germans that Philadelphians got the "Tincture of the Accent in their speech."[41]

Together freedom of worship and the variety of cultures help account for the lag of enthusiasm in Philadelphia for independence. At first glance the opposite would seem true. For, as one traveler noted, Philadelphians, "as they consist of several nations, and talk several languages, they are aliens in some respect to Great Britain."[42] But thin ties with Britain did not necessarily promote the idea of change. Most who came to Philadelphia had flourished. In little had they been forced to conform. They had kept their native languages and customs, they had religious freedom, they were legally the equal of any man in the city, and, with all this, they had prospered.

This strange mixture of peoples hindered any mass movement either for or against independence in another way. Philadelphia was a fragmented society. The blend of races Crèvecoeur anticipated had only begun. Similarities between Quakerism and the German pacifist sects had opened the door for intermarriage for some. Sally Wister, for instance, was a Quaker girl whose ancestors were German.[43] But for the most part such intermixing appears to have been rare, and cultural barriers remained high. Catholics reacted first as Catholics and only after reflection as Philadelphians. The Quakers viewed public affairs through the eyes of their religion. The Germans stubbornly held to their native language, supported their own German-language newspaper, and for the most part lived only among their own kind. Until something occurred that cut through these various barriers and touched

---

[41] Padelford, *Dr. Honyman's Journals,* 20.
[42] Burnaby, *Travels,* 97.
[43] Frederic Klees, *The Pennsylvania Dutch* (New York, 1950), 149, says there was considerable intermarriage between English Quakers and Germans, especially among the more prosperous Germans in Philadelphia. He writes: "Wister and Wistar, Gummere, Shoemaker, Lukens, and Yerkes are good Quaker names that were once Pennsylvania Dutch."

directly the lives of all the city's inhabitants, forcing them to react as Philadelphians and not as Germans or Presbyterians or Quakers, the city would continue to be balanced between the poles of reconciliation and independence. Twice in 1775, but each time only for an instant, the city had reacted as one — when Benjamin Franklin had returned home from England and when the New England delegates had returned to Philadelphia shortly after the battle of Lexington and Concord. But the moment passed as quickly as it came. The May election showed that nothing had occurred to unite this fragmented society into acting decisively one way or another. As long as things were going well, the consensus seemed to be, there was no great need for a change.

And things *were* going well for Philadelphia in the spring of 1776. To some extent this judgment depended on whom a visitor talked to. By March two men-of-war — the *Roebuck* and the *Liverpool* — had taken up patrolling stations at the mouth of Delaware Bay and effectively sealed up Philadelphia shipping. "All our vessels that were going out are returned, and our harbour is completely shut up," one man wrote.[44] Two days before the May election the port was still so tightly bottled up that one merchant reported: "We know not of a single Person willing to adventure out, excepting two or three Vessels that have been loaded some weeks, and are now lying by till a good Opportunity to sail." None of these vessels had been able to get shipping insurance, so great was the risk they ran. In short, concluded the merchant, "there is no trade."[45]

Thus, some people would have found it hard to say that business prospered. Philadelphia merchants owned 63 per cent of the shipping and 72 per cent of the tonnage that moved in and out of the port and this ownership was spread among at least one

---
[44] Joseph Reed to Charles Pettit, March 30, Reed, *Life of Reed*, I, 182.
[45] Letter to Stephen Cooper, April 30, Reynell-Coates Letterbook, HSP.

hundred thirty-five businessmen.[46] These men saw little to be cheerful about in the economic situation. But these men were a small segment of the voters. For the city as a whole the blockade had made no serious dent in a pleasant prosperity. It had only lessened, not silenced, activity along the wharves. The ropewalks, ship chandlers, and grogshops still thrived. River traffic still flourished the length of the bay and northward along the Delaware. Shipbuilders had more business than they could handle, for most of the embryonic continental navy was being built in Philadelphia shipyards.

The ships left in port had released a small flood of sailors on the city. This floating body of foot-loose toughs could have had an unsettling effect on city affairs if they had remained long unemployed. A demagogue could have conjured up a mob with a finger snap. Fortunately, the sailors appear to have been quickly absorbed into the wartime prosperity. At least when William Bradford, Jr., went hunting for a man to handle a shallop he "searched all the most probable places I hear of, for seamen; but without any success."[47]

For all their importance, shipping and commerce remained only two of the city's diversified ways of making a living. Philadelphia was accustomed to economic well-being. There had been a mild depression between 1766 and 1769, when prices dropped 17 per cent. But for six years—1770 to 1776—the city had enjoyed a phenomenal stability in which price rises were confined to only 4 per cent.[48] The war only brightened this picture. The news of Lexington and Concord had stimulated the city's prosperity and this made up for the effects the blockade might have had. Both the province and Congress had passed out hundreds of war contracts. The armies needed guns, cannons, ammunition, canvas for

---

[46] Anne Bezanson, "Inflation and Controls, Pennsylvania 1744–1779," *Journal of Economic History,* Supplement, 1948, 4.
[47] Bradford, Register, May 31 (misdated June 1).
[48] Anne Bezanson, *Prices and Inflation During the American Revolution—Pennsylvania, 1770–1790* (Philadelphia, 1951), 12.

THE CITY

tents, shoes, blankets, uniforms. Philadelphia was the best-equipped spot in America to handle these contracts. Prior to the war the city had had too many craftsmen for its needs and many of them had drifted into farming. The war brought their skills into demand again and with no urging they left the farms and turned to casting cannons, weaving cloth, making shoes. By mid-1776 labor was in such short demand that it was said some four thousand women were employed in their homes spinning and weaving cloth.[49]

By the time of the May election a mild inflation had begun to set in. Within a few weeks its effects would begin to hurt the workingman, shopkeeper, and artisan, but in late April its effects were negligible and hardly noticeable. A shoemaker raised the price of his shoes but at the same time upped the wages of his journeymen six pence over the accepted rate in order to keep them. The value of the Continental dollar began to decline, but so slowly it was hardly perceptible to the man in the street.[50]

One reason inflation made such little headway was that many merchants, convinced by the blockade that Philadelphia was in for hard times, were shutting up their shops and moving to the country. They kept their prices low in order to clear their stocks quickly. John Elliott, for instance, who owned a "Looking-Glass" store on Walnut Street, advertised for someone to buy his house, store, "and the remaining stock on hand, which he will sell very low to such a purchaser."[51] Flour and lumber dealers with Philadelphia headquarters were relocating in the country and thus liquidating their stocks at reasonable prices.[52] The immediate effect of these shifts was to keep down prices and strengthen the illusion of prosperity in the average man's mind more than ever.

Luxury goods were the main items to feel inflation in the early stages, and here the price rises were artificial. Tradesmen took

---
[49] *Ibid.*, 17.
[50] *Ibid.*, 29, 30.
[51] *Pennsylvania Gazette*, May 22.
[52] Bezanson, *Journal of Economic History*, 6.

advantage of the blockade and upped prices on West Indies goods, molasses and sugar in particular. "The scarcity of some West Indies Goods in our opinion is an Artificial one," one merchant reported.[53] The city Committee worked hard to fix prices on rum, sugar, molasses, coffee, pepper, salt, cocoa, and chocolate. It had little success, but the lack of it did not strike the public perceptibly until mid-May or early June.

Philadelphia sacrificed little for this war-borne prosperity. One gentleman accustomed to Burton ale found he could not get it any longer and another's wife, who had her heart set on a certain shade of wallpaper, had to do without.[54] But the newspapers were still filled with advertisements for fine imported wines, tobacco, coffee, imported linens, books from England, tableware, and nearly any item that a Philadelphian might normally expect to find in the city shops. A few things only were in short supply. By March there was no "common English paper to be bought in the whole city," ran one report. Only American-made paper was available and that in small quantities.[55] This hurt mainly printers and newspapers. The *Pennsylvania Packet* had to cut back its size.[56] A recently arrived printer complained he had applied "to several printers since my arrival in town, but have not been able to get employ, the want of paper having rendered work very scarce."[57]

Only the pair of men-of-war at the mouth of Delaware Bay blemished this picture of prosperity. These reminded Philadelphia, if dimly, that it could soon be in the uncomfortable position in which Boston found itself. Up to now Philadelphia had remained untouched directly by the war. Parts of Massachusetts had been a battleground for nearly a year, with Boston until recently occupied

---

[53] Letter to Stephen Cooper, May 3, Reynell-Coates Letterbook, HSP.

[54] Joseph Shippen to Edward Shippen, January 15; Edward Shippen to Jasper Yeates, June 5, Shippen Papers, vol. 7, HSP.

[55] Joseph Shippen to Edward Shippen, March 12, Shippen Papers, vol. 7, HSP.

[56] The *Packet* reduced its size on April 15.

[57] William Prichard to Benjamin Franklin, June 10, Franklin Papers, American Philosophical Society. (Hereafter APS.)

by British troops. A British task force had razed the town of Falmouth, Maine. Virginians had burned Norfolk to keep it from British hands. Several seacoast towns in the South had been bombarded by British warships. New York momentarily expected an invasion and Washington was in the process of moving the continental army down from Boston to protect it. Philadelphia had thus far escaped injury, and a war out of sight placed it, for many, also out of mind. Nothing had occurred to dent the city's feeling of security and no flaw had yet appeared in the war-borne prosperity that affected the mass of people. Surely, to many Philadelphians, it must have seemed senseless to gamble away this state of well-being by casting a ballot for the Independents. Especially when in the midst of all this word still persisted that the King was sending peace commissioners. In mid-March Francis Alison, a Presbyterian divine and vice-provost of the College, wrote: "We expect commissioners every day with terms of accommodation from England. I pray God that they may be so just & responsible as to establish peace."[58] Rumors of the commissioners still flourished on election day. True, other rumors floated about that foreign troops were also on their way, but when a man can choose between his rumors he seldom selects the one that brings bad tidings, especially when he prospers.

William Bradford, Jr., believed that Philadelphia's location would have a lot to do with determining her reaction to the war. "It is happy for us that we have Boston in the front & Virginia in the rear to defend us," he wrote James Madison. "We are placed where Cowards ought to be placed, in the middle."[59] Put more charitably, Philadelphia took advantage of her location. She waited for the war to come to her rather than sallying out in search of it.

---
[58] Francis Alison to his cousin Robert Alison, March 16, Miscellaneous Collection, HSP.
[59] William Bradford, Jr., to James Madison, undated letter probably written in late February, 1775, Bradford Letterbook, 1775, HSP.

Philadelphia's central location had helped keep the city prosperous and contented and to that extent it helped defeat any agitation for independence. This central location, coupled with the city's diverse population, created active distrust of the idea of independence in another way, one involved with the intense sectional sentiments of the day. When a colonial American spoke of "my country" he generally referred to his home colony. Events of 1775 and early 1776 had to some extent diluted this feeling in the South and New England, where common suffering had, momentarily at least, created a sense of community. Philadelphia had not suffered and nothing had occurred to diminish the feeling of "apartness." In fact, much had taken place to re-enforce its dislike of Virginia and New England. What little animosity the people of Philadelphia could stir up in 1776 was directed, curiously, less against the British than against fellow Americans.

Philadelphians had no great antipathy toward Virginians personally. They joked about their penchant for turkey hash and fry'd hominy, and about their Southern accent,[60] but kept their quarrel on a diplomatic level between the officials of the two colonies. The roots of the dispute dated back to the early 1750's, but only in the 1770's did Virginia put a firm claim to the western country beyond the Alleghenies that Pennsylvania said belonged to her.

---

[60] Was there a Southern accent, or, for that matter, any regional accent in colonial America? Carl Bridenbaugh, *Myths and Realities* (Baton Rouge, La., 1952), says in his Preface (vii) that "there was not even any Southern accent." Nicholas Cresswell seems to agree. He writes in his *Journal*, 271: "No County or Colonial dialect is to be distinguished here, except it be the New Englanders, who have a sort of whining cadence that I cannot describe." On the other hand, Sally Wister mentions in her *Journal* that a man from Maryland "has the softest voice, never pronounces the R at all." (92); and when with some Virginians she said, "Ridiculed their manner of speaking. I took great delight in teasing them." (108). Virginians, in turn, took note of the grating Philadelphia accent. Dr. Honyman, we have seen, attributed it to German influence. Philip Vickers Fithian, incidentally, observed in his it to German influence. Philip Vickers Fithian, incidentally, observed in his *Journal 1775–1776* the oddities of speech among the Scotch-Irish. "This is an Irish Settlement," he writes of the village of Little Britain. "They speak in a shrill acute, Accent, & have many odd Phrases." (6)

Pennsylvania created Westmoreland County in 1773 to strengthen her hold on the area. She sent Arthur St. Clair over the mountains, ostensibly to act as prothonotary for the court there, actually to direct Pennsylvania's offensive against the Virginians. Virginia promptly retaliated by creating the District of West Augusta, which included approximately the same land as Westmoreland.[61] St. Clair had not been on the scene long before he was convinced that Virginia's Governor Dunmore was trying to steal the profitable Indian fur trade that Pennsylvania traders had worked up, and at the same time turn the Indians against Pennsylvania.[62] After Lexington the warmth of the dispute, surprisingly, increased rather than diminished and in September, 1775, the situation had reached such a point that Thomas Willing, speaking for the entire Pennsylvania delegation, tried to persuade Congress to interfere in settling a temporary line between Pennsylvania and Virginia.[63] Congress, after a long debate, refused, apparently on the ground that once such a precedent was established there would be no end of trouble and requests from colonies, pressure groups, and individuals to get Congress to settle local problems.

The dispute smoldered through 1775 and into 1776. Edmund Physick, the Penn family's agent in Pennsylvania, fanned it into flames again in early April, 1776. The Penns in England needed money and the quit rent, which every landowner in Pennsylvania theoretically paid the family, had become so difficult to collect that in recent years the income hardly covered the proprietary's administrative expenses. Physick advised Lady Juliana Penn that to get money the family must put up more land for sale. With Lady Penn's permission he proceeded to do that.[64] The Pennsylvania

---

[61] For a summary of the dispute see Solon J. and Elizabeth H. Buck, *The Planting of Civilization in Western Pennsylvania* (Pittsburgh, 1939), chapter 7.
[62] A full discussion from the Pennsylvania viewpoint is found in the correspondence of St. Clair in W. H. Smith, *The St. Clair Papers: Life and Public Services of Arthur St. Clair* (2 vols., Cincinnati, 1847), I, 257–362.
[63] "Diary of Richard Smith," *American Historical Review,* 1 (1896), 292.
[64] See the Penn-Physick Correspondence for March–April, 1776, HSP.

Land Office, under the aegis of the Penn family, announced in all the Philadelphia papers that tracts were up for sale in "the country to the westward, called INDIANA."[65] The day the advertisement appeared Carter Braxton called on Thomas Wharton, "to confer with me on the Subject of our Right to that Country as the same was within the Limits of Virginia."[66] Mr. Wharton immediately conferred with one of Pennsylvania's ablest politicians, Joseph Galloway. Galloway by now had determined to depart from America if she declared independence, but he still remained loyal to Pennsylvania's interests. He now advised Wharton "that We should not at any time Acknowledge Our Lands to be within the Colony of Virginia."[67] There the matter stood at the time of the May election.

The effect of this dissension on either Philadelphia or Pennsylvania backcountry voters is impossible to judge. Most of the negotiations were conducted behind the scenes and the public seldom knew enough to get worked up about the argument. Probably the most that can be said is that the dispute did not promote warm relations between the two colonies. Virginia leaders were shrewd enough to sense it would be a tactical error to push the matter just at a time when they were attempting to cajole Pennsylvania into the independence column. They sensibly dropped the dispute until after the declaration of independence had been forced through Congress.[68]

The effect of the New England quarrel on Philadelphia and Pennsylvania affairs was sharper, deeper, and more complex. The Virginia dispute was really one between lawyers and dealt in the main with the fine print in charters. The New England bitterness

---

[65] See the *Pennsylvania Gazette*, May 15, for a typical advertisement. This land, of course, was in western Pennsylvania, not modern Indiana.
[66] Thomas Wharton to William Trent, April 17, Wharton Letterbook, HSP.
[67] *Ibid.*
[68] For a summary of the Virginia arguments see Julian Boyd *et al*, eds., *The Papers of Thomas Jefferson* (16 vols. thus far, 1950–61), I, 235n, 389n, 462–65, 465–66, 594–95.

THE CITY 53

was between two bodies of people. There were times in late 1775 and early 1776 when it threatened to obscure completely the American quarrel with Great Britain.

Actually, this New England quarrel was several disputes rolled into one, each kept alive and nourished from the heat engendered by the others. One of the disputes—the major one—centered on the Wyoming Valley, which lay some hundred miles north of Philadelphia. In 1755 the Susquehanna Company of Connecticut, successor of earlier Connecticut land companies, purchased the land from the Indians.[69] Soon Connecticut settlers "invaded" the valley. In 1771 the Connecticut government gave official support to the settlement; the people sent representatives to the Connecticut legislature and were governed by that colony's laws. By 1775 feelings between Pennsylvania backcountry men and the New Englanders had reached the point where both sides verged on a full-scale war. Congress, on the pleadings of the Pennsylvania delegation, became involved and spent nearly two full weeks in December of 1775 discussing the matter.[70] As in the Pennsylvania-Virginia boundary dispute, Congress ultimately refused to step in.

While Congress temporized the dispute flared. A traveler in the backcountry in the summer of 1775 reported that the people of Buffalo Valley "are cordial & inveterate Enemies to ye: Yankees. . . ." The people of Buffalo Valley might have tolerated the Yankees if they had shown a willingness to stay in the Wyoming Valley, but rumor had it "they are intending to come into this Neighberhood & fix down upon the unsettled Land which exasperates the People grievously." The Pennsylvanians got so tense that in mid-July two strangers wandering through the backcountry

---

[69] The best summary of the dispute is in Boyd, *Jefferson Papers*, VI, 474n–476n. See also Julian Boyd, *The Susquehanna Company: Connecticut's Experiment in Expansion* (Tercentary Commission of the State of Connecticut, New Haven, 1935). The Indians' side of the story is told in Anthony F. C. Wallace, *King of the Delawares—Teedyuscung* (Philadelphia, 1949).

[70] " Diary of Richard Smith," *American Historical Review*, 1, (1896), 292–301, 504–14.

were tossed in the Sunbury jail "on Suspicion of selling here what they call the Yankee Rights of Land."[71]

The ill feeling between Yankee and Pennsylvanian did not let up. "There was a great Talk here," came a report from Sunbury in the late fall of 1775, "of going against the Yankees when I came up but it has subsided a good deal. The Snow & Severity of the Weather coming on has made it a little discouraging."[72] The weather apparently did not deter the backcountry farmers, for in January, 1776, news reached Philadelphia "of a Skirmish between the Pennsylvanians & the Connecticutt People in which Jesse Lukins was killed. . . ."[73]

The Wyoming Valley quarrel still thrived—and would continue to until long after the Revolution—at the time of the May election. No one dismissed the Connecticut invasion casually. The feeling persisted that this excursion only marked the prelude to further depredations. An inhabitant detailing the reasons why Pennsylvanians resisted independence remarked that "*above all they fear the New Englanders should the Americans gain the day.*"[74] This deep distrust went with men who marched with the army to New England. Even after extended meetings with the Yankees one Pennsylvanian, an officer in the continental army, could muster only contempt for them. "They are a set of low, dirty, griping, cowardly, lying rascals," he wrote. "There are some few exceptions and very few. . . . *You may inform all your acquaintance not to be afraid that they will ever Conquer the other Provinces (which you know was much talked of). . . .*"[75]

There were other aspects of the Philadelphia enmity toward New England. The Quakers had an ancient grudge. Some mem-

---

[71] Albion-Dodson, *Fithian Journal 1775–1776,* 57, 61.
[72] Edward Burd to James Burd, November 1, 1775, Shippen Papers, vol. 7, HSP.
[73] Marshall, Diary, January 3.
[74] "Some Extracts from the Papers of General Persifor Frazer," *PMHB* 31 (1907), 136.
[75] *Ibid.,* 135.

bers of the Society of Friends had emigrated to New England long before Penn inaugurated his "holy experiment," and the Puritans had persecuted them with enthusiasm. The General Court of Massachusetts forbade Quakers to enter the colony. Two women who did spent five weeks in a dingy cell waiting for a ship to carry them away from Boston. A William Brand ignored the order and for his temerity had his head and heels locked together with irons for sixteen hours, then later received one hundred and seventeen lashes from a tarred rope. In 1658 the Court ordered the death penalty for banished Quakers who persisted in returning to Massachusetts and under this ruling at least three members of the sect were hanged.[76] After Penn founded Philadelphia, many New England Quakers who had survived the Puritan persecutions moved down to Pennsylvania, bringing their bitter memories with them. When the Revolution began, New Englanders who were puzzled by Philadelphia's distrust of their "country" were quietly reminded of the treatment the early Quakers had received there.[77]

Philadelphia Catholics had their own reasons for despising Yankees. Among them was the memory of the vitriolic anti-Catholic campaign carried on in Boston newspapers against the Quebec Act of 1774. Also, there was Sam Adams' famous remark that "... what we have above everything else to fear is popery."[78] Philadelphia had the largest single concentration of Catholics in America,[79] and their vote was strong enough in the May election

---

[76] On the treatment of Quakers in New England see James T. Adams, *The Founding of New England* (Boston, 1921), 263–274. A summary of Adams' remarks appears in Louis B. Wright, *The Cultural Life of the American Colonies 1607–1763* (New York, 1957), 82–83.

[77] Frederick B. Tolles, *Meeting House and Counting House—The Quaker Merchants of Colonial Philadelphia 1682–1763* (Chapel Hill, N. C., 1948), 91n.

[78] *Boston Gazette,* April 4, 1768, quoted in C. H. Metzger, "Catholics in the American Revolution," *American Catholic Historical Society of Philadelphia Records,* 59 (1948), 197.

[79] Metzer judges Maryland had 16,000 Catholics spread through the colony and Pennsylvania 6,000 to 7,000, most of them in or around Philadelphia. These figures are toned down by John Tracy Ellis, "Catholics in Colonial America," *American Ecclesiastical Review,* 136 (1957). He notes that in 1757 there were 1,365 Catholics in Pennsylvania, of whom 949 were Germans and

to arouse Paine's ire. If, as Paine says, they voted almost as one against the Independents, their deep feeling against New Englanders must have helped shape their decision.

New Englanders knew of their Philadelphia reputation as persecutors and they may have sensed that this anti-New England sentiment had a hand in the Independents' May election defeat. On Sunday, May 12, Charles Wilson Peale reports he went "to the Roman Chapel in company with Mr. Adams and other New Englandmen."[80] A few days later the lead article in the *Pennsylvania Gazette* extolled at length the tolerant spirit of Massachusetts. The author, Christianus, said he feared Philadelphians "are from old histories possessed with a notion, that the people of New-England are of a persecuting spirit."[81]

Two days before the May election Philadelphians were advised to ask themselves before casting their ballot two questions: *"Is a change necessary,* and *Is this the time for it?"*[82] Almost exactly half the men who voted decided that for the time being no change was necessary. The Independents, in blaming their defeat on the Catholics, the "testimonizing Quakers," the "Tory non-conformists," and the "proprietary dependents," had failed to note the part played in the election by Philadelphia's unique character, its widespread prosperity, its distance from the battlefields, the bitter feeling toward New England and to some extent Virginia, and the continued rumors that peace commissioners were on their way.

---

the remaining 416 were English, Irish, or native Americans. Of this total, 378 Catholics lived in or about Philadelphia. Father Ellis takes these figures from " A List of All the Roman Catholicks in Pennsylvania, 1757," Samuel Hazard, ed., *Pennsylvania Archives, First Series, 1664–1790* (12 vols., Philadelphia, 1852–56), III, 144–145. Father Ellis adds (188) that by 1765 these figures had increased to " around 3,000 adults with approximately an equal number of children." His source is Father George Hunter to John Dennett, S. J., July 23, 1765, in Thomas Hughes, S. J., ed., *History of the Society of Jesus in North America: Documents* (Cleveland, 1908), I, 335–38, 351–52.

[80] Charles Wilson Peale, Diary, May 12, APS.
[81] Christianus, *Pennsylvania Gazette,* May 15.
[82] *Pennsylvania Packet,* April 29, quoted in Leonard W. Labaree, *Conservatism in Early American History* (New York, 1948), 161.

All this convinced a sizeable group of Philadelphians to give their votes to the Moderates, thus delaying—they thought—any prompt decision on the question of independence.

3 THE BACKCOUNTRY

Defeat in Philadelphia disheartened the Independents. A sharper disappointment hit them later in the week when the election results from the eight western counties began to arrive in the city. A final tally of the backcountry vote showed that even if the Independents had won every seat up for vote in the city, they still could not have gained control of the Assembly.

If, as historians have it, the Pennsylvania backcountry served as a breeding ground for independence, little sign of it appeared in the men it sent to the Assembly in the May election. York County, west of the Susquehanna, sent James Rankin, a Quaker who had left meeting to support the Revolution but eyed the prospect of independence with such distaste that he was eventually accused of being a traitor. Rankin was chosen "by so large a majority *as near two to one* against the opposition ticket."[1]

Northumberland County, the tense center of anti-Yankee sentiment in the backcountry, elected James Potter, its wealthiest, most distinguished resident. Potter defies the cliché of the fire-eating backcountry radical who was resentful against eastern domination and fervent for independence. He was one of the many educated and well-to-do backcountrymen who had impressed a touring New Jerseyite, whose approach to western Pennsylvania had been tinged with an easterner's contempt for the West and who had accepted the myth, current even in 1776, that all backwoodsmen lived mean

---
[1] James Rankin, *Pennsylvania Evening Post,* June 8.

and miserable lives. He found Potter living, almost in baronial splendor, in remote Penn Valley, where he owned "many thousand Acres of fine Land." More astonishing than his wealth or the comfort of his life was the library he had brought to the wilderness. "He has here a Number of Books—Justice Blackstone's celebrated Commentaries—Pope's Works—Harvey's Meditations—Many Theological Tracts &c—"[2]

Bedford County, over the Alleghenies and a presumed hotbed of frontier firebrands, sent Thomas Smith, who was a half-brother of Dr. William Smith, bulwark of the Moderates in the city. Thomas Smith lacked the outward graces; he had a rough tongue and favored a costume of boots and spurs and huge broadskirt coat that even fellow frontiersmen must have found eccentric. In 1776 he personified the Crown's and the Proprietary's rule in Bedford County. He held nearly every appointive office that the Governor could offer; and now he had won its highest elective office. Smith had inherited little of his brother's ability, which may be one reason he drifted to the backcountry, but the family resemblance turned up in his political convictions. He held no affection for the idea of independence, nor had the frontier environment imbued him with respect for leveling principles.

Northampton County's choice embarrassed the Independents even more. Here James Allen, one of *the* Allens, brother of Andrew and third son of the old Chief Justice, won in an unopposed contest 853 to 14. He did not win on his personality, to judge from the querulous self-portrait left in his diary. In January he had joined Colonel John Shee's battalion, partly because "a man is suspected who does not," and partly because "I believe discreet people mixing with them, may keep them in Order."[3] By March, to hear James Allen tell it, the Independents had won the hearts of all Pennsylvania. "The plot thickens; peace is scarcely

---

[2] Albion-Dodson, *Fithian Journal 1775-1776*, 85, 86. 1778," *PMHB*, 9 (1885), 186.

[3] "Diary of James Allen, Esq., of Philadelphia, Counsellor-At-Law, 1770-

thought of — Independancy predominates," he wrote. "Thinking people uneasy, irresolute & inactive. The Mobility triumphant." And yet a few weeks later he emerged from his gloom to find he was "now a political character," a member of the Assembly.[4]

Not long after the Assembly convened an affair arose to point up exactly how crushing the Independents' defeat in the backcountry had been. A dispute had broken out early in May between the Committee of Safety and the captains of the city's flotilla of row-galleys, as they were called — armed whaleboats designed to beat off any water-borne invasion aimed at Philadelphia. The dispute boiled away for weeks in the press, in taverns, and on street corners, until by early June a minor military matter had become a major political issue. By this time the Independents had taken up the galley captains' cause. The Committee of Safety had been appointed by the Assembly and thus represented the reactionary, the aristocratic element of the province; the galley captains embodied the virtues of the common people. One Independent wrote: "Several of the Committee of Safety are suspected Tories . . . and are highly improper to be at the head of the military secrets and affairs . . . ; and I cannot see how any man, especially a military man, holding independent principles, can think himself safe under the direction or authority of those who oppose them."[5]

Public pressure soon forced the Assembly to step in and investigate the charges and countercharges. Aware of the delicate situation it faced, the Assembly chose its investigating committee with care. The four new Moderate members from the city were purposely omitted. Twenty-seven men composed the committee, at least two from every county with deputies present at the current session of the Assembly.[6] All eleven of the new members from the backcountry — neither Thomas Smith nor John Procter from West-

---

[4] *Ibid.*, 186.
[5] "To the People," *Pennsylvania Gazette,* June 26.
[6] Neither Bedford nor Westmoreland County sent members to this session of the Assembly.

moreland County had bothered to make the long trip over the Alleghenies to Philadelphia—received seats on the Committee. After completing its investigation the committee wrote a final report that exonerated the Committee of Safety and handed it a vote of confidence.[7] The Independents promptly used the report in their attacks on the Assembly. No one, either then or since, has bothered to point out that eight of the eleven backcountry members signed the committee report and only three refused to do so.[8] The eight who signed implicitly disassociated themselves from the Independents by their action and were thereafter considered in the Independents' propaganda aligned with the Moderates.

What accounts for the strange success of the Moderates in the backcountry, an area that historians have pictured ablaze with fervor for independence? This, in turn, raises another question. Historians argue that the backcountry's affection for independence emerged in large part from an East–West estrangement. After the French and Indian War, so the argument goes, Philadelphia and the backcountry bickered continually over trade, taxation, representation in the Assembly, and proprietary control. The diversity of economic interests coupled with bitterness over racial and religious matters widened the rift.[9] Eventually the estranged West allied itself with the equally bitter, disenfranchised masses of Philadelphia. The revolution in Pennsylvania now became a two-fold movement in which the issue of home rule vied with the issue of who should rule at home.[10]

---

[7] The report is published in Gertrude MacKinney and Charles F. Hoban, eds., *Pennsylvania Archives, Eighth Series: Votes and Proceedings of the House of Representatives of the Province of Pennsylvania* (8 vols., 1931–1935, Harrisburg), VIII 7543–44. (Hereafter cited as *Votes*.)

[8] Those from the backcountry who signed the report were: Bartram Galbreath, Samuel Eddy (or Eddie), James Rankin, Jonathan Hoge, John Lesher, James Allen, Jacob Arndt, and James Potter. Those who refused to sign were: Robert Whitehill, Henry Haller, and Thomas Porter. (See *Votes*, VIII, 7544.)

[9] Charles H. Lincoln, *The Revolutionary Movement in Pennsylvania 1760–1776* (Philadelphia, 1901), chp. 3, " The Influence of the German and Irish Immigration," 23–39.

[10] Lincoln has never received the praise he deserves, for it was he who set

THE BACKCOUNTRY 63

Could it be that historians have argued from a false assumption, that there was no East-West split, or, if there was some anti-eastern sentiment, it was to a large extent counteracted by unifying forces hitherto ignored? From among several patterns that overlay the Pennsylvania backcountry—and by backcountry is meant those eight counties that received additional representation in the May

---

the pattern for interpreting the American Revolution as a twofold movement. Carl Becker, abler and a far better writer, picked up and polished Lincoln's approach in *The History of Political Parties in the Province of New York 1760-1776* (Madison, Wis., 1909). The Lincoln-Becker view of the Revolution proved so viable that it still flourishes today, notably in the writings of Merrill Jensen. This interpretation may test out for other colonies; so far as Pennsylvania is concerned it does not hold water. Now, perhaps eventually there was something like an East-West estrangement in Pennsylvania sentiments. This split may have appeared by 1783, for seven years of war can create deep changes in a society. There is, however, no sign that it existed in 1776 and no reason to conclude as does J. Paul Selsam, who follows the trail laid out by Lincoln, that the Pennsylvania Constitution of 1776 was the "outgrowth of years of patient suffering and smouldering antagonism; the culmination of class rivalry and sectional strife . . . ."

The flaw in Lincoln's interpretation developed from a situation no historian can hope to avoid. His ideas of the past, like all men's, no matter how detached they try to be, were shaped by his present. Note the publication date of his book—1901, smack in the middle of the Progressive era. Now, the Progressives tended to regard their reform movement as an internal revolution, for all its peaceful, lawful nature. They divided the nation into two groups. Among the virtuous were the people—or the "plain people," as they were called, carrying over a phrase from the Populist era that lacked the patronizing tone of "common people." Representing evil were the "special interests," who, it was said, controlled and corrupted the nation and held the people at their mercy. The Progressive crusade, then, was a battle between good and evil in which the people, with virtue on their side, would naturally win. Lincoln reflected this contemporary struggle in his book. The people—those in the backcountry, along with the mechanics, laborers, and small tradesmen of Philadelphia—face the entrenched special interests, represented by the Quaker oligarchy, wealthy merchants, lawyers, and other "respectable" persons. Lincoln favored words like "plain people," "trusts," and "monopolies" throughout his study, perhaps to point up his parallel. In the best Progressive sense, the people, once they had been told the truth—as Tom Paine told them in *Common Sense*—arise in anger to oust the corrupt special interest. The Constitution of 1776 was their triumph. This happy ending must have cheered Progressives who believed that history repeats itself. The persistence of the Lincoln interpretation of the Revolution may be due to the persistence of the Progressive attitude toward American society, past and present, among historians.

election — let us choose four: religious-cultural, historical, economic, and political. Perhaps these patterns, looked at separately and together, will explain why the backcountry sent moderate-minded men to the Assembly in May and at the same time throw new light on the supposed East–West split.

The religious-cultural composition of the backcountry was the same "strange mixture" found in Philadelphia. Only the proportions of the mixture differed. The Quakers were not, for the most part, backcountry people. They prevailed in the three eastern counties of Bucks, Philadelphia, and Chester. In a general way the Germans and Scotch–Irish split the backcountry between them.

In 1776 the population of the Pennsylvania backcountry was about 150,000 people.[11] Over a third and perhaps close to half this was German.[12] The word German is not sufficiently discriminating. There were at least three German cultures and several variations on these three.[13] First, there were the "plain people" — drably dressed Mennonites, mostly of Swiss stock; Amish, whose women favored brightly colored dresses and whose men wore

---

[11] "Answers to the Heads of an Enquiry on the Condition of the Province, 1775," *Pennsylvania Archives, First Series*, IV, 597, gives as part of an official accounting of the province for the Proprietors the figure 302,000 for Pennsylvania's total population. Half this sum seems a reasonable estimate of the backcountry's population.

[12] Franklin in 1766 estimated Pennsylvania's population as one-third German, one-third Quaker, and one-third Scotch–Irish. It was an off-the-cuff opinion and Franklin took care to note he did not "speak with authority." Still, it has been accepted as authoritative ever since. Even the scholarly "Report of Committee on Linguistic and National Stocks in the Population of the United States," *American Historical Association Report for 1931*, I, 107–408, bases all its figures for Pennsylvania on Franklin's estimate. I believe Franklin underestimated. Every town of importance in the backcountry, except for Carlisle, was predominantly German. Of the counties only Cumberland, Bedford, and Westmoreland, none of them heavily populated, clearly had more Scotch–Irish than German inhabitants.

[13] The remarks that follow are based largely on the account in Klees, *Pennsylvania Dutch*, a book written with wit, style, and great understanding. See also Ralph Wood, ed., *The Pennsylvania Germans* (Princeton, 1942), a collection of scholarly essays.

beards; and the smaller sects of Dunkards, River Brethren, and Schwenkfelders. They strove to shut themselves off from the world and lived only among themselves. They were pacifists and for the most part settled in Lancaster County, safely surrounded by a thick buffer of settlers more willing to fend off marauding Indians. The "plain people" refused to hold public office—that would entail mixing with the world—and from the time of the French and Indian War it appears that they refused even to vote.

The "church people," Germans who belonged to the Lutheran and Reformed Churches, comprised the bulk of backcountry Germans. The Reformed Church was often called the Dutch or German Presbyterian Church, an understandable error since John Knox adopted the Reformed organization as he had observed it in Switzerland almost unchanged for the Presbyterians. The "church people" were of the world's people. They did not believe in pacifism. Their stronghold was Berks County, on the northern frontier, but they could be found anywhere in the backcountry, especially where there was good farm land. In a day when a man's religion shaped his way of life the similarities in churches let the "church people" and Scotch-Irish live together in reasonable harmony. Neither group expressed fondness for the other—it was probably the Scotch-Irish who coined the phrase "dumb Dutch" —but they tolerated one another with only occasional flare-ups.

The Moravians, who centered in and around Bethlehem, were in many ways a blend between the "plain" and "church" people. They emphasized a life shed of ornaments but did not attempt to live apart from the world. They disliked war and worked to promote peace by sending missionaries among the Indians, but they would fight when pressed. They were, as they put it, neither *kriegerisch* (warlike), nor *Quäkerisch* (Quakerlike).[14]

These diverse German cultures cut diagonally across the Pennsylvania backcountry in a broad swath that began at Easton in the northeast, curved through Bethlehem and Lancaster, and ended

---

[14] Klees, *Pennsylvania Dutch*, 110.

west of the Susquehanna in the vicinity of York. Scotch–Irish were scattered all through this belt and around Easton and York the blend reached about half and half. The Scotch–Irish concentrated on the frontiers. From the Susquehanna they fanned out westward until they backed up against the early ridges of the Alleghenies. Probably most of the estimated fifty thousand settlers who had trickled over the mountains to settle in Bedford and Westmoreland counties were Scotch–Irish. Cumberland County was almost wholly theirs and Carlisle served as their western hub.

Scattered through this backcountry were "pockets" of English and Welsh Baptists; some Scotch Presbyterians; a few, very few Quakers; some Church-of-England English (they had a church in York); an indeterminate number of Negroes and Indians; and, south of Philadelphia, some Swedes, Finns, and Dutch, who had been on hand to welcome William Penn and had by 1776 become so absorbed with the English immigrants as to have lost any cultural distinctions.[15] There were also some Catholics—a congregation at Reading, at nearby Goshenhoppen, at Conewago, and Lancaster.[16] Most of these Catholics were Germans, except for a few slaves imported from the West Indies. They were tolerated, but reluctantly. A resident of Reading wrote: "We know that the People of the Roman Catholick Church are bound by their Principles to be the worst Subjects and worst of Neighbors. . . ." The same man reported they were "very numerous in this County." At the time he wrote the Catholic congregation of Reading numbered eighty-eight.[17]

From the cultural view, then, the backcountry comprised an expanded version of Philadelphia society, with one difference—the fragmentation of city life was even more pronounced in the

---

[15] For a description of Pennsylvania's cultural map as it existed around 1740 see Frederick B. Tolles, "The Culture of Early Pennsylvania," *PMHB*, 81 (1957), 134.

[16] Klees, *Pennsylvania Dutch*, 84–85, and J. Bennett Nolan, *The Foundation of the Town of Reading in Pennsylvania* (Reading, 1929), 152–156.

[17] Nolan, *Foundation of Reading*, 154, 153.

backcountry. Pressure of city life had begun to force cultural compromises on the diverse peoples of Philadelphia. German shopkeepers were forced to learn English if they wished to stay in business. Quaker merchants as they prospered became more worldly than their country brethren and some even drifted into the Church of England. Intermarriages between Mennonites and Quakers occurred occasionally. The accent of the city Irish, perhaps even their tempers, began to soften under daily contact with other people. But the backcountry strengthened rather than weakened the barriers between various cultures. As long as they obeyed the laws of the province, no one except the tax collector interfered with these people's lives. No pressures forced them to conform to any pattern but the one they themselves set. Germans in the backcountry resisted learning English. They saw to it that their sons were reared in the customs of the old country and trained to pass them along intact to their sons. The Scotch-Irish lived apart, drank their whiskey, and sent their sons, if they could, to school under a good Presbyterian preacher. Even in the backcountry towns and villages the various cultures refused to blend. A traveler in 1775 noted in his journal that Little Britain was "an Irish settlement" and that in York "the inhabitants are Dutch." Traveling southward along the Great Waggon Road from York he came to the village of Abbotstown ("One Dutch Lutheran Church with a Cupola; All the Houses built with Square Logs—an old, kind, Dutch Landlady gave our Horses, for Breakfast a dish of '*Spelts*.'"). then next to New Oxford, "another Settlement of the Scotch-Irish."[18]

Little or nothing in the religious-cultural pattern of the backcountry fostered an East-West split. The split, culturally at least, was more within the backcountry itself than between East and West. The Scotch-Irish and Germans went separate ways and the Germans themselves broke down into several distinct cultures. An Irishman in York felt more kinship, had more in common with

---

[18] Albion-Dodson, *Fithian Journal 1775-1776*, 6, 7, 8-9.

a fellow Irishman in Philadelphia than with his predominantly German neighbors. A Mennonite in Lancaster County felt closer to his brethren in Germantown than to a German neighbor who belonged to the Lutheran Church.

The backcountry had no religious-cultural reasons to complain against the East nor any reason to desire a change. In no way had their cultures been repressed. Backcountry Irishmen in the South did have cause from this standpoint to yearn for a change, as did the Baptists in Massachusetts who, as they saw it, were taxed for the state-protected church in that colony. In Pennsylvania no sect and no race could or did complain against any domination from the East over their religious or social life.

Much has been made of the historical pattern overlaying the backcountry to explain the area's supposed affection for independence. The argument goes like this: with the coming of the French and Indian War the backcountry appealed to the Quaker-dominated Assembly for military aid. None was forthcoming. The backcountry banded together in voluntary Associations to defend themselves. Bitterness toward the East still persisted when the war ended and it festered for the next twenty years, finally erupting in 1776 in a united backcountry drive for independence. Behind this push for independence was the desire to overthrow the eastern-dominated Assembly and set up a government in which the backcountry had a major voice.

No doubt the backcountry had grievances against the Assembly dating back twenty years and more. But how much did this historical pattern shape the opinions of backcountry people in 1776? For the past to have an overwhelming influence on the present assumes a sense of continuity, an awareness of history, which is a risky assumption about Americans of any period. It also assumes a stability that the backcountry lacked. Men were constantly on the move; new people with no knowledge of old grievances kept flowing into the backcountry right through 1775 and 1776. A visitor to Sunbury in mid-1775 wrote: "Two Waggons, with Goods, Cattle, Women, Tools &c, went through Town to Day from East-Jersey, on their Way to Fishing Creek up this River [the west branch of the Susquehanna], where they are to settle; rapid, most rapid, is the growth of this County."[19]

Even among the old-time residents the backcountry's historical pattern seemed to have little influence. Edward Biddle, of Berks County, fought in the French and Indian War. A gift of five thousand acres of land probably blotted out any bitterness he might have had toward the Assembly.[20] After the war he became a prosperous Reading lawyer and eventually a member of the Assembly. As late as 1776 he still could not make up his mind about independence. "The subjugation of my country," he would tell friends, "I deprecate as a most grievous calamity, and yet sicken at the idea of thirteen, unconnected, petty democracies: if we are to be independent, let us, in the name of God, at once have an empire, and place Washington at the head of it."[21]

John Montgomery, of Cumberland County, also fought in the French and Indian War.[22] This, along with his Scotch–Irish background and his position as elder in the Presbyterian Church, should have caused him to hate the East and become an early enthusiast for independence. But Montgomery returned to Carlisle from the war and prospered. He became a moderate-minded man with deep contempt for all leveling principles. He was elected sheriff of the county and later sent to the Assembly. As a member of the Assembly he helped push through the equal representation bill. He said it was a measure he had "much at heart."[23] He looked out for his county's welfare but held none of the enmity toward the

---

[19] *Ibid.*, 62, The entry is dated July 19, 1775.
[20] Craig Biddle, "Edward Biddle," *PMHB*, 1 (1877), 101.
[21] Graydon, *Memoirs*, 265.
[22] The best biographical sketch of Montgomery is Whitfield J. Bell, Jr., "The Other Man on Bingham's Porch," in *John and Mary's College* (Carlisle, Pa., 1956), 33–59.
[23] *Ibid.*, 36.

East nor, even in early 1776, affection for independence that the historical pattern of the backcountry was supposed to have instilled in him.

All this is not to say that the past had no influence on the backcountry. No doubt the Independents' propaganda to the backcountry recalling the bloodshed and atrocities of the French and Indian War stirred the emotions of some and revived the memories of others. The influence of this historical pattern, however, can be and possibly has been exaggerated.

The economic pattern—or patterns, for there were at least two of them—gave another shape to backcountry attitudes. The first economic belt fanned out from Philadelphia to Wilmington on the south, Lancaster on the west, and Reading and Easton on the north.[24] The economy of these areas was tightly bound to Philadelphia. With many of the farmers in Bucks, Chester, and Philadelphia Counties the ties were direct. In the early hours of market-day morning their wagons could be heard rumbling through the city, and by dawn as many as seventy wagons from the country lined Market Street alone.[25] The ties became less direct but not weaker for farmers more distant from the city. Those surrounding Reading and Easton floated their flax and rye and wheat down the Schuylkill and Delaware. Harvests from Lancaster bumped over the Great Wagon Road, a reasonably good highway in fair weather, from July onward. This trade from Lancaster, went one report, "is carried on by means of large covered waggons, which travel in great numbers to Philadelphia, (sometimes, as I have been informed, there being above one hundred in a company) carrying down the produce of the country, and returning with all kinds of stores and merchandize."[26]

---

[24] Mary Alice Hanna, *The Trade of the Delaware District before the Revolution* (Northampton, Mass., 1917), discusses this economic belt in detail. On roads connecting this area see 242–243; on products and industries of the Delaware District, as Hanna calls it, see 248–260.

[25] "Dr. Solomon Drowne," *PMHB*, 48 (1924), 236.

[26] [Duché], *Observations*, 69.

THE BACKCOUNTRY

Lancaster was the largest inland town in America, an eminence achieved in spite of the fact—and most travelers remarked on this—it was not located on a navigable stream. The highway tie with Philadelphia, several conveniently close iron plantations, and an abundance of skilled workmen accounted for the town's size and prosperity. In the double role of manufacturing center and supply depot Lancaster served as the hub of the second economic belt of the backcountry. Lancaster, however, lacked the tight grip on *its* backcountry that Philadelphia held over its domain. She competed with Baltimore for the trade of farmers settled along the Susquehanna and over the Alleghenies. The merchants were quick to complain to the Assembly "that on account of the Inattention paid to public Highways," they and their Philadelphia colleagues were losing a lot of business to Maryland.[27]

Reading, on a smaller scale, served as the economic hub of the northern and northwestern part of the backcountry. The town specialized in the manufacture of wool hats—"sometimes called Ram's Beavers"[28]—but had the usual collection of mills and shops and over thirty taverns to serve the surrounding farmers.[29] Reading merchants had few worries about competition for the upcountry trade. Here again the main problem was bad roads. It generally took a farmer at least a week to make the trip into Reading, sell his produce, and return home.

The economic domain of Lancaster and Reading stretched westward to a string of towns either on or just beyond the Susquehanna. On the south stood York, already "a considerable Village" which had emerged from the log-house stage and now had a main street "near half a Mile in Length, the Houses a great Part of the Way very near & joining each other, many of them . . . large & fine; some three Stories high."[30] To the north the less sedate

---
[27] From a 1774 petition to the Assembly, quoted in Lincoln, *Revolutionary Movement*, 69.
[28] M. S. Richard, quoted in Nolan, *Foundation of Reading*, 170.
[29] *Ibid.*, 171.
[30] Albion-Dodson, *Fithian Journal 1775–1776*, 7–8.

Scotch–Irish village of Carlisle thrived on the growing trans-Allegheny trade. Still further north, at the forks of the Susquehanna, lay Northumberland and Sunbury. Sunbury, barely four years old, was a village of some hundred log cabins, except for the house of William McClay, "which is of Stone, & large & elegant."[31]

McClay's elegant house set amid a cluster of log cabins exemplified the most startling feature of these wilderness villages to Philip Vickers Fithian, a young Presbyterian who traveled westward in 1775 apparently expecting to find that the backcountry had leveled all men to a barbarous existence. He found instead that while he had to endure the filthy huts and flea-ridden beds that he had expected, he also visited a lady who received him in "a well finished Parlour, with many Peices of good Painting" and a gentleman on the Juniata who "lives elegantly — In the Parlour where I am sitting are three Windows each with twenty four Lights of large Glass!"[32] An evening with a drunken lout who dined on a scupper full of whiskey came as no surprise, but he was astonished to find himself one evening in the wilderness "in the Company of Gentlemen where there is no Reserve" and where "Books & Litterary Improvements were the Subject."[33]

Fithian perceived that though a surprising number of the amenities of life had been preserved the wilderness had worked deep changes on the settlers. For one thing, they dressed differently. "It is the Custom in these back Woods," he noted, "almost universally with Women, to go barefooted — Men in Common I observe wear *Mockisons,* or Indian Shoes." For another thing, old-fashioned formalities were giving way "to the greatest Plainness & Familiarity in Conversation; Every Man in all Companies, with almost no Exception, Calls his Wife, Brother, Neighbor, or Acquaintance, by their proper Name or Sally, John, James, or Michael, without every prefixing the customary Compliment of 'My Dear,' 'Sir,'

---

[31] *Ibid.,* 63.
[32] *Ibid.,* 47, 36.
[33] *Ibid.,* 65.

'Mr.' etc." This familiarity and feeling of equality that went with it was not a male prerogative.

"Peggy," a man named Thompson said one night when the hearth fire began to flicker out, "bring in some Bark to save the Fire."

"Indeed, Tom," said Peggy, "I am tired, pulling Flax all Day & cant."

"Well, then," said Thompson, "run out & call in the Neighbours to see it *die*."[34]

These new habits and attitudes did not kill old ones the settlers brought with them. The democracy of daily life did not dent the tradition of electing only men from the elite to public office. No one hinted that women should share the vote. The old ideas would die only when a new generation arose.

The prosperity of the wilderness settlements impressed Fithian as much as their customs. A brisk river traffic in wheat and rye plied between the forks of the Susquehanna and Middleton, where the grain was transferred to wagons bound for Philadelphia. This prosperity was not recent nor unusual. It dated back over a decade for all parts of the backcountry.[35] Between 1764 and 1772 Philadelphia's West Indies trade doubled that of New York's and exceeded Boston's by a third. Her South European trade was nearly four times greater than New York's and fifteen times that of Boston's.[36] Pennsylvania's backcountry, of course, profited immensely from these favorable balances. Since 1772 Philadelphia merchants had further expanded the overseas grain market and each year as prices kept rising Pennsylvania farmers put more and more land to wheat and rye. Throughout these years the farmers in all parts of the backcountry voiced no economic complaints at all against the city. In fact, any bitterness between city and country came from city dwellers. Listen to this comment from a Philadelphia

---
[34] *Ibid.*, 117, 95.
[35] See William S. Sacks, " Agricultural Conditions in the Northern Colonies Before the Revolution," *Journal of Economic History*, 13 (1953), 274–290.
[36] *Ibid.*, 285.

merchant in 1773 : ". . . tho' the last Crop is said to be a tollerable good one yet the Farmers having been used a long time to great prices the most of them are become wealthy, and therefore will keep back their supply unless they can obtain what they call a good price."[37]

By the spring of 1776 some backcountry farmers may have begun to regard their economic ties with Philadelphia as a mixed blessing. Prices began a slow decline in mid-1774 as the foreign market began to dry up. The decline picked up speed when the *Roebuck* and *Liverpool* arrived at their patrolling stations at the mouth of Delaware Bay and by late April it hovered close to the bottom of the trough, or about one-half the top level reached in 1772. The price of flour between February and April, when shipping was sealed up in port, dropped from fourteen to twelve shillings a hundredweight.[38]

While grain prices dropped retail prices rose. One country store owner began to wonder why he had gone into business. "You in the wholesale way," he wrote his Philadelphia dealer, "can scarcely form an idea how disagreeable it is now to sell goods in our way." He went on : "Some say they will muster no more till the price of goods cease rising; others threaten."[39] It was the high price of salt, the one commodity that every backcountry farmer had to buy, that infuriated most. Once, when farmers got word that a sloop at the head of the Elk was loaded with salt, they trooped down to the wharf, ripped away the hatches, and retailed off the cargo at what they considered a fair price.[40]

This economic discontent can be exaggerated. Aside from salt, depending on the outside world. Mint tea from the kitchen garden the occasional purchase of a scythe, an ax, an iron kettle, or a gun, nearly all backcountry farms could go through the year without

---
[37] Stocker and Wharton to C. Champlin, August 6, 1773, quoted in *ibid.*, 288.
[38] Bezanson, *Prices and Inflation . . . Pennsylvania 1770–1790*, 74–75, 80, 82.
[39] Bezanson, *Journal of Economic History* (Supplement, 1948), 7.
[40] *Ibid.*, 8.

made a palatable brew; roasted rye could substitute for coffee; wine was homemade and if the supply of rum was closed off there was always whiskey; honey and maple sugar took the place of sugar; flax, hemp, and wool provided the cloth for clothes; shoes, candles, soap could be, and were, made on the farm.[41]

There was even a bright side of the picture for those farmers who depended on a little cash coming in. In January, 1776, the demand for fodder started prices up. In February the price of meat began to rise sharply. By April pork was selling at its highest price in the colonial period.[42] The price of both flax and hemp was also on the upswing.

The slump in grain prices in 1776 produced no strong economic arguments that encouraged either the idea of independence or a bitterness toward the East. It would take a more serious downturn to wipe out a decade and more of good prices. Besides, few Pennsylvania farmers specialized to the extent that they depended solely on grain crops for their incomes. Most combined general farming with livestock raising. The Germans, and probably by 1776 a lot of the Scotch–Irish, diversified their crops in order to rotate them. Those who diversified could balance the decline in wheat and rye prices with the rise in meat prices and in flax and hemp. It is hard to see how this mixed economic situation, with its blend of rising and falling prices, could have had any overwhelming effect on the way the backcountry farmer voted in the May election.

The political pattern that overlay the backcountry was, in many ways, not much clearer than the economic pattern. Many generalizations have been based on few facts, for little is known about

---

[41] For a detailed and fascinating picture of how self-sustaining a backcountry farmer's life could be see Joseph Doddridge, *Notes on the Settlement and Indian Wars* (2nd edition, Pittsburgh, 1912). See also Stevenson W. Fletcher, "The Subsistence Farming Period in Pennsylvania Agriculture," *Pennsylvania History*, 14 (1947), 185–195.

[42] Bezanson, *Prices and Inflation . . . Pennsylvania 1770–1790;* for corn prices see 113, chart on 335; for meat prices, 128; for pork prices, 129.

what went on in backcountry politics during early 1776. It is not clear, for instance, that the May election created the sharp feeling in the counties that it did in Philadelphia. Nor is it clear that men in the counties split into Moderate and Independent parties and each ran on separate tickets. James Allen, for example, ran unopposed. (The fourteen votes against him were for no particular candidate, but only against Allen.)

It may be that our judgment of the political temper of the backcountry has been warped by the fears of Philadelphia gentlemen, who saw the ferment in the city and assumed something similar was brewing in the backcountry. Promptly after the Assembly agreed to enlarge its membership Edward Shippen, Jr. dispatched a letter to his friend Jasper Yeates, one of the substantial gentlemen of Lancaster. "There is certainly a design on foot," he wrote, "to reduce the Affairs of this province to as great a State of Anarchy as will put us on a level with some of the Colonies to the Eastward." He went on to urge Yeates to run for one of the two seats created for Lancaster County. Good men were needed "to support our tottering Constitution." Yeates, a known quantity, would "be particularly useful" at this time in the Assembly and Shippen was eloquent in his pleas for him to stand for the office, "if you can think it any way consistent with the good of your private Affairs."[43]

Shippen's letter indicates that the political pattern of the backcountry was not something Philadelphia left to chance. The gentlemen of the city had over the years built one of the most effective political machines in America. Even if the cultural, historical, or economic patterns had put the backcountry in the mood for independence the provincial political machinery could most likely have slowed the stampede, at least temporarily.

---

[43] Edward Shippen, Jr., to Jasper Yeates, March 11, Shippen Papers, vol. 7, HSP. Yeates did not run, for reasons not known. He continued to give generously of his time to public affairs; in a few weeks he journeyed to Pittsburgh for Congress to negotiate with the Indians. Perhaps he refused because he supposed both Thomas Porter and Bartram Galbreath, who eventually won the seats, were safe, substantial men.

In September, 1775, some of the leading lights of Lancaster aired their irritation at Philadelphia politicians. The Lancaster County Committee had received orders from the city Committee to hold new elections for its members. "I cannot help observing that this Desire below [*i.e.* Philadelphia] of interfering in our Politics is not generally relished amongst us here," Jasper Yeates wrote to a friend. "The Step is viewed with Jealousy & manifest Dislike. It is thought some Kind of Controul on the Freedom of elections, & many do not scruple to say [it]." These, of course, were not Yeates's views. "I speak the Sentiments of others," he said. "I carefully avoid the Subject myself, in Conversation."[44]

Yeates held back his views because he knew that Philadelphia interference in backcountry affairs was nothing new. He had been in Lancaster politics long enough to lose his innocence. New people, less skilled at their avocation, were easing into control of Philadelphia affairs. What the old hands managed to achieve discreetly, without rumpling sensitive backcountry tempers, these new people bungled. The old machinery operated awkwardly in their hands.

Philadelphia had controlled backcountry politics almost from the day William Penn stepped ashore at Upland in 1682. Historians have tended to ignore this control of provincial affairs by a few of the elite because politicians of the day obscured it so well. Charles Thomson talked much about the glories of Pennsylvania's local self-government without mentioning how much of the affairs of the backcountry was shaped by the hidden hand of Philadelphia politicians.[45]

The formal government over Pennsylvania was relatively clear-cut and simple. All official posts in theory received their authority from the King, but the Crown's direct appoitive power extended only to the court of Vice-Admiralty, the Comptroller,

---

[44] Jasper Yeates to James Burd, September 22, 1775, Burd Papers, vol. 7, HSP.
[45] Charles Thomson to W. H. Drayton, Stillé, *Life of Dickinson,* 348.

and the customs collector in every county. The Proprietors, with the King's approval, selected the Governor, the Secretary of the Land Office, and the Keeper of the Great Seal. The Governor, in turn, appointed the Provincial Council, the Supreme Court, the Attorney General, and in each county the Register of Wills and Prothonotary of the courts. The people elected the Assembly and in their home counties the sheriff and coroner.[46] Since the outbreak of war in 1775, there had been only one basic change in this structure. Governor John Penn had returned home to England and to fill this gap the Assembly "appointed a Council or Committee of Safety and invested them with executive powers of government, reserving to themselves the legislative authority, which they exercised by resolves."[47]

On paper political power seemed reasonably well distributed. In fact power was concentrated in the hands of a few men. The essential problem the government faced was to somehow get intelligent, competent, and moderate-minded men into the backcountry; through these men political control could be extended over a vast area. The story of Arthur St. Clair illustrates how neatly the government solved its problem. St. Clair was an ex-British army officer who in 1776 was forty years old. He had fought with Wolfe at Quebec, then, about 1760, drifted down to Boston and there married Miss Phoebe Bayard, who was notable, if for nothing else, for the fourteen-thousand-pound dowry that came with her. Though now a man of wealth, St. Clair traveled with his wife over the Allegheny Mountains in 1764, and eventually settled down at Ligonier. There he built a fine house and a grist mill. What attracted St. Clair from the comforts of Philadelphia, where his wealth would have allowed him to lead an easy, pleasant life, over the mountains to one of the wildest and most western settlements in America? More

---

[46] For details see E. R. L. Gould, "Local Self-Government in Pennsylvania," *PMHB*, 6 (1882), 156–173.

[47] Charles Thomson, "The Papers of Charles Thomson," *Collections of the New York Historical Society for 1878* (New York, 1879), 285.

than a love of mountain scenery seems involved. Soon after his arrival Bedford County was erected. St. Clair, though a professional soldier, was made a justice of the court, recorder of deeds, clerk of the orphan's court, and prothonotary of the court of common pleas. He was handed all these assignments again when Westmoreland County came into being in 1773.[48] (Note how neatly the government used these posts as magnets to draw able men farther west. When St. Clair departed for Westmoreland, Thomas Smith was attracted away from Carlisle by the offer of the posts he had vacated.) From Ligonier he conducted all of Pennsylvania's dealings with settlers, Indians, and infiltrating Virginians. He was, so to speak, the province's *ex officio* governor of the transmontane region, charged with the delicate job of fending off Virginian attempts to take the territory from Pennsylvania. St. Clair's unobtrusive advancement to this post had been no accident. The Allens seem to have been the hidden power that shaped his fortune. "You know," he wrote William Allen in 1776, "the obligations I have to your family — obligations which no change of circumstances can ever cancel." [49]

The notable thing about this Pennsylvania political machine, and the main reason that it remained so long in control of events, was that it was not a closed affair. If aristocratic, then it was an aristocracy composed of the ablest talent in the province. The men who ran it were always on the alert for intelligent, capable men. In 1766 John Hughes suddenly found himself out of a job.[50] His friend Franklin had generously arranged to make him collector of revenues from the Stamp Act, but what was meant to be a plush post served to send Hughes into retirement. He settled down on his country estate, Walnut Grove, and with plenty of free time began to call on his neighbors, among them a Quaker farmer named

---

[48] Most of the above material on St. Clair is drawn from Smith, *St. Clair Papers*, vol. I.
[49] St. Clair to William Allen, September 1, *ibid.*, I, 375.
[50] On Hughes see Edmund S. and Helen M. Morgan, *The Stamp Act Crisis* (Chapel Hill, N. C., 1953), 238–257, 297–299.

Jonathan Roberts. Roberts had served in the Assembly when living in Bucks County, but since moving to Philadelphia County had not returned to politics. Hughes' favorable opinion of Roberts "soon induced him to lend his good offices to have him return'd to the assembly." He began to canvass the county for his friend. Each time he returned from a tour he said jokingly: "Mr. R., where have you liv'd, I find nobody here who knows you."[51] Mr. R. was soon well enough known, however, thanks to Hughes, that he was elected to the Assembly at the next election and remained in office until 1776, when his Quaker beliefs forced him to leave.

Both St. Clair and Roberts were mature men when they were drawn into politics. Often a man's initiation into the intricacies of Pennsylvania politics began in his youth; the skill for operating the political machinery was acquired slowly, like the facts of life. Sometimes a young man being groomed for his part had trouble adjusting, or even understanding exactly how to conduct himself. Take, for example, the problems young Edward Burd faced.

Neddie Burd began his career as a lawyer in Reading. Edward Shippen and Jasper Yeates of Lancaster got him off to a decent start. They arranged through Andrew Allen for his appointment as prosecuting attorney for the Crown in the new county of Northumberland.[52] Though the post was in Sunbury, young Burd continued to live in Reading. Now, though Reading was only a country town sin flourished there almost as well as in Philadelphia. In 1774 "a Set of Sharpers" infiltrated the town and set up gaming tables in one of the local taverns. Neddie Burd promptly found his way to the scene and just as promptly lost more money than he could afford. His uncle, Edward Shippen, Jr., a Philadelphia lawyer, arrived in town and learned of the debacle. He reprimanded the boy, reminding him that with a bright future ahead he could not afford to gain the reputation of a wastrel. "What

---

[51] Klein, "Memoirs of Jonathan Roberts," *PMHB*, 61 (1937), 468, 469.
[52] Edward Burd to Jasper Yeates, April 24, 1772: "Mr. Allen was so kind as to consent to my prosecuting for the Crown in the new County at Uncle's request." In Nolan, *Neddie Burd's Reading Letters*, 38.

regards *you* in this matter," he concluded, "is yet a Secret to all the Gentlemen from Philadelphia but myself; I hope it may remain a Secret. . . ."[53]

Uncle Edward had not finished with the matter. Sheriff Nagle obviously knew about the gaming table, in fact had lost some half-joes there. Now, the sheriff was one of the county officers that the people elected — so they thought. Custom had it, however, that the Governor chose between the top two candidates; he, supposedly, selected the people's choice. Uncle Edward made clear the custom was more than an empty gesture of authority. "I told Nagle," he wrote, "it was well for him that this was the last year of his office, otherwise it would be impossible that he could either get Security for his performance of it or that the Governor could intrust any Men with the Office of Sheriff who played for half Joes."[54]

Neddie Burd erred again in 1775. He decided he had had enough of being the King's attorney in the backcountry, and told his friend Jesse Ewing he would get the office turned over to him. He told his grandfather, Edward Shippen of Lancaster, about this, and asked him to pass the word along to Jasper Yeates, who, in turn, would be so kind as to tell Andrew Allen, the attorney general. Grandfather Shippen wrote that Mr. Yeates would not speak to Mr. Allen and he, the grandfather, agreed with the Yeates decision. "I think on reflection you ought not to have proposed the Office to any body until you had consulted those Gentlemen."[55] Neddie Burd now began to comprehend the facts of political life in Pennsylvania. He ceased to play the game by his own rules. Eventually he became Prothonotary of Pennsylvania.

Neddie Burd's painful years as a novitiate in Pennsylvania politics trained him to conform to the pattern. But Burd would

---

[53] Edward Shippen, Jr., to Edward Burd, May 28, 1774, Edward Burd Papers, HSP.
[54] *Ibid.*
[55] *Ibid.*

have matured into a cautious, moderate-minded man despite these experiences, regardless of the career he chose. His family would have seen to that. What about a man like James Wilson? What shape would his ideas have taken if he had matured outside the political machine?

Wilson emigrated to America in 1765, the same year as James Cannon. The two men had much in common. Both were Scotsmen, both came to Philadelphia in their early twenties. They were about the same age — Cannon thirty-six, Wilson thirty-four in 1776. Both were shrewd, intelligent, and ambitious. Both began as tutors at the College of Philadelphia — Cannon in mathematics, Wilson in Greek. In 1776 Cannon was still teacher of mathematics at the College. He had eased into politics through his posts as Secretary of the Committee of Privates, as Secretary of the United Company of Philadelphia for Promoting American Manufactures, and as a behind-the-scene manipulator of the Committee of Inspection and Observation. He was an early and vitriolic fighter for independence. Timothy Matlack, Tom Paine, and Dr. Thomas Young were his closest friends. Wilson in 1776 had become one of Pennsylvania's leading lawyers. The Assembly had chosen him as a delegate to Congress. He opposed independence up to the moment he realized it was prudent to change his views if he wished to preserve his political future. Wilson matured within the political elite; Cannon matured outside of it.[56]

John Dickinson was Wilson's legal mentor. After a year of study in Dickinson's office, he was dispatched to Reading and there, equipped with the proper references and introductions, room was made for him in the already crowded ranks of Berks County lawyers. Friends in Philadelphia tried to see that the bright young man prospered. When Franklin's wife wanted a backcountry debt

---

[56] Charles Page Smith, *James Wilson—Founding Father* (Chapel Hill, N. C., 1956), argues that Wilson in his early years was a great democrat. I side with Merrill Jensen, who, reviewing Smith's book in *PMHB*, 80 (1956), 521–523, points out that "the difficulty with the picture of Wilson as a democrat is his career in Pennsylvania politics" (522).

collected, she was referred to Wilson. There were too many lawyers in Reading for Wilson to make his way, even with these assists from friends. He moved to Carlisle and there among fellow Scotsmen and the contentious Scotch–Irish his law business flourished. The substantial men of Cumberland County immediately accepted him as an equal. Soon he was in politics.[57].

Wilson's personal and professional life exemplify how neatly the political machine knit the fragmented backcountry into a tight unit. He married Rachel Bird, daughter of a Reading patriarch. He lived in Carlisle, practiced in York and Lancaster, and occasionally traveled to Philadelphia to argue a case before the Supreme Court. He was at home everywhere in the province. He knew all the substantial citizens in the backcountry. If Andrew Allen happened to ask who might be an able man for sheriff of, say, the newly created Bedford County, Wilson surely had a candidate to suggest whom Allen knew would be acceptable; this was the man the people usually found themselves electing, just as John Hughes' candidate Jonathan Roberts was the man Philadelphia County elected to the Assembly.

Pennsylvania's efficiently managed political machine gave a predictable element to the course of politics in the backcountry. Appointive offices went to moderate-minded men like Arthur St. Clair. Elective offices were subtly controlled. An unwanted man, like Sheriff Nagle, could be eased out of office, and a desired candidate like Jonathan Roberts could be skillfully advanced to office. The people cooperated in all this, for this was a time when voters accepted as one of the facts of life the leadership of the elite. The elite, after all, had the time and they were trained to run the colony's affairs and it seemed senseless to accept second-rate men. Thus, when in 1774 Committees of Inspection and Observation were being set up in the backcountry, it was Wilson's friends, the substantial, prosperous men, who served on them.

---

[57] See the readable account of a backcountry lawyer's life in Smith, *James Wilson*, 29–61.

When citizens formed their military Associations, it was Wilson's friends again who did the organizing and were elected as officers of the battalions. The men who had been running backcountry affairs for years still remained in control and the firebrands, if they existed, were held firmly in check. The results of the May election gave proof of that.

Politicians like Dickinson and Wilson knew that so long as the political machine continued to operated smoothly no one need fear that Pennsylvania would rush headlong into independence. The religious-cultural, historical, and economic patterns indicated no signs of mass discontent in the backcountry. The one major complaint—unequal representation—had been relieved. Any other grievances that remained could be contained by the political machine—if, that is, the machine continued in sound working order. But there were signs it might soon collapse, or be replaced by another machine. The Independents had captured control of Philadelphia's Committee of Inspection and Observation, the most powerful political organization in the province, aside from the Assembly. The city Committee had already challenged the old machine—in February, when it sent out a call for a convention—and it backed down only because it felt certain of winning the May election. The Independents had lost the election but not control of the Committee.

The threat from the city Committee was increased by a series of changes in the backcountry. Men who had long managed local affairs were being drawn from the scene. Wilson spent most of his time in Philadelphia, St. Clair had entered the army. Age and illness had removed some men, like Edward Biddle of Reading, from politics. Others, like Edward Shippen, Jr., and his brother Joseph, rather than fight the trend of events, had retired to private life. The shift in power was apparent on every Committee of Inspection and Observation in the backcountry. Zealous Independents like Robert Whitehill of Carlisle and James Smith of York were moving into politics for the first time. Along with these changes the enlisted men in the military battalions were being organized into Committees of Privates and these many separate committees were being welded into a single unit by James Cannon back in the city.

The signs indicated that the old political machine might soon be fighting for its life, but in May of 1776 there was still no great cause for pessimism. In 1775 Fithian had found the backcountry nearly unrestrained in its eagerness to see America declare its independence. Some villages mustered their able-bodied youth on the commons every morning at five to drill them in the arts of war. This sort of frenzied enthusiasm for war pervaded the backcountry that summer. The next year Fithian found on his tour that the people were much calmer. The fever had burned itself out. Why? Simply because such a high pitch cannot be long maintained. The fever must soon pass or the patient dies.[58] An exhausted backcountry found it hard in the spring of 1776 to work up much enthusiasm for independence.

The old machine had other reasons not to fear the future too much. The backcountry had no overwhelming economic problems. Perfect spring weather indicated the province would have one of the greatest harvests in its history. In the midst of this cheerful setting rumors of peace commissioners still went the rounds. The Wyoming Valley affair still boiled away; this might be sufficient to stem, for a while at least, anxiety for independence in the tier of northern counties—Northampton, Berks, and Northumberland —where bitterness against New Englandmen was highest.

And, finally, there still remained the powerful moderating effect of the frontier on the minds of men in the backcountry. When men move into isolated areas they strive to hold on to what little they can salvage from the past; they cling to the old, conventional way of doing things and experiment only when forced to. This

---

[58] The analogy is borrowed from Edwin Scott Gaustad, *The Great Awakening in New England* (New York, 1957), 62.

force alone might be enough to ward off any great upheaval.[59]

There were strong forces, then, working against change and the idea of independence in both the city and backcountry. But at least half the people in Philadelphia and probably an equal share in the counties were convinced, to judge by the May election returns, that there was merit in independence and much to be said for change. What shaped their ideas? What were the forces at work that counterbalanced the Moderates and won the Independents considerable public support?

---

[59] Too much attention has been given to the "radical" effects of frontier life on the minds of the people, and not enough to the conservative, or perhaps preservative is the word, effects. Leon Howard's study of the writings of Sally Hastings, a frontier lady, shows that "conventional modes of expression were probably maintained with a rigidity not found among equally sensitive people in a more civilized environment." (*English Literary History*, 7, 1940, 68–82.) What holds true for writing might well hold true for a frontiersman's political ideas. Louis B. Wright, *Culture on the Moving Frontier* (Bloomington, Ind., 1955), makes out a good case for the conservative effect the frontier had on men's ideas, though he overemphasizes the English influence it seems to me.

4 THE COUNTERBALANCE

Philadelphia, we have seen, was a fragmented society. Rarely did an event occur that overrode racial, religious, and economic differences and united the people to act as one. Two such events took place in May of 1775. The first was the return from England of Benjamin Franklin, whose arrival on May 6 "was announced by ringing of bells, to the great joy of the city."[1]

The city quickly regained its composure, only to lose it again four days later when the New England delegates rode into town for the opening of the second session of the Continental Congress. Philadelphia, filled with sympathy for beleaguered Boston, greeted them solemnly and "every mark of respect that could be was expressed." Thousands of citizens watched silently from the curbs as several miles of carriages and horsemen and soldiers with swords at salute position moved at a solemn pace through the streets, accompanied by the tolling of the muffled bells of Christ Church. "Philadelphia is wholly American," remarked a Tory, "strong friends to Congressional measures."[2]

The warmth of the moment was promptly dissipated when Congress went into secret session and lost its hold on the people. Occasionally it emerged with pretentious pronouncements which were dutifully printed in the papers. These could have had little

---

[1] George Atkinson Ward, ed., *The Journal and Letters of Samuel Curwen, An American in England, From 1775 to 1783* (4th edition, Boston, 1864), 28.
[2] *Ibid.*, 29, 30.

effect on a public that read little and understood less of the subtle revolution in constitutional relations that Congress was attempting to bring about with England. In the year past, when Congress had met in Carpenters' Hall, the delegates had given the city librarian there a busy time. The librarian told William Bradford, Jr., that "Vattel, Burlemagiu, Locke & Montesquie seem to be the standard to which they refer either when settling the rights of the Colonies or when a dispute arises on the Justice or propriety of a measure."[3] Such a body of high-minded lawyers and philosophers would have a hard time of it swaying the people of Pennsylvania.

Franklin, if he had wished, could have perhaps maintained the unity, the intensity of feeling in Philadelphia displayed on his return. He, if anyone, could have molded the opinions of that diverse population. If, within a few days of his return, he had announced he stood for independence, Philadelphia at that instant might have followed his lead. But such an "if" would require Franklin to act against his nature. He had never been a man to hurry a decision and now, at seventy, he was even less prone to haste. Nor was he anxious to find himself on the losing side. "Didst thee ever know Dr. Franklin to be in a minority?" a Quaker once asked rhetorically.[4]

So Franklin held his peace until he saw what was best for both America's and his own interests. The first month and a half of his return he kept to his home and went abroad only on public business. In Congress he kept completely silent.[5] The Moderates hoped he would use his influence to make Congress listen to reason. Rumor had it he was scheduled to return soon to London.[6] Franklin's long silence evoked gossip of another sort. The word was

---

[3] William Bradford, Jr., to James Madison, October 17, 1774, Bradford Letterbook, HSP.
[4] Quoted in William C. Bruce, *Benjamin Franklin, Self-Revealed* (2 vols., New York, 1917), II, 98n.
[5] Carl Van Doren, *Benjamin Franklin* (New York, World reprint edition, 1948), 529–30.
[6] Ward, *Curwen Journal*, 28.

whispered about the city that the delegates in Congress "begin to entertain a great Suspicion that Dr. Franklin came rather as a Spy than as a friend, & that he means to discover our weak side to make his peace with the ministers by discovering information with regard to affairs at home, but hitherto he has been silent on that head & in every respect behaved more like a spectator than a member."[7] These rumors had died by July of 1775, for by then Franklin had ended his silence. He had told his friend Joseph Galloway and his son William, governor of New Jersey, that he favored independence.[8] Bradford passed the reassuring news to James Madison: "The suspicions against Dr. Franklin have died away; whatever his design at coming over here, I believe he has now chosen his side, and favors our cause."[9]

But Franklin did little or nothing outside Congress to promote independence. He made no public speeches, wrote no articles for the papers. The people must decide the question without his help. Deprived of his leadership, the unity of Philadelphia in early May, 1775, evaporated. The city slipped back into routine habits. About the only constant sign to remind the city that America was at war was the groups of Associators to be seen drilling on the commons. Shiploads of immigrants from Northern Ireland and Scotland continued to arrive at the wharves along Front Street.[10] The shops were filled with goods. Prices remained steady.

As the months passed hope for reconciliation slowly began to wane among some of the people. Letters and essays in the newspapers indicate that the idea of independence was being nourished by news of the King's charge that the colonists were seeking independence, although they had insisted up to now that they sought

---
[7] William Bradford, Jr., to James Madison, June 2, 1775, Bradford Letterbook, HSP.
[8] Van Doren, *Franklin*, 527–28.
[9] William Bradford, Jr., to James Madison, July, 1775, Bradford Letterbook, HSP.
[10] See Marshall, Diary, for the later months of 1775 and in the Philadelphia newspapers note the arrival and departures of ships and advertisements for indentured servants.

only to protect their rights as Englishmen; by an act of Parliament removing the colonies from the Crown's protection, prohibiting trade with them, and permitting seizure of their ships at sea; and by persistent rumors that agents of the King were inciting slaves to revolt.

James Madison sent this last up to Philadelphia. "It is imagined our Governor has been tampering with the Slaves," he wrote, "& that he has it in his contemplation to make great Use of them in case of a civil war in this province." If the British did stoop to using slaves Madison feared Virginia would "fall like Achilles by the hand of one who knows that Secret."[11] At least one Negro among the two or three thousand in Philadelphia expected the British to make use of his race. This man had insulted a "gentlewoman" on the street one night and when she reprimanded him, according to the brief newspaper report, he answered: "Stay you d——d white bitch, till Lord Dunmore and his black regiment come, and then we will see who is to take the wall."[12]

The idea of independence was further nourished on January 9, 1776, when Tom Paine's anonymous pamphlet *Common Sense* appeared in the shop of Robert Bell, the publisher. Gentlemen who had gingerly talked of independence with trusted friends behind closed doors now found a reckless spirit blustering forth with the idea in print. Genteel minds reacted to it as to a piece of bawdy house pornography—they read it, fascinated, finished it in disgust. Sam Adams put it mildly when he said "it has fretted some folks here more than a little."[13]

This pamphlet sold so briskly that two weeks after publication Bell had a second printing on the bookstalls. Paine, meanwhile, had decided to make additions and revisions. Bell's eagerness to cash in on a best-seller before it was pirated peeved Paine, who

---

[11] James Madison to William Bradford, Jr., June 19, 1775, Bradford Letterbook, HSP.
[12] *Pennsylvania Evening Post*, December 14, 1775.
[13] Sam Adams to James Warren, January 10, *Warren-Adams Letters* (2 vols., Boston, 1917, 1925), I, 204.

loved mankind but found it hard to get along with people. In anger he turned publication rights over to William Bradford, Sr., then aired his grievances against Bell in a newspaper advertisement. Bell, in injured tones, answered "this noisy man."[14] Despite the fuss, or perhaps in part because of it, the pamphlet still sold so well by the end of the month that both publishers could afford half-page advertisements in the *Evening Post,* along with smaller ads in the city's four other papers.

If books can convince, this one did—or so it would seem. Dr. Benjamin Rush, without checking his fondness for hyperbole, said "it burst from the press," and "with an effect which has rarely been produced by types and paper in any age or country."[15] Evidence seems to support the doctor. Ten days after Bell had placed it in his bookstalls copies of *Common Sense* had reached Alexandria, Virginia, and were already making "a great noise."[16] Edmund Randolph said that "the public sentiment which a few weeks before had shuddered at the tremendous obstacles, with which independence was environed, overleaped every barrier." But at the same time he added that *Common Sense* only "put the torch to combustibles which had been deposited by the different gusts of fury. . . ."[17] Perhaps the pamphlet's effectiveness elsewhere in America should be distinguished from its influence in Pennsylvania. The combustibles present in Virginia, whose coasts had been bombarded and whose slaves might revolt at any moment, and in Massachusetts, which had been fighting the British for a half year, were certainly not present in Pennsylvania to the same degree. True, when *Common Sense* was translated into German in March, one report said that it "Works on the Minds of those People

---

[14] The heart of the Bradford-Bell-Paine dispute over publication rights to *Common Sense* appears in advertisements in the *Pennsylvania Evening Post* for January 23, 25, 27, and 30.

[15] Benjamin Rush to James Cheetham, July 17, 1809, Butterfield, *Rush Letters,* II, 1008.

[16] *Journal of Nicholas Cresswell,* 136.

[17] "Edmund Randolph's Essay on the Revolutionary History of Virginia, 1774–1782," *Virginia Magazine of History and Biography* 43 (1935), 306, 307.

amazingly."[18] And another gentleman was equally convinced that it "seems to gain ground with the common people." In fact, he went on, "this Idea of an Independence, tho sometime ago abhorred, may possibly by degrees become so familiar as to be cherished."[19] The influence of Paine's work in shaping or clarifying the minds of Pennsylvanians cannot, of course, be determined Obviously, it was not negligible, but in the light of the May election results it would be a mistake to exaggerate it.

Regardless of the effect of *Common Sense* on men's minds, events — or rather, rumors — soon abetted the pamphlet's aim. In mid-January gossip which was quickly scooped up and spread by the press began to drift into port with every inbound ship from Europe that the British contemplated sending mercenary troops to America, that these foreign troops had not only been hired to fight Englishmen in America, as all but the Germans in Pennsylvania regarded themselves, but had been offered bounties for every colonist killed or wounded. The day *Common Sense* appeared James Wilson moved that "Congress may expressly declare to their Constituents and the World their present Intentions respecting an Independency, observing that the Kings Speech directly charged Us with that Design." Wilson received such equally balanced support and opposition that his resolution got nowhere. But during the debate "Several Members said that if a Foreign Force shall be sent here, they are willing to declare the Colonies in a State of Independent Sovereignty."[20]

The possibility of a "Foreign Force" coming to America stirred up much talk about the need for a declaration of independence. "It is in every body's mouth as a thing absolutely necessary in Case foreign Troops should be landed, as if this Step alone would enable us to oppose them with Success," one extreme Moderate said. Men

---

[18] Edward Burd to James Burd, March 15, Shippen Papers, vol. 7, HSP.
[19] Edward Shippen to Jasper Yeates, January 19, Shippen Papers, vol. 7, HSP.
[20] "Diary of Richard Smith," January 9, *American Historical Review* 1 (1896), 307.

who recoiled from the arguments in *Common Sense* now began to give thought to the virtues of independence. "Whatever Objections we & thousands of others may have to . . . Independence," said another strong for reconciliation, "it appears to me, beyond a Doubt, that a public Declaration of it will be made as soon as it is fully ascertained that a large Army of Foreigners has been taken into British pay to be employed against the Colonies."[21]

Even one of the Allens — William — felt, as a friend remembered his words, that "if foreign troops were employed to reduce America to absolute submission, that independence or any other mode was justifiable."[22] If the rumors became fact, Great Britain clearly meant to fight the war to the end and not attempt reconciliation. But worse, it meant that she no longer meant to prosecute a gentlemanly war in which, once defeated, the obstreperous children would be mildly punished and then welcomed back to the family. Nor could those unfriendly to the war expect to sit it out and be well treated after it ended, for the use of foreign troops, in their minds, meant America would be indiscriminately ravaged by soldiers who made it their business to profit from war. Homes would be looted and towns plundered and the property of no man, regardless of his political convictions, would be safe. Such, it would seem, were the thoughts of many men of property. These men were convinced the mercenaries would not be able to distinguish "betwixt friends and foes" and that "foreign avarice and rapacity would not be glutted [even] with the indiscriminate spoils of both."[23] Clearly, Great Britain's plan to use foreign troops, influenced many on the need for independence. Arthur St. Clair was convinced that "many worthy men would not have wished to go as

---

[21] Edward Shippen to Jasper Yeates, January 19, Shippen Papers, vol. 7, HSP; Joseph Shippen to Edward Shippen, May 11, quoted in J. Paul Selsam, *Pennsylvania Constitution of 1776* (Philadelphia, 1936), 105, from the Shippen Papers, 1727–83, Library of Congress.
[22] Arthur St. Clair to William Allen, September 1, Smith, *St. Clair Papers*, I, 375.
[23] *Ibid.*, I, 376.

they have done," except that when the rumor of mercenaries became fact "that fatal proceeding has cast the die."[24] The coming of foreign troops was still in the rumor stage the day of the May election. Documents substantiating the rumors as true arrived in late May.[25] If they had reached Philadelphia three weeks earlier the results of the May election might well have been quite different.

The past is often pictured in terms of people resolutely facing the great problems of their times. Epochal events like the appearance of *Common Sense,* the issue of foreign troops, the decision of the Assembly, of Congress, and of the Committee of Inspection and Observation are usually considered sufficient to explain why Americans slowly swung over to independence. The minds of many were doubtless shaped by these events and decisions. But it is often forgotten that in times of crisis, when great decisions are in the making, even so-called "thinking people" remain deeply involved with the minutiae of life. Young Bradford worried less when the Independents were defeated than when he "indulged in bed till almost 8" or when he stole time from his law books and had to admit "this has been an idle day: . . . played billiards & drank Tea."[26] The war surely became a petty affair for Mrs. Jasper Yeates after a friend had "dropt a hint . . . that the former Inhabitants of your House left it well stocked with a disagreeable Animal called a bug."[27] Mrs. Christopher Marshall's thoughts centered on her husband's well-being, on her garden, on getting to market before the best cuts of meat had gone, and on inhibiting the habits of her servant Polly, "who had taken to running away with men."[28]

Only when war begins to impinge on daily concerns are pam-

---

[24] *Ibid.,* I, 376.
[25] The rumors became fact for most people by May 15 and for all on May 24 when both the *Pennsylvania Journal* and the *Gazette* published two-paged supplements of the treaties with German princes for troops.
[26] Bradford, Register, May 24, 30.
[27] Edward Shippen to Jasper Yeates, June 5, Dreer Collection, HSP.
[28] Marshall, Diary, April, May, and June, *passim.*

phlets and the decisions of politicians effective. By the spring of 1776 the war had begun to cut through and reshape old habits and daily routines. May, for instance, had once been a gay month for the city. The horse races held at Centre Square — George Washington had enjoyed them enough to travel up from Virginia to attend[29] — had been cancelled for the duration, and so, too, had the annual mid-May fair.

Not too long ago Jacob Duché, sitting in a room overlooking the Delaware, described the scene from his window for an English friend: "Whilst I am writing this, three topsail vessels, wafted along by a gentle southern breeze, are passing by my window. The voice of industry perpetually resounds along the shore; and every wharf within my view is surrounded with groves of masts, and heaped with commodities of every kind, from almost every quarter of the globe."[30] In mid-1776 the British blockade of Delaware Bay had not stopped the traffic of river boats plying between the Pennsylvania–Jersey shores and up and down the Bay, but the sight of the majestic topsails of vessels gliding in from every quarter of the globe was gone. The wharves were no longer heaped with goods from Europe and the West Indies. The thick groves of masts remained, only now the masts were unrigged.

Signs of war cropped up everywhere. Bookstores advertised among their best sellers such tracts as *Simes's Military Guide,* designed to instruct the erstwhile civilian how to prepare for army life.[31] Members of the Free Masons, either preoccupied with war duties or fearful of public censuring, no longer gathered for convivial lodge meetings.[32] After electing a new set of officers in

---

[29] Allen, Diary, *PMHB* 9 (1885), 180.
[30] [Duché], *Observations,* 3–4. The above quote comes from a letter written in 1771.
[31] See advertisement in *Pennsylvania Gazette,* May 15.
[32] Norris S. Barratt and Julius F. Sachse, eds., *Freemasonry in Pennsylvania, 1727–1907* (2 vols., Philadelphia, 1908), I, 208, say no meetings appear to have been held between February 14 and October 15, 1776 of Lodge Number Two in Philadelphia.

January, the American Philosophical Society had ceased to hold official meetings.[33]

A man out for a relaxing evening at the theater could escape neither the war nor talk of independence. The Southwark Theater still operated but now on the boards, in lieu of a polished Sheridan comedy, was *The Fall of Tyranny or American Liberty Proclaimed,* an awkward five-act production filled with twenty-six scenes—among them "a pleasing scene, a droll scene, a very bleak scene, a patriotic scene." The play was advertised as "a truly dramatic Performance, interspersed with wit, humour, burlesque, and serious Matter."[34] The audience supposedly left the theater with these words ringing in their ears:

> Are we not men? Pray, who made men, but God?
> Yet men made kings—to tremble at their nod!
> What nonsense this! let's wrong with right oppose
> Since naught will do but sound, impartial blows.
> Let's act in earnest, not with vain pretense;
> Adopt the language of sound COMMON SENSE,
> And with one voice proclaim—INDEPENDENCE![35]

Occasionally newspaper advertisements indicated that the war had left some things untouched. Dr. L. Butte, Surgeon-Dentist, continued to remind the public that he "cleans teeth, however bad, so radically, that in half an hour they look as white as snow; and has tooth drops which cureth the toothache in a few minutes. Also a plaister which cures corns in the toes in twenty-four hours."[36] Maredant's anti-scorbutic drops—they cured scurvy, struma, sistules, piles, ulcers "and by purifying the blood, prevent malignant humours of every kind from being thrown upon the lungs"—were

---

[33] *Proceedings of the American Philosophical Society: Minutes 1743–1838* (Philadelphia, 1884), 98. After listing the new officers the printed version of the Minutes reports: "Many blank pages follow."

[34] Advertisement in the *Pennsylvania Gazette,* June 19.

[35] Quoted in Moses Coit Tyler, *The Literary History of the American Revolution* (2 vols. New York, 1897), II, 207. Tyler gives a full discussion of the play, II, 198–207.

[36] *Pennsylvania Evening Post,* May 30.

still being prepared by Mr. Norton, Surgeon, and he had a testimonial to prove their miraculous powers:

> I was afflicted with a most shocking leprosy, attended with violent rheumatic pains, so that my life was quite miserable; I tried everything that could be thought of for my relief in vain. I am now perfectly cured by the use of Maredant's drops, as my neighbors can testify, who knew the shocking condition I was in.[37]

The cheering news in these advertisements ran against the general trend. The stream of immigrants that had continued into early 1776 had now stopped, thanks in part at least to the two men-of-war stationed at the mouth of the Bay. Until the warships appeared the papers had been filled with advertisements spreading the virtues of indentured servants to be had at reasonable prices. By May the standard advertisement went like this:

EIGHT DOLLARS REWARD

Run away from the subscriber . . . an indented servant lad, named *James Hannach*.

FOUR DOLLARS REWARD

Runaway . . . a German servant BOY, named George Ferver.[38]

Indentured servants were taking full advantage of the war and quietly, effectively working a great change on the city. Labor was already in short demand and as servants began to disappear into the army the problem became more severe. Now when a good worker or a volunteer for the army turned up the usual probing questions were often overlooked. The standard greeting of the West of a later America — "What name you travelin' under, stranger?" — would have been appropriate for Philadelphia in 1776.

Congress inadvertently became entangled in Philadelphia's social problems. In late January a petition "was produced from the Debtors in Philad. Goal [sic] praying that the several Colony Assemblies may be directed to devise Methods to free all Prisoners

---

[37] *Pennsylvania Gazette*, June 26.
[38] *Ibid.*, May 15

for Debt[.] this Petition was not read the President thinking it coram non Judice."[39] A few days later a disturbed Congress passed and ordered published a report against "Apprentices, small Debtors and Infants inlisting." Thomas McKean tried to get the report reconsidered but failed.[40] The good intentions of Congress achieved little. In February the shipwrights of Philadelphia pleaded with Congress "to stop their Servants and Apprentices whom they cannot hinder from going on the Expedition tomorrow to N York...."[41] Again Congress dutifully passed a resolve telling the servants and apprentices to stop running away.

Persifor Frazer held a sour view of these lofty resolves, to him empty gestures that did nothing to retrieve his runaway servant. Frazer entered the army with divided feelings. He was equally anxious to find his departed servant Jacob Down as to defeat the British. "I always expected to see him in the army," Frazer wrote, "and there has been scarce a guard, Company or Battalion collected on this ground but I have had my Eyes employ'd looking out for him." Perseverance paid off. At Ticonderoga Frazer "espy'd Jacob Down that ran away from Us." Jacob played dumb when caught. "I laid hold of him, ask'd him if he knew me, he deny'd he had ever seen me, when I told him my name, after a considerable time he thought proper to recollect me."[42] After a couple of days haggling with Jacob's captain, the army agreed to pay Frazer fifty-one dollars for his servant. It was one of those rare bargains that satisfied all parties. Frazer got "abt the sume he Cost me." The army for a reasonable price held on to a soldier. Jacob had his freedom and had earned for his progeny the right to become members of the Daughters—or Sons—of the American Revolution.

---

[39] " Diary of Richard Smith," January 27, *American Historical Review*, 1 (1896), 496.
[40] *Ibid.*, January 30 and 31, 497, 498.
[41] *Ibid.*, February 14, 502.
[42] " Some Extracts from the Papers of General Persifor Frazer Paper," *PMHB* 31 (1907), 113–14.

By early spring in 1776 the counterbalancing forces had stirred up enough discontent to make the idea of independence look attractive to quite a few people in Pennsylvania. *Common Sense* had convinced many. Social changes fomented by the war had adjusted others to the idea of a complete change. The continued denouncement of the colonies by King and Parliament, the persistent rumors of foreign troops had decided still others.

These counterbalancing forces still lacked the power to unite Pennsylvania's fragmented society, both in the city and in the backcountry, and create a mass demand for independence. The May election had proved that. Much of the discontent had been contained, quieted, or cancelled out by Cato's answers to *Common Sense*, by the continued rumors of peace commissioners en route with acceptable proposals, by the lack of sharp discontent in the backcountry and the presence of general prosperity in the city. All this left the people uneasy and confused but not yet sold on the glories of independence.

The city's Committee of Inspection and Observation deliberately set out to exploit the people's confusion and uneasiness when, with the suddenness of an explosion, it turned on its supposed ally, the Assembly, and voted to call a provincial convention. What drove the Committee to this action? Sixty-eight of the hundred men on the 1776 Committee had served on the 1775 Committee. Why were these citizens, so docile in 1775, suddenly moved to bold action in February, 1776?

Innocence may to some extent account for the Committee's action. In December, 1774, the Committee, then under John Dickinson's leadership, had sent out a call for a provincial convention in order that "the Sense of the Province may be obtained." With equally commendable vagueness the new Committee had called for a convention to take into "consideration the present state of the province."[43] Many new members may not have realized

---

[43] *Pennsylvania Gazette,* December 28, 1774; *Pennsylvania Evening Post,* March 2,

that in 1774–75 gentlemen controlled Pennsylvania politics and any convention was certain to travel along a safe and moderate route; in 1776 the gentlemen were notably out of control on the city Committee. Considerably more than half of the Committee members were in politics for the first time. Many of these men perhaps voted cheerfully for a convention without realizing they were, in effect, sanctioning an overturn in government.

Innocence, in an age known for the lack of it, hardly accounts for the Committee's rash action. A glance at the membership may give more light. Shopkeepers, artisans, and merchants predominated on the Committee — men like Nathan Brown, a blacksmith; Sharpe Delaney, a druggist; Christopher Ludwig, a German baker; John Bayard, Francis Gurney, Charles Massey, and Jonathan B. Smith, all merchants. In age these men averaged out in their late thirties and early forties.[44] They were in their prime, still on the way up but at a point in life where they had begun to prosper. Suddenly, in 1776 the work of a lifetime began to disintegrate. The war by February had reduced trade from Europe and the West Indies to driblets. Servants and apprentices began to vanish into the army. The loss of a servant might irritate a wealthy man, but only as a minor inconvenience. The loss of a trained apprentice struck a printer, a druggist, a blacksmith as a disaster.

More than economic pressure swung these men to independence. Their view of the future conditioned their actions. This more than anything emboldened these essentially moderate-minded men to risk that "leap in the dark" — a declaration of independence. This set them apart from the lawyers and wealthy merchants, who were conspicuously absent in any force from the Committee. The lawyer looks at the future through the eyes of the past. He is trained to look backward, to settle the affairs of the present by rules garnered from the past. The future distresses him only when it appears

[44] These remarks are based on a study of eighty-two of the Committee's hundred members. It is difficult to draw precise conclusions about the political ideas of the members, when they swung to independence and why, for information on most of these little-known men is, at best, brief.

about to veer from the old track; he works only to set it back on that track, not a new one. The successful businessman lacks the lawyer's affection for the past. He views the future in terms of the present. He has too much investment in the present to welcome any swift, radical changes. Wealth insulates him from shocks that afflict less prosperous colleagues, and thus he is slow to find the present intolerable. The young businessman still on his way up attends little to the present, less to the past. He lives with hope for a bright future. The slightest blemish on that future agitates him. At the same time he feels distress quicker and looks about more promptly for ways to relieve it. Deprived of a heavy investment in the present, he hesitates less to gamble on a brighter future.

Certainly not all shopkeepers and artisans in Philadelphia favored independence in February of 1776. But nearly all the thirty-two new members elected to the Committee did. When Charles Thomson, Thomas Wharton, Jr., and Robert Morris— three who would have had a moderating influence on any decisions—decided not to stand for re-election, their places were taken by men like the high-spirited Benjamin Rush—"prudence is a *rascally virtue*," he once said[45]—and Samuel Simpson, chairman of the Committee of Privates, warm for independence, and known to some about the city as "a drunken shoemaker."[46]

It was no accident that mainly Independents filled the vacant seats. The February election had been carefully planned. On January 20, nearly a month before the election, Christopher Marshall reports he met "a few friends to America at fountain Tavern in chestnut Street in order to Consult & Consider of proper persons to be Elected. . . ."[47] On February 7 Marshall and James Cannon went together to another caucus meeting, this time at Joseph Stiles's schoolroom. At the final caucus a week later, just

---

[45] Benjamin Rush to Horatio Gates, June 12, 1781, Butterfield, *Rush Letters*, I, 264.
[46] "Extracts from the Diary of Dr. James Clitherall, 1776," *PMHB*, 22 (1898), 471.
[47] Marshall, Diary, January 20.

two days before the election, a ticket was finally settled on. Now, a caucus to select candidates was nothing new in Philadelphia politics.[48] In the past gentlemen had called these meetings and decided whom to put up for office. They no longer did. The new inner circle comprised such men as Joseph Stiles, William Davidson, John Wilkins, Samuel Simpson, William Adcock, William Thorne, Andrew Epley, John Chaloner, James Langley, and a number of others about whom little or nothing is known. None of these men had been previously active in politics; none either during the Revolution or later became prominent in public affairs.

Clearly, a new political machine was being built in Philadelphia with new men at the controls. The key men behind this new machine were James Cannon, Christopher Marshall, Timothy Matlack, Tom Paine, Benjamin Rush, and Thomas Young. They were an odd assortment—two doctors, a journalist, a college teacher, a retired druggist, a retailer in bottled beer. Their ages varied from thirty-one (Rush) to sixty-five (Marshall), though the spread was less among the other four (Cannon was thirty-six, Paine thirty-nine, Young forty-four, and Matlack forty-six). Two came from Quaker backgrounds, two were Presbyterians, and two were, or soon would be, deists.

A unity of sorts emerges from this diversity. All six were intelligent and, except possibly Marshall, extremely able. None were men of great property. The six, for the time being, got along well with each other, quite an achievement for six men with warm tempers and quick to take offense. Rush had been one of Paine's earliest friends in Philadelphia, had chosen the title for *Common Sense,* and had helped find a publisher for the pamphlet. Cannon, Young, and Marshall were constant companions. A day seldom passed that they did not meet for afternoon coffee, for dinner, or for an evening of political talk. Rush, as late as July, still thought

---

[48] See the article signed A Brother Chip, *Pennsylvania Gazette,* September 27, 1770, wherein the complaint is raised that the workingmen and shopkeepers do not have a say in nominating men for the party tickets.

highly enough of Cannon and Matlack that when a new Council of Safety was elected, he wrote: "A majority of them are *good* men. Cannon and Matlack are among them! ! !"[49]

"The craving to change the world," it has been said, "is perhaps a reflection of the craving to change ourselves. The sick in soul insist that it is humanity that is sick, and they are the surgeons to operate on it."[50] The aphorism seems to apply to these six men. All, in varying degrees, had reason to be discontent with themselves and with the way the world had treated them. Marshall, for instance, did not get along well with his sons or their wives. He carefully noted in his diary what he considered examples of their ill-treatment in order, he said, that posterity might know what thankless offspring he had reared. Also, Marshall was a devout man denied spiritual nourishment. He had been disowned from Quaker meeting years earlier for associating with counterfeiters.[51]

Timothy Matlack was the son of a hapless merchant who died bankrupt and severely criticized by his Quaker meeting. When he was twenty-six Matlack rounded up enough money to open a hardware store. Cockfights, bull baits, and horse racing intrigued him more than business. By 1765 he was both bankrupt and disowned from meeting for "frequenting company in such manner as to neglect business whereby he contracted debts, failed and was unable to satisfy the claims of his creditors."[52] Matlack was never allowed to forget that Friends had bailed him out of debtor's prison. One day while on his way to battalion drill in his uniform, a sword swinging at his side, a Quaker of his acquaintance stopped him and said:

---
[49] Benjamin Rush to his wife, July 23, Butterfield, *Rush Letters*, I, 106.
[50] Eric Hoffer, *The Passionate State of Mind* (New York, 1955), 66, 68.
[51] According to the Minutes of the Philadelphia Monthly Meeting, Marshall had "spent much time and pains in attempting the Transmutation of Metals." He was found innocent of the "grosser parts of the accusation," but, as Tolles puts it, "disowned for having given cause for reproach to be cast upon the Society of Friends." Tolles, *Meeting House and Counting House*, 79–80.
[52] From the Minutes of the Philadelphia Monthly Meeting, quoted in A. M. Stackhouse, *Col. Timothy Matlack — Patriot and Soldier* (Privately printed, 1910), 6.

"Where art thou hurrying so fast with this thing dangling by thy side?"

Matlack said: "I am going to fight for my property and my liberty."

The Quaker said: "As for thy property thou hast none—and as for thy liberty, thou owest that to the clemency of thy creditors, me amongst the rest."[53]

A second business venture, this time selling bottled beer, appears to have succeeded sufficiently to keep his family alive. In 1775 Congress appointed him clerk to Charles Thomson, the Secretary. By this time he was deeply involved with the independence movement, which, understandably, he viewed as an opportunity to sweep the old guard from power in order to put in power new men with fresh visions.

Benjamin Rush had not received much better treatment than Matlack from Philadelphia. He returned from studying medicine at Edinburgh to find none of the city physicians willing to help him get started. In those first years of practice not "one of my brethren ever sent a patient to me," he said in later life, "and yet several of them had more applications daily than they were able to attend to."[54] In 1772 he published an anti-slavery pamphlet and for his efforts received "the most virulent attack that ever was made upon me."[55] Though his youth was hardly behind him he was sensitive to the fact that "by the persons who called themselves great in the city, I was at this time neglected or unknown."[56]

Neither Paine nor Young could blame their troubles on Philadelphia. Paine reached Philadelphia in 1774, a wrecked marriage and a string of failures behind him.[57] Young arrived about the

---

[53] *Ibid.*, 23.
[54] Corner, *Rush Autobiography*, 81–82.
[55] Benjamin Rush to Noah Webster, December 29, 1789, Butterfield, *Rush Letters*, I, 529.
[56] Corner, *Rush Autobiography*, 85.
[57] The best sketch of Paine is Crane Brinton's in the *Dictionary of American Biography*. The best biography is Alfred Owens Aldridge, *Man of Reason* (Philadelphia, 1959).

same time, by way of Albany, Boston, and Newport. Public pressure had encouraged his departure from each town. In Albany he had been involved in the Stamp Act fight. In Boston he became a good friend of Sam Adams, a member of the first Committee of Correspondence, and a participant in the Boston Tea Party.[58] No patriot of the day could equal his long and devoted fight for independence. He was remembered for years in Boston as "a Firebrand, an Incendiary, an eternal Fisher in Troubled Waters . . . a Scourge, a Pestilence, a Judgment."[59] He was condemned not only for his politics but for his deism. He was, said one, a man who had rebelled not only "against his Sovereign, but against *his God;* — he makes a mock at the merits of his Redeemer, and uses his God only *to swear by.*"[60]

James Cannon, probably the ablest of these six, made less noise than any. He lived for eleven years in Philadelphia quietly teaching school, not once creating a public stir. For eleven years he watched James Wilson rise while he remained at the same job, slowly accumulating a bitter feeling toward the world around him. With the outbreak of war his ambition and energy began to find outlets. When "The United Company of Philadelphia for Promoting American Manufactures" was organized, Cannon became the Secretary. He helped to organize the first battalions of Associators in the city. The Committee of Privates seems to have been his creation. Once organized he had himself appointed the Committee's Secretary. Cannon never ran for public office, as if fearful of the abuse he might meet. He remained until July the organizing genius behind the scenes.[61]

---

[58] Henry H. Edes, "Memoir of Dr. Thomas Young, 1731-1777," *Publications of the Colonial Society of Massachusetts,* 11, (Boston, 1910), 2-54.

[59] John Adams to Benjamin Rush, February 8, 1789, *Old Family Letters: Copied from the Originals for Alexander Biddle* (Philadelphia, 1892), 30.

[60] Dr. Thomas Bolton on Young, in a speech in Boston in 1775; in Edes, "Memoir of Dr. Young," 29.

[61] Except for William H. Egle's brief and almost useless sketch of Cannon in *PMHB* 3 (1880), 198-199, I have found nothing written about Cannon. The *Dictionary of American Biography* ignores him.

None of these six men believed he had yet found his place in the world. Each believed his talents were going to waste, unrecognized by society. Each detested the present and found happiness only in the future — "when freedom shall prevail without licentiousness, government without tyranny, and religion without superstition, bigotry, or enthusiasm. Oh happy days!"[62] Out of the depths of their frustration and faith in the future emerged their passionate attachment to independence. And out of their innocence developed their common belief that this perfect world would come quickly, instantly once evil had been crushed. The leaders of a mass movement "must be wholly ignorant of the difficulties involved in their vast undertaking. Experience is a handicap."[63] Again these six filled the bill. None had ever been in politics. Three — Cannon, Paine, and Young — were still not in politics officially, for none were members of the city Committee nor held any public elective office. Marshall had been on the Committee since 1774, Matlack since August, 1775, and Rush only since February, 1776.

Ignorance of the obstacles kept them from despair. Wiser men could have told them how little new their better world would be. But wise men often do not make history. By May of 1776 these innocent six had laid a solid foundation for a political machine to oppose the old guard's control of Pennsylvania politics. Rush and Marshall, with Matlack leading, worked within the city Committee. Usually at least a third of the hundred members and often half were absent from the weekly Tuesday-evening meetings of the Committee, held at the American Philosophical Society's hall. Matlack, Rush, and Marshall were invariably present, constantly prodding less dedicated members to bolder action.

Cannon, meanwhile, had developed a way to shape opinion in the backcountry. In early February, when there was much dissatisfaction about the articles for the military Associations drawn up by the Assembly, he had suggested that the Committee of Privates

---

[62] Benjamin Rush to his wife, May 29, Butterfield, *Rush Letters*, I, 99.
[63] Eric Hoffer, *The True Believer* (New York, 1951), 11.

create a Committee of Correspondence which "would gladly enter into a friendly correspondence with the privates of those battalions throughout the province which sign the articles, that they may know the sense of the Associators in general on any part of the articles . . . and that any future application to the Honorable House of Assembly may express the desires of the whole body of Associators."[64] The gentlemen's control of the backcountry was about to be circumvented for the first time. Cannon had found a way of exploiting in every town and village in the backcountry an uneasiness which up to now had been nicely contained. And he would deal with just the men who would have plenty to complain about — young enlisted men who would be finding the restraints of army life an unpleasant experience, to put it mildly.

The city Independents by now had picked up two men to help them win over the backcountry — James Smith of York and Robert Whitehill of Carlisle. Smith was a man of wit and seemingly easy-going temperament. He was fifty-seven years old. He had been admitted to the bar in 1745, spent five years in Cumberland County trying to work up a practice with no luck, then returned to York. The lack of clients turned him to iron manufacturing in 1771; he had lost five thousand pounds in business by 1776.[65] Whitehill, a native of Cumberland County, was thirty-eight. He, like Smith, had studied under Francis Alison, but seems to have remained a farmer. He saw the world in blacks and whites and was a hard man to turn. "Even were an angel from Heaven sent with proper arguments to convince him of his error," said Robert Morris, "it would make no alteration with him."[66] These two men neatly complemented in temperament and discontent with the present the Independent leaders in the city. They held the same

---

[64] Open letter " to the Privates of the Military Association . . ." signed by James Cannon, in the *Pennsylvania Evening Post*, February 1.
[65] James H. Peeling, article on Smith in *Dictionary of American Biography*.
[66] Mathew Carey, *Debates . . . on Annulling . . . the Charter of the Bank* (1786), quoted in James H. Peeling's article on Whitehill in the *Dictionary of American Biography*.

faith in the future, the same dislike of the present, and the same ignorance of politics.

The Independents lost their battle in the May election to control the Assembly partly because the Moderates' machine was still too strong, partly because the people were not ready for any abrupt change. "The leader," it has been said, "cannot create the conditions which make the rise of a movement possible."[67] The equal strength of the Moderates and Independents left both the city and the backcountry suspended in delicate balance in early May, and no amount of behind-the-scenes manipulating by the politicians of either side seemed able to swing the balance to one side or the other. Only some event that touched the lives of all the people would do the trick. Sam Adams saw this and mentioned it the day before the May election, as if sensing that the Independents were going to lose. "We cannot make Events," he wrote. "Our business is wisely to improve them. . . . Mankind are governed more by their feelings than by reason. Events which excite those feelings will produce wonderful Effects. . . . The burning of Norfolk & the Hostilities committed in North Carolina have kindled the resentment of our Southern Brethren who once thought their Eastern Friends hot headed and rash. . . . There is a reason that wd induce one even to wish for the speedy arrival of the British Troops that are expected at the Southward. I think our friends are well prepared for them, & one Battle would do more towards a Declaration of Independencey than a long chain of conclusive Arguments in a provincial Convention or the Continental Congress."[68]

Obviously, by the time of the May election the event that would shape the people's minds had not occurred. When they stepped up to vote they remained puzzled and undecided about this idea of independence. Things had not changed too much from the day

---

[67] Hoffer, *True Believer*, 109.
[68] Sam Adams to Samuel Cooper, April 30, Harry A. Cushing, ed., *The Writings of Samuel Adams* (4 vols., New York, 1904–1908), III, 284–85.

late in 1775 when a confused young lady wrote a letter to the editor of the *Evening Post*:[69]

Dear Mr. Towne,

I am a young lady, who delights much in politics; and, if I know my own heart, am a warm friend to America. But my misfortune is, that some times, whilst I am contending for what I think is true liberty, I am told that I am a Tory; and perhaps the next day, expressing the same sentiments, that I am an outrageous Whig. As there are many of my acquaintance labouring under the same inconvenience I should be glad any of your correspondents would favor me with a clear definition of the above characters, that I may conduct my conversation in future, as becomes

A REASONABLE WHIGESS

Even "thinking people" remained confused in the spring of 1776. Joseph Reed, usually of a clear mind on public affairs and among the first and warmest supporters of American rights, spoke the sentiments of the city when he told a friend: "like many others, I am waiting to see how the chapter of accidents will turn out. . . ."[70] Reed went on in his letter to mention that the two ships at the mouth of the Bay had caused some uneasiness. Many people had packed up and left the city, "but the alarm is not so great as I should have expected." He spoke of the "terrible wordy war waging on the subject of independence" in the newspapers—the Cato-Cassandra-Forester battles—but added that "the city seems desirous they should all have fair play." Tolerance still pervaded the air. Papers continued to print both sides of the controversy, and so long as the city's sense of fair play persisted Philadelphia would remain outside the war emotionally and unprepared for independence. "I never felt so much puzzled how to act," Reed continued. "I am perplexed with the scene of which

---

[69] *Pennsylvania Evening Post*, November 16, 1775.
[70] Joseph Reed to Charles Pettit, March 30, Reed, *Life*, I. 182.

one can yet see so little. I think a little time must give us more light."

Clearly, events and not politicians alone would settle the people's minds. But the politicians could wisely improve upon the events, and that is what John and Sam Adams prepared to do.

5   AN EPOCHA

John Adams could never accommodate himself to man's perversity. He never, for instance, could calmly accept the fact that the age he had tried so hard to shape came to be called the Age of Reason, after the book by that "disastrous meteor" Tom Paine.[1]

"I am willing you should call this the Age of Frivolity as you do," he wrote at an unmellowed seventy-one, "and would not object if you had named it the age of Folly, Vice, Frenzy, Fury, Brutality, Daemons, Buonaparte, Tom Paine, or the Age of the burning Brand from the bottomless Pitt: or any thing but the Age of Reason. I know not whether any Man in the World has had more influence on its inhabitants or affairs for the last thirty years than Tom Paine. There can be no severer Satyr on the Age. For such a mongrel between Pigg and Puppy, begotten by a wild Boar on a Bitch Wolf, never before in any Age of the World was suffered by the Poltroonery of mankind, to run through such a Career of Mischief. Call it then the Age of Paine."[2]

Adams' contempt for Paine's ideas did not emerge late in life. It appeared in full fury in 1776 when he first met up with Paine's thoughts in *Common Sense*. He had liked the arguments for independence in that pamphlet, but found in the remarks on government "some whims, some sophisms, some artful addresses to superstitious notions, some keen attempts upon the passions. . . ."[3]

---

[1] Charles Francis Adams, ed., *The Life and Works of John Adams* (10 vols., Boston, 1850–1856), II, 507.
[2] Worthington Chauncey Ford, ed., *Statesman and Friend — Correspondence of John Adams with Benjamin Waterhouse, 1784–1822* (Boston, 1927), 31.
[3] John Adams to his wife Abigail, March 19, Adams, *Familiar Letters*, 146.

What Adams held most against Paine were his "absurd democratical notions." This was the essential, most disastrous ingredient in an age that was to be so painful to him. Paine wanted all property qualifications for voting ended. Also, he favored a government designed to be promptly responsive to the will of the people, one with a single, supreme legislature, unchecked by a cautious upper house, or by a strong executive or judiciary. "'Common sense,' by his crude ignorant Notion of a Government by one Assembly," said Adams in the spring of 1776, "will do more Mischief, in dividing the Friends of Liberty, than all the Tory Writings together. He is a keen Writer but very ignorant of the Science of Government."[4]

It is clear—without attempting at the moment to note further ingredients—that John Adams claimed no credit for shaping the era he called the Age of Paine. It is equally clear that Adams helped shape the age more than he was willing to admit or able to see. Out of a brief, uneasy alliance with the Philadelphia Independents in 1776 John Adams became, so to speak, the unwilling midwife at the birth of the Age of Paine—at least, its birth to political power in Pennsylvania.

John Adams' role in Philadelphia politics can be exaggerated, mainly through his own doing. For instance, when the city Committee forced the Assembly to enlarge its membership, he tells of a rumor floating about the city that John Adams had master-minded these pressure tactics. "I am flattered with it," he writes. ". . . I am inclined to hope, that a small Portion of this Merit is due to me."[5] He does not add that an equal, if not larger, portion of merit was due to his cousin Sam Adams. Between the Committee election and the vote for a convention Christopher Marshall stepped up the pace of his occasional visits to the "brace" of Adamses. On February 17, 20, 24, and 26 he stopped by the lodgings of Sam

---

[4] John Adams to James Warren, May 12, *Warren-Adams Letters*, I, 243.
[5] John Adams to James Warren, March 21, *Warren-Adams Letters*, I, 213, 214.

and John. Clearly, he came to discuss with Sam, one of the ablest politicians in the country, ways to maneuver the convention resolution through the Committee. Sam Adams and Marshall were good friends. They were about the same age and both viewed the war as a religious crusade. Marshall often stopped off by Sam's rooms to drop such tracts as George Stonehouse's *Universal Restitution* and *Universal Restitution Further Defended*.[6] The two saw eye to eye on everything. One day when Marshall heard that a ball was being planned in Mrs. Washington's honor, he hurried to the State House and had the doorkeeper call out Sam Adams. Sam saw at once the impropriety of such gaiety in these "melancholy times" and used his influence to have the ball cancelled.[7] Sam's advice and experience would be even more useful in helping the city Independents, for the problems they faced in Philadelphia were similar to those Adams had confronted and surmounted in Boston. An added certainty that Sam's advice and techniques would be used was that Dr. Thomas Young, one of his right-hand assistants in Boston, was among the leaders of the city Independents. Sam Adams' hidden hand—hidden because only oblique references remain to indicate his part—was probably involved in every decision made by the city Committee between February and July of 1776. If John's role looms disproportionally large, it is only because he left plenty of "tracks" behind that make it easier to reconstruct his part in affairs.

From the day in May, 1775, when Congress gathered in Philadelphia for its second session both John and Sam Adams were determined to guide America toward a declaration of independence. By May of 1776 the project had not made much headway, but by then John had devised a precise, three-part plan to lead the country toward the goal.[8] The first step was to get each of

---

[6] Marshall, Diary, March 18, 1775.
[7] *Ibid.* November 24, 1775
[8] John Adams mentions this three-part plan several times in letters of this period. See his letters to John Winthrop, May 12, *Massachusetts Historical Society Collections* (hereafter *MHSC*), Series 5, vol. 4, 301–302; to James

the thirteen colonies to establish its own government, free from all royal control and influence. "I have reasons to believe," he said, "that no colony, which shall assume a government under the people, will give it up. There is something very unnatural and odious in a government a thousand leagues off. A whole government of our own choice, managed by persons whom we love, revere, and can confide in, has charms in it for which men will fight."[9] Once royal influence had been swept aside, he saw America ready for the second step of his plan — colonial confederation. That done, the colonies would then be strong enough to openly declare their independence — the final step in his plan.

This was the strategy. The tactics were more involved. They concentrated on Pennsylvania, America's economic "keystone," or, to use Robert Morris' analogy, "what the heart is to the human body in circulating the blood."[10] America could not move toward independence until the leaders of Pennsylvania accepted the idea, or were forced by the people to accept it. For a year these Pennsylvania leaders had thwarted all of John Adams' plans. Now, Adams in the best Philadelphia sense was a moderate gentleman — if not in temper at least in politics. His ideas of liberty and government squared with those of John Dickinson. He believed with Dickinson that the colonies' war with England was aimed at preserving a way of life, not at creating a new way of life.[11] The split came over how best to preserve it. Those in Dickinson's camp stood firmly for reconciliation, insisting that only within the Empire could the rights

---

Warren, May 15, *Warren-Adams Letters,* I, 245–247; to his wife, May 17, Adams, *Familiar Letters,* 173–174; to Patrick Henry, June 3, Adams, *Works,* IX, 413.

[9] John Adams to his wife, May 17, Adams, *Familiar Letters,* 174.

[10] Robert Morris to John Hancock, February 4, 1777, quoted in Bezanson, *Prices and Inflation . . . Pennsylvania 1760–1790,* 18.

[11] Still the best discussion of the patriots' " reactionary " desire to restore a political situation that supposedly existed in the past is Randolph G. Adams, *Political Ideas of the American Revolution* (Durham, N.C., 1922), 54–103. See also Merrill Jensen, *Articles of Confederation* (Madison, Wis., 1940), 54–103; and Daniel J. Boorstin, *The Genius of American Politics* (Chicago, 1953), 66–98.

and liberties they treasured be maintained. John Adams, convinced that Great Britain was bent only on enslaving the colonies, demanded independence.[12]

When the British attacked Lexington and invaded Boston, he had spoken out bluntly that reconciliation was a hopeless dream. "What is the reason, Mr. Adams," asked John Dickinson one July afternoon in 1775, finding his opponent in the State House yard, "that you New-Englandmen oppose our measures of reconciliation? . . . Look ye! If you don't concur with us in our pacific system, I and a number of us will break off from you in New England, and we will carry on the opposition by ourselves in our own way."[13] Adams held his temper then, only to lose it later in a letter home. "A certain great Fortune and piddling Genius, whose Fame has been trumpted so loudly, has given a silly Cast to our whole Doings," he wrote of Dickinson.[14] The British got hold of the letter and published it. For months thereafter in Philadelphia John Adams was "an object of nearly universal detestation."[15]

On the eve of the May election Dickinson still obstructed any move to break the ties with Britain. The prevailing opinion among the Independents held him "timid to the last Degree, & for putting off [independence] till Commissioners come, tho' he has little Expectation from them, but then he thinks the way will be more clear."[16] Adams and the Independents failed to see that Dickinson,

---

[12] Curtis Nettels, *George Washington and American Independence* (Boston, 1951), 115–120, insists the militant views of Adams and others resulted to a great degree from Arthur Lee's reports from London which, Nettels implies, Dickinson did not see. Dickinson did see these letters and he was as fully informed as Adams on the situation in London. Several of the Lee letters addressed to Dickinson are in the Dickinson Papers, Library Company, Ridgeway Branch.
[13] Adams, *Works*, II, 410.
[14] John Adams to James Warren, July 24, 1775, *Warren–Adams Letters*, I, 88.
[15] Corner, *Rush Autobiography*, 142.
[16] Franklin Bowditch Dexter, ed., *The Literary Diary of Ezra Stiles* (3 vols., New York, 1901), II, 10. Stiles here reports the opinion in Philadelphia of Dickinson as he received it from " Francis Dana Esq. late from London and last from Phila."

timid or not, reflected rather than lagged behind sentiment in Pennsylvania. The results of the May election made this clear.

The election results clearly blocked John Adams' hopes for a quick decision on independence. He knew that Pennsylvania set the pace for the Middle Colonies and that her continued faith in reconciliation only bolstered the faith of moderate-minded men in New York, New Jersey, Delaware, and Maryland. It was after the election that Adams devised his three-step plan which approached independence with more deliberation than he liked. (Perhaps "accepted" is more apt than "devised"; the striking thing about Adams' plan is that it is identical to the one John Dickinson had argued for and kept pleading for up to the day the Declaration was finally passed.)[17]

Hard after the election, while the results from the backcountry were still coming in, the seemingly settled situation changed abruptly. First came definite news about the foreign troops. "You will see," Caesar Rodney of Delaware promptly reported to his brother, "that our (Much talk'd of) Comissioners are turned into Men of War and foreign troops."[18] Richard Bache hurriedly sent the news to Franklin, absent in Canada on a mission for Congress. "You will see by the Papers," he wrote, "what a formidable Armament we are daily to expect—45,000 *Commissioners* at least, of different Nations, that is to say, Hessians, Hanoverians. . . ."[19]

On the heels of this news word arrived in the city on May 6 that the *Liverpool* and *Roebuck* had left their patrolling stations and were coming "up our Bay & River sounding & filling water & it is thought were making themselves acquainted with the Channel for no good purpose."[20] Early in the afternoon the "Alarm Guns,"

---

[17] See Dickinson's speech to Congress, J. H. Powell, ed., " Speech of John Dickinson Opposing the Declaration of Independence, 1 July, 1776," *PMHB* 65 (1941), 458–481.
[18] Caesar Rodney to Thomas Rodney, May 8, Ryden, *Rodney Letters*, 76.
[19] Richard Bache to Benjamin Franklin, May 7, Franklin Papers, APS.
[20] Clement Biddle to George Tayler, May 12, typescript copy in Society Collection, HSP.

which were fired only when an attack was imminent, echoed through the city. They "put the Town into some Consternation for a short time."[21] William Bradford, Jr., was in the midst of dinner when he heard the guns. The ships, as he got the news, had sailed above Chester and burned Newcastle. He and Thomas Mifflin marched their company of Associates to the State House, "where we got the Guns marked for cartridges," but by late afternoon the report of an attack had proved false.[22] Bradford that night seemed unconcerned by the day's events. He spent some time with a Miss Fisher and Miss Standley, then returned home to read "A Dialogue on Civil Liberty" by Dr. John Witherspoon, president of the College of New Jersey. The rest of the city seemed less calm. Several members of the Fellowship Fire Company announced "they will be under the necessity of removing into the country. . . ."[23]

During the afternoon excitement Congress continued in session. John Adams, perhaps spurred to action by the sound of the alarm guns, hoping they might panic timid members, asked Congress to recommend that all colonies which had limited the power of their delegates to vote for independent-minded acts to "repeal or suspend those instructions for a certain time."[24] The motion was defeated.

May 7 passed quietly in Congress and through the city. Bradford spent most of the day studying his law books. The next day, too, started off calmly, but when Bradford got down to his office "I found the young lad is very much alarmed with the firing of Cannon down the river. I listened & could hear them very distinctly. . . . I hastened home where I received orders to take out the Company provided with Ammunition."[25] The news that evening was good. The *Roebuck* had been forced aground and the city's armed row-galleys had her surrounded. During the night the *Roe-*

---

[21] Richard Bache to Benjamin Franklin, May 7, APS.
[22] Bradford, Register, May 6, HSP.
[23] J. J. Jordan, "The Fellowship Fire Company of Philadelphia," *PMHB* 27 (1903), 481.
[24] Quoted in Lincoln, *Revolutionary Movement in Pennsylvania*, 249.
[25] Bradford, Register, May 8.

buck drifted free on the high tide. The battle resumed again the next day, this time farther up the river, closer to the city. The sound of the booming guns resounded through the town. Thousands of citizens turned out along the shores to watch the galleys cautiously lob their shots in from great distances toward the slow-moving warships.[26] The battle was carried on halfheartedly during the early afternoon; toward sunset the tempo picked up and the "firing was very heavy; we counted distinctly 60 in seven minutes."[27] The firing ceased around seven o'clock, then, admitting to a draw, the warships slowly swung about and sailed back down the river to their patrolling stations.

They left behind an undamaged but changed city. Edward Shippen, Jr., immediately canceled his planned tour of the county courts, for "my family are too much alarmed to make it eligible for me to be absent."[28] Joseph Pemberton put his house up for sale.[29] A visitor to the city found his friends Mr. Duché and Mr. West absent because "the appearance of the King's Ships so far up the river made them hurry their families out of town."[30] The Library Company called a meeting to decide what to do with its books in the event of invasion.[31] Jane Mecom said the "Alaram hear to Day . . . Almost Determins me to Sett out for NewEngland Directly. . . ."[32] William Bradford, Jr., packed up some law books to send out of town, "for tho' I hope this City is in little Danger yet we are not free from alarms. . . ."[33] The feeling of all was that "a larger force will come against us. . . ."[34]

---

[26] Accounts of the battle appear in the *Pennsylvania Evening Post*, May 11; the *Pennsylvania Journal*, May 15.
[27] Bradford, Register, May 9.
[28] Edward Shippen, Jr., to Jasper Yeates, May 9, Balch Papers, vol. 2, HSP.
[29] Advertisement in *Pennsylvania Gazette*, May 29; manuscript of the ad in the Pemberton Papers, HSP, is dated May 6.
[30] Clitherall, Diary, *PMHB* 22 (1898), 468.
[31] See notice in *Pennsylvania Gazette*, May 15.
[32] Jane Mecom to Catharine Greene, May 8, W. G. Roelker, ed., *Benjamin Franklin and Catharine Ray Greene—Their Correspondence 1755–1790*. (Philadelphia, 1949), 71.
[33] Bradford, Register, May 11.
[34] Clement Biddle to George Tayler, May 12, Society Collection, HSP.

On May 10 John Adams, undeterred by past defeats, made a bold move in Congress. Whether the timing was accidental or calculated is unimportant, though it is hard to believe this shrewd little lawyer, with an even shrewder cousin at his side, left much to chance. The point is that the timing was perfect. The news that mercenaries were on their way had been substantiated. Less than twenty-four hours earlier all Philadelphia and probably most of Congress, too, had been jarred from complacency by the sounds of battle. While the city and Congress strove to recover their composure, John Adams offered a resolution which read:

That it be recommended to the respective assemblies and conventions of the United Colonies, where no government sufficient to the exigencies of their affairs have been hitherto established, to adopt such government as shall, in the opinion of the representatives of the people, best conduce to the happiness and safety of their constituents in particular, and Americans in general.[35]

The key phrase here is "where no government sufficient to the exigencies of their affairs have been hitherto established." John Dickinson, still firm for reconciliation, announced, doubtless to John Adams' astonishment, that he agreed entirely on the necessity for such a resolution.[36] The colonies needed stable governments to carry out the imminent summer campaign. Furthermore, he felt "that it would not prevent but perhaps promote a more speedy reconciliation" because the longer the colonies let the royal government exist "the more firm that Government would be, & therefore the more difficult to effect a reconciliation."[37] Of course, added Dickinson, this resolution did not apply to Pennsylvania, which already had a government "sufficient to the exigencies of their affairs," and one which the voters had just given a mandate of approval. The liberties and rights the colonies now fought to preserve were amply protected in Pennsylvania by the Charter of

---
[35] E. C. Burnett, *The Continental Congress* (New York, 1941), 157.
[36] See John Adams to John Winthrop, May 12, *MHSC*, Series 5, vol. 4, 301–302.
[37] Thomas Rodney to Caesar Rodney, May 19, Ryden, *Rodney Letters*, 82.

Privileges of 1701, which, among other things, gave the Assembly the right to initiate all legislation. The Assembly functioned so smoothly that Pennsylvania's contribution to the war in men and materials exceeded that of any other colony. Thus, with John Dickinson's unexpected blessing the resolution, now enervated since it clearly did not apply to Pennsylvania, promptly passed Congress.[38]

John Adams refused to be out-maneuvered. All important resolutions of Congress were dignified with a high-sounding preamble before giving them to the public. Adams used this device effectively to plug the loopholes Dickinson had discovered in his measure. On the pleasantly warm spring morning of May 15 the delegates assembled in the State House to debate his handiwork.[39] The entire day was given over to the matter. The usual reading of the daily letters from General Washington and his commanders in the field with which President Hancock opened each session was dispensed with.[40] Promptly after the chamber's pine-paneled doors had been swung shut and the doorkeeper had taken up his post outside, to assure secrecy for the discussion within, the preamble was read aloud. It stated, in essence, that "it appears absolutely irreconcileable to reason and good Conscience, for the people of the colonies now to take the oaths and affirmations necessary for the support of any government under the crown of Great Britain, and it is necessary that the exercise of every kind of authority under the said crown should be totally suppressed...."[41]

The preamble was unquestionably aimed at Pennsylvania, where the Assembly still took oaths of loyalty to the Crown, where the King's justice was still practiced in the courts, and where the general official tone of the colony was one that recognized still the King's

---

[38] John Adams to James Warren, May 12, *Warren–Adams Letters,* I, 242: "Congress have passed a Vote with remarkable Unanimity for assuming Government in all the Colonies, which remains only for a Preamble."
[39] See Marshall, Diary, May 15, for the weather.
[40] See Ford, *Journals of Congress,* IV, 357.
[41] *Ibid.;* IV, 358.

authority. The formidable job of presenting Pennsylvania's views against the measure fell on thirty-three-year-old James Wilson. (John Dickinson was absent. He would soon take up a second set of political duties when the Assembly convened next Monday, May 20; he had left Congress for a short vacation at his farm near Dover, Delaware, assuming that for a few days at least John Adams had been effectively silenced and the drive for independence momentarily stopped.)[42] Without hedging, James Wilson put full responsibility for future events in Pennsylvania directly on Congress if it passed this measure. "In this Province," he said, "if that preamble passes, there will be an immediate dissolution of every kind of authority; the people will be instantly in a state of nature. Why then precipitate this measure? Before we are prepared to build a new house, why should we pull down the old one, and expose ourselves to all the inclemencies of the season?"[43] (These words would soon have ironical significance for John Adams, now doing so much to pull down Pennsylvania's house. Within a few days he would hear of many disconcerting democratic "innovations" in Massachusetts. Such innovations had no part in his plan for independence. "Many of the projects that I have heard of," he wrote with sadness, "are not repairing, but pulling down the building, when it is on fire, instead of laboring to extinguish the flames.")[44]

If the plight of Pennsylvania had been the sole issue at stake, there would have been little reason to spend a full day in anguished debate over the preamble. There were more compelling reasons for opposing it. In the first place, Congress had no authority to interfere in any colony's internal affairs. This was clearly stated in the

---

[42] See Thomas Rodney to Caesar Rodney, Ryden, *Rodney Letters*, 82. The evidence is all but positive Dickinson was absent from Congress May 15. He obviously did not speak at the debate or Adams would have mentioned it. His calm remarks to Rodney on May 19 in Dover indicate he was unaware of the Adams preamble.
[43] Adams, *Works*, II, 491.
[44] John Adams to John Winthrop, June 23, *MHSC*, Series 5, vol. 4, 310.

instructions every delegate carried from his colony. This had been the argument used twice against Pennsylvania when she asked for aid in settling her boundary disputes with Connecticut and Virginia. James Duane of New York — a prosperous, plump lawyer, slightly squint-eyed and, in John Adams' judgment "a sensible, an artful, and an insinuating man"[45] — rose to make this point. "You have no right to pass the resolution, any more than Parliament has," he said.[46]

Furthermore, the theoretical implications of the preamble trod new and dangerous ground. The focus on His Britannic Majesty was awkward. To deny the legality of Parliament's law the colonies, in their constitutional debate with Great Britain, had been forced to deny Parliament's right to legislate for them. The effort to work out a scheme that permitted the colonies to exist within the framework of the British Empire without being responsible to Parliament had by now led to the theory that the colonies owed allegiance only to the King, that they were equals within the Empire and could make their own laws, levy their own taxes as Englishmen in Britain did through Parliament.[47] The King, then, remained the last link between England and the colonies. To demand the complete suppression of his authority, as the preamble did, meant in effect to declare independence. Such a declaration, though only implied, came at a lamentable time — to Duane's way of thinking, at least — for rumors of the coming peace commissioners still continued. "Every account of foreign aid is accompanied with an account of commissioners," Duane said. "Why all this haste?" he asked. "Why this urging? why this driving?"[48]

Sam Adams, who seldom spoke in Congress, marked the im-

---

[45] For contemporary descriptions of Duane see Edward P. Alexander, *A Revolutionary Conservative* (New York, 1938), 93, 149, 150. The Adams quote comes from *Works*, II, 354, 350.
[46] Adams, *Works*, II, 490.
[47] R. G. Adams, *Political Ideas*, gives the best discussion of the shifting political theories developed by Congress to clarify America's relations with Great Britain. See particularly 40–61.
[48] Adams, *Works*, II, 490.

portance of the debate by rising to answer Duane. His white hair and creased face, the congenital trembling of his hand and head made him appear older than his fifty-seven years. Mr. Duane, he said, had asked Congress not to act until its petitions to the King had been answered. "Our petitions have not been heard, yet answered with fleets and armies, and are to be answered with myrmidons from abroad," Adams said. "We cannot go upon stronger reasons than that the King has thrown us out of his protection. Why should we support governments under his authority? I wonder that people have conducted so well as they have."[49]

Other arguments were advanced to overcome Wilson's and Duane's objections. One was the ridiculous, humiliating aspect of pretended loyalty to a King who treated his subjects as rebels. "The Continuing to Swear Allegiance to the power that is Cutting our throats, and attesting jurors to keep the Secrets and Try offenders against the peace of our Sovereign Lord the King &c is Certainly absurd," Caesar Rodney said.[50] Such absurdities pervaded the colonies. While Congress debated war measures within the State House the King's Arms hung without over the entrance. Delegates who visited Christ Church listened to Jacob Duché read a liturgy that still offered up prayers for the King's well-being.[51] Even in John and Sam Adams' Massachusetts writs were still issued in the King's name.

The approaching summer campaign offered a forceful reason for ending royal influence in the colonies. The river battle of the past week hinted at what was to come. The May 15 issue of the *Pennsylvania Gazette* reported a late dispatch from London — only three months old — that said a fleet of fifty-seven warships and

---

[49] *Ibid.*, II, 490.
[50] Caesar Rodney to John Haslet, May 17, Ryden, *Rodney Letters*, 80.
[51] Frank M. Etting, *The Old State House of Pennsylvania* (Philadelphia, 1891), 103n–104n. Duché kept the prayer in his service until the day independence was declared. Charles Wilson Peale notes in his diary on June 2: "Went to Christ's Church, hiss'd the Minister for praying for the King as in the Littany." Peale Diary, 1776, APS.

three armies totaling thirty-five thousand men were enroute to the colonies. The summer would be the testing-time for America. "... the ensuing campaign is likely to require greater exertion than our unorganized powers may at present effect," said Thomas Jefferson, who had returned to Congress only a day ago, after a four-month absence in Virginia.[52] Stable, effective governments were impossible, so the argument went, so long as royal influence persisted.

John Adams' preamble forced the delegates to balance the plight of Pennsylvania, the illegality of the measure, and its theoretical implications of independence against the evident necessity for strong, regular governments in all the colonies, a necessity which even Pennsylvania admitted was valid. Pennsylvania insisted that the body of the resolution cleared the way for creating new governments in colonies that lacked them but that the preamble only threatened those colonies — notably Pennsylvania — that already had effective governments.

The preamble came up for vote in the early afternoon. The ballots were cast, as usual, by colonies. The result was close. Six colonies (the four of New England, plus Virginia and South Carolina) voted in favor of the measure, and four (North Carolina, New York, New Jersey, and Delaware) voted against it. Georgia was absent, Pennsylvania and Maryland abstained.[53]

Maryland did more than abstain. After the voting, her delegates gathered up their papers and walked from the chamber. "[They] gave us to understand," said Carter Braxton of Virginia, "they should not return nor deem our farther Resolutions obligatory, untill they had transmitted an Acct. of the Proceedings to their

---

[52] Thomas Jefferson to Thomas Nelson, May 16, Boyd, *Jefferson Papers*, I, 292.
[53] Carter Braxton to Landon Carter, May 17, E. C. Burnett, ed., *Letters of the Members of the Continental Congress* (8 vols., Washington, 1921–1936), I, 454. Braxton reports the vote as six to four, which means the colonies were divided as stated above. James Allen, *PMHB*, 9 (1885), 187, states the vote was seven to four. If that is true, then Pennsylvania must have voted rather than abstained and North Carolina voted with the majority.

Convention and had their Instructions how to act or conduct themselves upon this alarming occasion. This Event is waited for with Impatience and while it is in agitation the assembly of this Province [Pennsylvania] will meet and it is not impossible but they may join in this extraordinary proceeding. What then will be the consequence God only knows." [54]

It would seem in retrospect that until Maryland left the meeting room many of the delegates who had voted for the preamble were unaware of exactly what they were voting for. The measure's proponents had skillfully emphasized in the day-long debate its utility—stable governments were needed to fight the "myrmidons from abroad"—and implied that timid delegates exaggerated the overtones of independence. (The skill and organization with which the proponents presented their side of the case suggests the directing hand of Sam Adams. "He was constantly holding caucuses . . ." Jefferson once said, "at which the generality of the measures pursued were previously determined on, and at which the parts were assigned to the different actors who afterwards appeared in them. John Adams had very little part in these caucuses; but as one of the actors in the measures decided on in them, he was a Colossus.")[55] Once Maryland had left the hall many of the delegates began to see that the measure held more than met the eye at first glance. "You will say [it] falls little short of Independence," Carter Braxton wrote a friend. "It was not so understood by Congress but I find those out of doors on both sides the question construe it in that manner."[56] Caesar Rodney had been among those who at the time of voting had noted only the preamble's practical virtues. Two days later he wrote: "Most of those here who are *termed the Cool Considerate Men* think it amounts to a declaration of Independance. It Certainly savours of it," he added, still not positive of

---

[54] Carter Braxton to Landon Carter, May 17, Burnett, *Letters of Congress*, I, 454.

[55] Quoted in James K. Hosmer, *Samuel Adams* (Boston, 1885), 364.

[56] Carter Braxton to Landon Carter, May 17, Burnett, *Letters of Congress*, I, 453–454.

its implications, "but you will see and Judge for Your Self. . . ."[57]

A few days before the preamble passed John Adams had warned a friend at home not to let Massachusetts move too rapidly toward independence; her boldness might separate her from the other colonies. "The Union is our defence, and that must be most tenderly cherished," he said.[58] He had now forced a crack in that union. If Maryland's defection spread to Pennsylvania and from her to the other Middle Colonies, that crack might widen into an irreparable split. More than ever now depended on the turn of events in Pennsylvania. "But, above all, let us see the conduct of the middle Colonies," James Duane cautioned his friend John Jay back in New York, "before we come to a decision: It cannot injure us to wait a few weeks: the advantage will be great for this trying question will clearly discover the true principles & the extent of the Union of the Colonies."[59]

Word spread quickly through the city of the new resolution and its preamble.[60] Down on Front Street at the London Coffee House the news temporarily ended talk about the river battle and interest in the pieces from the British warships which had been found floating in the Delaware and brought to the Coffee House for display.[61] Philadelphia's social life to a large extent centered at the Coffee House, which offered patrons a wider choice of drink than its name implied (". . . some people may be desirous at times to be furnished with other liquors besides coffee," William Bradford, Sr., the proprietor, had said when applying for a government license). Merchants, farmers, mechanics, and politicians met here. Ship captains stopped by to write up their reports, their vessels tied up at the wharves only a few hundred feet to the east at the foot

[57] Caesar Rodney to Thomas Rodney, May 17, *ibid.*, I, 455.
[58] John Adams to John Winthrop, May 6. *MHSC,* Series 5, vol. 4, 300–01.
[59] James Duane to John Jay, May 18. Henry P. Johnson, ed., *The Correspondence and Public Papers of John Jay* (2 vols., New York, 1890), I, 61.
[60] William Bradford, Jr., wrote in his Register for May 15 (misdated May 14): " This evening the resolve of Congress . . . came out."
[61] Marshall, Diary, May 15.

of High Street. It was an informal post office for itinerants, a clearing house for gossip, where even the bickerings behind the closed doors at the State House were often open secrets.[62]

Soon after it passed Congress William Bradford, Sr., read aloud the measure that John Adams would hereafter refer to as "an epocha, a decisive event."[63] "One man only huzzaad," James Allen reported. "In general it was ill-received. We stared at each other. My feelings of indignation were strong, but it was necessary to be mute. This step of Congress, just at the time commissioners are expected to arrive, was purposely contrived to prevent overtures of peace. . . . Moderate men look blank, & yet the Majority of the City & province are of that stamp."[64]

---

[62] J. Thomas Scharf and Thompson Westcott, *History of Philadelphia 1609–1884* (3 vols., Philadelphia, 1884), I, 279n–281n.
[63] Adams, *Works,* III, 44.
[64] Allen, Diary, *PMHB* 9 (1885), 187.

6 AN ENTERTAINING MANEUVER

After May 15 Benjamin Rush channeled a good part of his energies into politics. He soon convinced himself — correctly — that the success of the drive for independence in Pennsylvania depended on a select few, among whom he was one. He wrote: "General Mifflin and all the delegates from the independent colonies rely chiefly upon me," then lined out "me" and continued, "Colonel McKean and a few more of us for the salvation of this province."[1]

By "salvation" Rush of course meant independence, and to achieve that he and "a few more of us" were scheming to bring about a revolution in government. Their chances of success had improved greatly since the May election. The river battle had bolstered the confidence of Philadelphians. ("British ships of war will not be thought so formidable," one Independent wrote.)[2] More than that it forcefully reminded inhabitants, as they heard the thundering guns and faced the threat of bombardment, that whether they liked it or not they were in a shooting war in which their lives and property were at stake.

The river battle, backed up by news of foreign troops, provided the "combustible" which, if ignited might swing Philadelphia into the independence column. How was this new mood to be ex-

---
[1] Benjamin Rush to his wife, May 29, Butterfield, *Rush Letters*, I, 99.
[2] George Read to Caesar Rodney, May 10, Ryden, *Rodney Letters*, 76.

ploited? The city only a few days earlier had voted down the Independents' candidates. In 1776 the tradition had already developed that regardless of the bitterness of any campaign, regardless of how wide the split between contending factions, the results of any election were accepted by both sides. This did not mean that the loser ceased to oppose. It did mean he carried on his opposition within the accepted political framework and did not threaten, because he had lost, to overthrow the government. This was the spirit in which William Bradford, Jr., had accepted the election results posted at the State House. The Independents in the city and, curiously, in Congress, too, decided to ignore this tradition.

Many of the Independents in Congress, all moderate-minded men, encouraged a revolution in Pennsylvania, often at the same time they were denouncing every sign of political innovation in their own "country." Independence lacked all chance of success until Pennsylvania could be forced into line. These otherwise cautious, prudent men willingly adjusted means to the end to achieve that. They could join in disrupting Pennsylvania affairs with a light heart; they would not have to live with the results of their machinations. They, like most visitors, were not hindered by any special affection for Pennsylvania. Some, like the Virginians, merely disliked the colony. Others, like John Adams, had deep contempt for both the province and its leaders. Late in life Adams said: "William Penn was the greatest land-jobber, that ever existed; & that his successors in the administration of that government, had continued the same policy."[3] These sentiments summed up Adams' feelings for Pennsylvania.

Support from Congress comforted and encouraged the "steering committee" of city Independents. Cannon, Rush, and their friends turned readily in the next month to those delegates anxious to help

---

[3] From an interview with Adams noted in the diary of Elihu Hubbard Smith, *PMHB* 73 (1949), 93.

whenever the revolution in Pennsylvania seemed to falter.[4] On May 3, as election results rolled in from the backcountry, Marshall, Cannon, and Young spent several hours together, then in the evening went out to talk with Thomas McKean; later they trooped over to Samuel Adams' lodgings and "stay'd a good while in Conversation with him. . . ."[5] On May 10, the day John Adams' original resolution had passed Congress, Cannon and Marshall again visited McKean and "thence to Saml. Adams Lodgins."[6] Three days later James Langley, Marshall, Cannon and Matlack stopped by again to see the Adamses. A caucus meeting scheduled for that night probably prompted the visit. Neither John nor Sam was home. The group traveled over to the Coffee House. They failed to find the two men there. That evening, deprived of Adams' advice, the caucus agreed that Tom Paine, Benjamin Rush, Timothy Matlack, Benjamin Harbison, James Cannon, and Christopher Marshall would "call upon Sundry other persons to mett to morrow night at Burnsides Schoolroom at 8 to take into Consideration & to Concert a plann necessary to be adopted on the meeting of our assembly next 2d day."[7]

The "steering committee" fumbled around for a way to deal with the Assembly, puzzled and confused how to circumvent the election results. Somehow the Assembly must be discredited in the eyes of the people, for "mass movements do not usually rise until the prevailing order has been discredited. The discrediting is not an automatic result of the blunders and abuses of those in power, but the deliberate work of men of words with a grievance."[8] It was natural, then, for Paine to set the tone and lead the attack, as he did on May 8. In the election the aim had been to elect enough Independents to the Assembly to control it. Failing in that,

---

[4] See Benjamin Rush to Richard Henry Lee, May 22, Lyman Butterfield, "Further Letters of Benjamin Rush," *PMHB* 78 (1954), 14–15.
[5] Marshall, Diary, May 3.
[6] *Ibid.*, May 10.
[7] *Ibid.*, May 13.
[8] Hoffer, *True Believer*, 129.

Paine now set out to discredit that body completely. The Assembly must go because its authority stemmed from the Crown, not the people. We are got wrong, said Paine; how shall we get right? "Not by a House of Assembly; because they cannot sit as *Judges in a case,* where their *own existence* under their *present forms and authority is to be judged of.*" Increasing the Assembly's membership solved nothing, for that merely "would *encrease* the *necessity* of a convention.*" Why? "Because, the more any power is augmented, which derives its authority from our enemies, the more unsafe and dangerous it becomes to us."[9]

The inconsistencies in this new line perturbed Paine and his friends little. But it would take time to develop this approach and spread it among the people, who so recently signified their approval of the Assembly's decisions by sending the Moderates additional support. Further delay meant continued frustration, postponement of the bright future. The delay, sad to say, would have to be endured until a better weapon than newspaper articles turned up to attack the Assembly. The "steering committee" settled down to turning out propaganda for the new line. In the evening of May 14 Cannon, Paine, Marshall, with others, met "to Draw up heads of a Protest to be brought tomorrow night for approbation" of the Committee of Inspection and Observation.[10] (All planning up to now had been conducted outside the city Committee, which, in fact, now served mainly as a front organization for decisions predetermined in the caucuses of the "steering committee," several of whose members — Paine, Young, and Cannon among them — were not members of the Committee of Inspection and Observation.)

The next night, May 15, the Protest had been abetted by Congress. John Adams' preamble had given the Independents a weapon tailored to their needs. Congress, as if prompted by Paine's newspaper article, had recommended that all royal authority in the colonies "be totally suppressed." The Assembly represented royal

---
[9] The Forester, *Pennsylvania Journal,* May 8.
[10] Marshall, Diary, May 14.

AN ENTERTAINING MANEUVER 133

authority; thus Congress had ordained, thanks to John, and doubtless Sam Adams, that the Assembly must go. A paragraph of words backed up by the authority and dignity of the Second Continental Congress had discredited the Assembly, achieving in an instant what might have taken the city Independents weeks, even months to accomplish.

The evening the preamble passed the city's Committee met at the Philosophical Hall and with "a large number of people" on hand the measure was debated from seven o'clock until past ten. No decision was reached how to use the measure. Further discussion was postponed until three o'clock the next afternoon.[11] By the next day the measure had already "occassioned a great alarm" throughout the city, "& the cautious folks are very fearful of its being attended with many ill consequences next week when the Assembly are to meet."[12] Meanwhile, the Independents—that is, those on the "steering committee"; the Independents' solid front now began to split—decided on a bold move: to prevent the Assembly from even meeting. At three o'clock Marshall went to James Cannon's home, then, properly advised, he went down to the Philosophical Hall "to consider of what steps might be necessary to take on the Dissolution of Government as published this Day. it was concluded to call a Convention with speed to Protest against the present assembly doing of any business in their house untill the sence of the Province was taken in that Convention to be called, &c. . . ."[13]

Chance now handed the Independents another opportunity. Two months earlier Congress had designated Friday, May 17, "a day of HUMILIATION, FASTING and PRAYER; that we may with united hearts confess and bewail our manifold sins and transgressions. . . ."[14] Ministers throughout America were urged

---

[11] *Ibid.,* May 15.
[12] Robert Livingston to John Jay, May 17, Johnston, *Jay Papers,* I, 60.
[13] Marshall, Diary, May 16.
[14] *Pennsylvania Gazette,* March 20.

to use their eloquence and prestige to invigorate flagging spirits. On a normal Friday, merchants would have been in their shops and workmen at their jobs. On this Fast Day — or Congress Sunday, as the people called this day of rest ordained by the politicians — people had the leisure and, after listening to their ministers, the inclination to talk politics. During the day Independents moved through the city gathering names on a petition which urged that "a general call be made of the inhabitants of the City and Liberties to meet next Monday at 9 o'clock forenoon at the State House in order to take the sense of the people respecting the resolve of Congress. . . . "[15] The next night the city Committee voted, with only five members dissenting, that a mass meeting should be held on Monday, May 20, the day assigned for the Assembly to convene.[16]

The next problem was to make sure people turned out for the meeting. May 19, God's Sunday, proved no day of rest for the Independents. "The town has been in a ferment to day about a change of Government," William Bradford, Jr., wrote.[17] During the day a broadside titled "The Alarm" — apparently written and in type before the city Committee had sanctioned the mass meeting — was delivered throughout the city. The project had been carefully planned. Even a German translation had been printed and spread among those who still faltered with English.[18] "The Alarm" — or "Der Alarm" — did not aim to calm jittery nerves. It said that since Congress had decreed the suppression of all royal authority any new government should be established *"on the authority of the people*, in lieu of the old one which were established on the authority of the Crown." The Assembly could not possibly suppress the royal authority because that is something that can only "be done *to them,* but cannot be done *by them."* And

---

[15] Broadside Collection (1776), HSP.
[16] Marshall, Diary, May 18.
[17] William Bradford, Jr., to Joshua Wallace, May 19, Wallace Papers, vol. 1, HSP.
[18] See "Der Alarm," Broadside Collection (1776), Item 59, HSP.

how were the people to go about this? The broadside, perhaps written by Paine, continued to paraphrase the ideas in the Forester's article of May 8. The people must form a new constitution and "CONVENTIONS, my Fellow-Countrymen, are the only proper bodies to *form* a Constitution. . . ." A convention of men "of known reputation for wisdom, virtue and impartiality, is . . . a far more probable, nay the only possible, method for securing the just Rights of the people, and posterity."[19]

At least one delegate in Congress who voted for Adams' preamble viewed all this noise in Philadelphia with dismay. "The Recommendation of Congress," wrote Caesar Rodney, "was certainly meant to go to the Assemblies, where there were such who had authority to Set."[20]

"We have had an entertaining maneuver this morning in the State House yard," John Adams wrote on May 20. "The weather was very rainy and the meeting was in the open air like the Comitia of the Romans. A stage was erected *extempore* for the moderator and the few orators to ascend. Col. Roberdeau was the moderator; Col. McKean, Col. Cadwalader, and Col. Matlack the principal orators. It was the very first town meeting I ever saw in Philadelphia and it was conducted with great order, decency, and propriety.

"The first step taken was this: the Moderator produced the Resolve of Congress of the 15th inst. and read it in a loud stentorian Voice that might be heard a Quarter of a Mile. 'Whereas his Britannic Majesty, etc.' As soon as this was read, the Multitude, several Thousands, some say, tho so wett, rended the Welkin with three Cheers, Hatts flying as usual, etc."[21]

The meeting had been well planned. By ten o'clock some four thousand people had crowded into the brick-walled yard.[22] Dr.

---
[19] "The Alarm," Broadside Collection (1776), Item 18, HSP.
[20] Caesar Rodney to Thomas Rodney, May 29, Ryden, *Rodney Letters*, 85.
[21] John Adams to James Warren, May 20, *Warren–Adams Letters*, I, 250.
[22] Marshall, Diary, May 20.

James Clitherall, a visitor from South Carolina, felt, contrary to Adams, that "the people behaved in such a tyrannical manner that the least opposition was dangerous." After Roberdeau had read aloud to the throng several resolves, carefully prepared before the meeting, Thomas Cadwalader suggested some minor changes. "Col. Cadwalader, one of their favorites," said Clitherall, "was grossly insulted for proposing a different form, preserving at the same time the sense of the resolves."[23]

The first resolve said that the Assembly's instructions "have a dangerous tendency to withdraw this province from that *happy union* with the other colonies, which we consider both as our *glory* and *protection*." It passed unanimously.[24] The second said that since the Assembly lacked the authority of the people it would be assuming arbitrary power if it sat this session. One man, Isaac Gray, a grocer,[25] alone among the throng voted against this.[26] Mr. Gray was "abused and insulted," Clitherall said. "I therefore thought it prudent to vote with the multitude."[27] Next, it was agreed unanimously that the present government was not "competent to the exigencies of our affairs." Finally, the crowd voted as one to call a Provincial Conference of county committees which would draw up plans for a Constitutional Convention.

One of the delegates who watched these proceedings was impressed how neatly the intent of Congress had been twisted. The compelling argument in the preamble's favor had been the necessity for regular governments. The throng at the mass meeting had voted to demolish their regular government. "By their mode it will be impossible for them to have any Government for three months to Come," said Caesar Rodney, "and during that time much Confusion — If the present assembly Should take order in the

---

[23] Clitherall, Diary, *PMHB* 22 (1898), 470.
[24] *Pennsylvania Gazette*, May 22.
[25] Scharf and Westcott, *Philadelphia*, II, 886n.
[26] Marshall, Diary, May 20.
[27] Clitherall, Diary, *PMHB* 22 (1898) 470.

the matter, the work would be done in one Quarter of the time."[28]

But the Independents—at least some of them—did not expect confusion in government to follow. Daniel Roberdeau ended the meeting reading aloud a Protest that summed up the arguments against the Assembly carrying out Congress' May 15 resolution. Buried in the Protest was this tortuous sentence:

> In thus protesting against the authority of the House for framing a new government, we mean not to object against its exercising the proper powers it has hitherto been accustomed to use . . . until such time as a new constitution originating from and founded on, " *the authority of the people* " shall be finally settled by a Provincial Convention to be elected for that purpose, and until the proper officers and representatives of the people shall be chosen agreeable thereto and qualified to succeed this House.[29]

For Roberdeau the Assembly was not a discredited body. It would continue to function while the source of power was transferred from the Crown to the people. The transfer would be orderly. Roberdeau and those he spoke for failed to see in their political innocence what a politician like Rodney knew from instinct—you cannot destroy confidence in an institution and expect it to continue functioning with public support. Paine and his friends were more logical. The Assembly was discredited in their eyes; they were against the Assembly doing any business.

Roberdeau's remarks unobtrusively marked the first open sign of a split in the ranks of the Independents. The party had embraced both moderate- and radical-minded men from the start. The common desire for independence had kept their differences submerged and until the goal had been achieved they would remain submerged. Roberdeau's words indicated that unwittingly the moderate men among the Independents were headed down one road and the radicals down another. Only when independence had been won would either faction be aware that the paths diverged. As the

---

[28] Caesar Rodney to Thomas Rodney, May 22, Ryden, *Rodney Letters,* 83.
[29] *Pennsylvania Gazette,* May 22.

throng in the State House yard dispersed through the rain, the Independent party remained united, ready to do battle against the Moderates. The political machines of both groups prepared for a struggle that would make the recent election campaign look like a genteel discussion.

7 PROTEST AND REMONSTRANCE

The Moderates refused to be intimidated or cowed to silence by the mass meeting. The next day, May 21, they had an answer written to the Protest Daniel Roberdeau had read to the multitude in the dripping rain. This Remonstrance, as it was called, put forth some effective arguments for those willing to listen. It reminded citizens that Congress had hitherto carefully refrained from interfering in the domestic policies of a colony, and therefore "the Representatives of the People are left as the sole Judges, whether their Governments be 'sufficient for the Exigencies of their Affairs.'" It pointed out that in Pennsylvania "Courts of Law are open, Justice has been administered with a due Attention to our Circumstances, and large Sums of Money issued. . . ." It bolstered its argument with a reference to New England: "Nor can we now see any Thing, in our Situation, which requires such an unequal Sacrifice, while other Colonies, particularly *Connecticut* and *Rhode Island,* the Authority of whose Assemblies is the same Way derived by Charter as ours, continue their ancient Forms of Government, by these Bodies, without Conventions." The Independents had made much of the idea that the new government would be established on the authority of the people. The Remonstrance noted that "Six Parts in seven of your Body are, by our inestimable Charter, vested with the Power of determining in this Matter."[1]

---
[1] *Votes* prints the entire Remonstrance, VIII, 7524–7526.

The Remonstrance was "carried by number two by two into allmost all parts of the town to be signed by all (tag, long tail, & bob), and allso sent into the country & much promoted by the Quakers."[2] Some six thousand people—among them the now completely confused though still independent-minded Joseph Reed[3]—signed it, half again as many as attended the protest meeting in the State House yard.[4] (Not to be outdone, the city Committee's propaganda material had by now raised attendance figures from the original four thousand to seven thousand.)[5]

The Moderates did not neglect the backcountry. Dr. William Smith sent copies of the Remonstrance, along with petitions for citizens to sign, to Phineas Bond in Lancaster. Bond, in turn, handed part of this packet of papers over to two young men to take down to York.[6] They were to give them for distribution to Samuel Johnson, the prothonotary, and Charles Lukens, the sheriff of York County and a member of the county Committee. Meanwhile, by another route Charles Stedman—a lawyer, a Scotsman, and also "a man of reading and erudition, though extremely magisterial and dogmatical in his cups"[7]—also headed for York with additional copies of the Remonstrance and petitions. From York he planned to travel up to Sunbury, seat of Northumberland County, where William McClay, the prothonotary there, who lived in the town's single "large & elegant" stone house, would take over. And, finally, James Rankin, the newly elected Assemblyman from York, wrapped up a packet of Remonstrances and petitions and dis-

---

[2] Marshall, Diary, May 24.

[3] Allan Nevins, *The American States During and After the Revolution* (New York, 1924), 106. The authority for the 6,000 signatures is James Rankin, *Pennsylvania Evening Post,* June 8. In the same paper, June 11, A Freeman doubts Rankin's figure and adds that even if true only 461 of the signers reside in the city and liberties of Philadelphia.

[4] *Pennsylvania Gazette,* June 12.

[5] "To the Publick in all Parts of the Province," in Peter Force, ed., *American Archives: Fourth Series* (6 vols., Washington, 1837-46), VI, 522.

[6] A full account of events in York County is given in the county Committee's letter of May 28, printed in the *Pennsylvania Evening Post,* June 4.

[7] Graydon, *Memoirs,* 94.

patched them with a letter to Henry Wolfe, urging him to do what he could to get this material out among the people.[8]

The effects of these efforts gave the Moderates little to cheer about. Let Benjamin Rush tell what happened: "It gives me great pleasure to inform you," he writes his wife, "that our cause continues to prosper in nine out of ten of the counties in our province. Two emissaries from the proprietary party were detected at Lancaster and York with the Remonstrance. One of them fled; the other was arrested by a county committee and obliged to go off without gaining a single convert to toryism. The Remonstrance was burnt as treasonable libel upon the liberties of America in Reading in Berks county. Many hundreds who signed it in Philadelphia county have repented of their folly and scratched out their names. A German we are told in Oxford township (a spot watered with the tory dew of the Reverend Dr. Smith's ministry) came up to the man who had by direct falsehood prevailed upon him to sign the Remonstrance, and begged him to erase his name. The man refused it. The German in a passion took the paper out of his hands and tore it into a thousand pieces, saying at the same time, 'Now, sir, you tell me d——d lies again.' The Remonstrance had 86 names subscribed to it."[9]

Rush's enthusiasm does not seem to have outrun the facts. Two Germans took space in the press to say that "being imposed upon by misrepresentations" into signing the Remonstrance they now "publicly disclaim against the sentiments therein contained."[10] Edward Shippen, Jr., told Jasper Yeates that his letters from Lancaster "have given me a full Insight into the politics of your County and shew the hard necessity you were under disguising your Sentiments at a Critical Conjuncture — While it may alter its Course the Stream runs so rapidly there is no stemming it; possibly

---

[8] Rankin's letter to Wolfe together with his own answer to the York Committee's rebuke to him is printed in the *Pennsylvania Evening Post,* June 8.

[9] Benjamin Rush to his wife, June 1, Butterfield, *Rush Letters,* I, 101.

[10] The notice, signed by John Tobias Rudolph and Christian Shaffer, appeared in the *Pennsylvania Gazette,* June 12.

before every thing valuable is swept away by it; in patient expectation of this, every moderate thinking Man must remain silent and inactive."[11]

In twenty days, give or take a few, the minds of the people, it would seem, had been shaped to take a decisive stand against the Moderates. The Remonstrance and the men who carried it out to the backcountry were received with abuse, threats, and even injury. What had occurred to inflame the people — some people, at least — who so recently voted to keep the Moderates in power?

Events since May 1 had put the Moderates in an awkward position. The river battle and news of the mercenaries, coupled with the nonappearance of peace commissioners, helped swing the backcountry from a wait-and-see attitude to one more favorable to independence. Even a moderate man like James Read, of Reading, had reached the point where he could hardly contain his fury. He wrote: "I imagine that all the Commissioners which are coming are Soldiers and Sailors, *determined*, if they can, to exterminate us. There is too much Hatred and Bitterness towards us in the Court of Britain to leave us any Hopes of Reconciliation."[12]

The Moderates adjusted to these events. The Remonstrance completely side-stepped the question of independence, and in so doing implied that the issue was a dead one, that independence was now all but a fact. The Remonstrance only asked that the people not overturn their government. It did not debate the virtues or defects of independence. But their past reputation clung to the Moderates. The Independents spread about the idea, without referring to the contents of the Remonstrance, that it was a "treasonable paper." It was easy to make the idea stick. People do not read petitions. They judge its contents by the people behind it, by the man who hands it to them. Had not the Moderates only a few days earlier campaigned on the platform of reconciliation? When a Moderate stepped up and asked a man for his signature he knew

[11] Edward Shippen, Jr., to Jasper Yeates, June 5, Shippen Papers, HSP.
[12] James Read to Edward Shippen, May 18, Shippen Papers, vol. 7, HSP.

what the Remonstrance said without glancing at it. And if he read it, he might regard this business about saving Pennsylvania's government as just another politician's trick to delay independence.

The Moderates' apparently stubborn refusal to give even token respect to the May 15 resolution of Congress killed any chance they might have had to shake their reputation as reconciliationists. James Biddle, prothonotary for Philadelphia County, still issued writs in the King's name, stamped with the King's seal, and made it clear he would "continue to do so till some Alteration shall be made either by the Assembly or Convention agreeable to the Recommendation of the Congress."[13] Jurors continued to take an oath to uphold the King's justice and judges to deliver their opinions in the name of the Crown. Reverend Duché still prayed for the King's health, only now his prayer provoked hisses from his congregation.[14]

The ticklish question of treason occupied the thoughts of men in public life. Jonathan Roberts sat in the Assembly in 1776 knowing, as his son put it, he "enter'd into measures technically treasonable, & acted in a body, (as he remark'd), with halters about their necks."[15] If James Biddle ceased to issue his writs in the King's name and if the British presently subdued the American rebellion, he might soon find himself judged a traitor. The devout Duché risked being defrocked for omitting the prayer for the King. In 1774-75 the Church of England in Philadelphia had supported the American stand against Great Britain. One churchman had tried to calm the fury of the Bishop of London by pointing out that "had our Clergy acted a different Part on the late Occasion, we should have ruined the Church Interest here."[16] The Bishop had

---

[13] Edward Shippen, Jr., to Edward Shippen, Sr., May 23, Shippen Papers, vol. 7, HSP.

[14] " June 2, Sunday—Went to Christ's Church, hiss'd the Minister for praying for the King as in the Littany," Charles Wilson Peale, Diary, 1776, APS.

[15] Klein, " Memoirs of Jonathan Roberts," *PMHB* 61 (1937), 469.

[16] Reverend William Barton to Dr. Hind, Secretary to the Society for Propagating the Gospel, August 28, 1775, William Smith Papers, vol. 6, HSP.

accepted the explanation then, but now the time for compromise had ended. Even a bold divine, and Duché was far from bold, would hesitate to risk his career in the church by dropping the prayer for the King. Better to endure a few hisses than to tread treasonable ground.

The strain of a past reputation and the awkward position of Moderates in public life might have been surmounted. The protest meeting in the State House yard gave the Moderates a more serious setback. People in the backcountry were sensitive to their isolation, and often in letters to city friends they pleaded for full accounts of what was going on in public affairs. They depended, unconsciously, on the city to help shape their opinions. The city Independents knew this. "Our situation makes us a kind of sentinel for the safety of the Province," the city Committee said in its propaganda to the backcountry.[17] Suddenly, from this sentinel of safety word came that four thousand — or was it seven thousand? — citizens had turned out in the rain to protest against the Assembly meeting, to demand a change in government and a set of pro-independent instructions for Pennsylvania delegates in Congress. So that was how the city felt — or at least that part of the city which, said the Committee, "consisted of that Class of men which are most to be depended on in time of danger."[18]

The Moderates in the city found themselves forced by events to strengthen the emotionalism engendered by the mass meeting. A few days after the meeting the Committee of Safety, long a target of the Independents, dispatched an open letter to the backcountry, asking for a prompt report "of the Number of Associators composing your Battalion and their State & Condition with Respect to Fire Arms & Accoutrements. The Great Preparation making in England both by Land & Sea to invade the Colonies require the use of every Precaution by the Spirited Sons of America, which

[17] Force, *American Archives*, VI, 522.
[18] *Pennsylvania Evening Post*, June 13.

may enable us to repel the Attacks of our unnatural Enemies."[19]

The events between May 1 and May 20 had given Pennsylvania every reason to both turn against the Moderates and swing over to independence. But were people in the backcountry being swept along by the tide? Did they rebuff the Moderates and their Remonstrance? It is worth noting that not a single copy of the Remonstrance nor of the petitions sent out from Philadelphia reached the people of York. The Independents were waiting for Charles Stedman when he arrived. Orders "were issued forthwith for securing Mr. Stedman's portmanteau, and keeping an eye on his person, till he might be examined." Stedman, having admitted the purpose of his trip, was hastened out of town. His departure "was attended with such circumstances, as caused two young men who came with another large packet of these treasonable papers . . . to decamp with precipitation."[20] Rankin's packet, too, was intercepted, and Rankin himself, when he later returned to York after the Assembly had adjourned in early June, was arrested; his release hinged on making "suitable concessions" and giving "sufficient surety for his good behaviour in future. . . ."[21]

The high feelings in York did not emanate from the people. This display of warmth came from the town of York's—not the county's—Committee of Inspection and Observation, and the leader was James Smith. The full county Committee had not been involved in what had happened in York. Smith had no doubt that when the county Committee assembled to discuss the resolves of the protest meeting in Philadelphia it would give its approval. "You may depend upon the event of this meeting," Smith said, "to be favorable to the cause of liberty, as the sense of the town militia was taken yesterday, and I am happy in being able to assure you that not a single dissentient, or even cool person, appeared in four

---

[19] Letter headed " In Committee for Lancaster—to all the commanders of the Battalions," May 28, Yeates Papers, HSP.
[20] James Smith's report to the Philadelphia Committee, dated May 28, in *Pennsylvania Evening Post,* June 4.
[21] Report of York County Committee, July 12, in York County Papers, HSP.

large companies."²² Smith was right. When the county Committee gathered the fifty-four members present approved the city resolves and voted to send delegates to a Provincial Conference.²³

James Smith's manipulation of York County sentiment was not an isolated example. The same thing was happening in Berks and Lancaster counties. The pattern repeated itself throughout the backcountry with little variation because the entire campaign was being planned and directed from one spot—Philadelphia. With two months of electioneering behind them, the Independents had acquired by now sufficient experience and organization to exploit every advantage offered them.

The backcountry campaign began soon after the mass meeting broke up. The city Committee met at the Philosophical Hall, "where were confirmed the resolves at State House & directions with proper persons apointed to goe with the said resolves to the different Countys."²⁴ Thomas McKean headed up to Reading.²⁵ Robert Strettel Jones and Joseph Watkins carried the Protest up to Bucks County.²⁶ The Moderates, alert to what was going on, passed the word to Lancaster that "a certain New England Man called Doctor Young of noisy fame together with Jacob Barge," were on their way "to endeavour to persuade the people there to join in the late Attempt to dissolve our Assembly. . . ."²⁷ On May 25 Christopher Marshall found that his friend Cannon "was gone out this morning with Tim. Matlack, Benja. Harbison, Lieutenant Chambers, William Miles to mett sundry [Philadelphia] county members at Norrington this afternoon."²⁸ On the same day the Committee of York, according to its report later to the city

---

[22] James Smith in *Pennsylvania Evening Post,* June 4.
[23] *Pennsylvania Evening Post,* June 4.
[24] Marshall, Diary, May 20.
[25] At least he was in Reading in May 29, for George Read writes, " I take an opportunity by Mr. McKean of writing . . . ." Shippen Papers, vol. 7, HSP
[26] Report of the Bucks County Committee, *Pennsylvania Evening Post,* June 15.
[27] Edward Shippen, Jr., to Jasper Yeates, May 23, Balch Papers, vol. 2. HSP.
[28] Marshall, Diary, May 25.

Committee, "was favored with the company of several of your respectable body, joined by others the worthy citizens of Philadelphia, who laid before our Town Committee immediately assembled for that purpose, the letters, votes and proceedings of the city and liberties of the capital."[29] Charles Stedman arrived the same day but only after the York Committee had been properly briefed by the city Independents about the "treasonable papers" the Moderates were flooding the backcountry with.

Each of these delegations traveled with bundles of propaganda material. Between May 20 and May 22, when the first of these delegations set out, the Protest and resolves passed at the mass meeting were printed; an open letter to be circulated among the county committees was written and printed; several hundred copies of a brief statement "for circulation by broadcasts and posters through the Province" were run off the press.[30] All this material was tailored for the backcountry. No mention occurred about the need for lowering suffrage qualification, as sometimes did in the Independents' propaganda in the city. One circular letter reminded the backcountry of woes endured in the past.

> We have seen and some of us have felt, the melancholy effects arising from the opposing interests of the Proprietary and the people. Who can recollect the horrors of the late Indian War, and not shudder at the idea it brings to his mind. Fire, sword, desolation, and *death in the most infernal forms,* will be presented to our view — Parents and children weltering in their blood — Infants torn with savage brutality from their mothers wombs, and made the food of dogs ! ! ![31]

The broadside warned that the question at issue would probably be "disguised or misrepresented to you, by designing persons." It pointed out that the only question was the union of the colonies and "seven thousands, who appeared at the State House, and have

---

[29] *Pennsylvania Evening Post,* June 4.
[30] The broadside appears in Force, *American Archives,* VI, 522.
[31] This Circular letter to the backcountry appeared in the *Pennsylvania Packet,* June 17. The letter is dated May 21.

sworn to support the Union."[32] The open letter, on the other hand, emphasized the county Committees' duty to elect delegates for a Conference in Philadelphia to decide on a new government for Pennsylvania.[33]

The common aim through all this material was to discredit the Assembly. This explains the gory reminder of the French and Indian War. Now, propaganda cannot on its own "force its way into unwilling minds; it penetrates only into minds already open. . . ."[34] It is possible that recent events had persuaded a majority of the backcountry of the merits of independence. There is no indication that the backcountry had sufficient grievances against the Assembly to wish its overthrow. The people's grievances were directed against England. But there was a group of men in the backcountry — the Associators — with an abundance of grievances. All military men, especially those in a volunteer army, have grievances — against the food, civilians, sergeants; the list is endless. In a disciplined army the officers keep these grievances subdued. The Pennsylvania Associators lacked discipline. (Richard Peters, asked how many men he commanded, said: "Not one, but I am commanded by ninety.")[35] Furthermore, the officers helped publicize the enlisted men's grievances. The assembly had worked up a set of Articles for governing the Associators. Anthony Wayne, speaking for his men, told the Assembly that as things stood "the burthen of the Association falls chiefly on the poor and middling sort of the inhabitants, — whilst the more opulent are, for the most part, exampt." The burden was excessive on patriotic shopkeepers, artisans, and the like who packed their apprentices off to a company. The master not only lost the apprentice-soldier's services; he had to pay for the boy's gun and other equipment. Wayne felt

---

[32] Force, *American Archives*, VI, 522.
[33] *Pennsylvania Packet*, June 17.
[34] Hoffer, *True Believer*, 103.
[35] Quoted in *PMHB* 25 (1901), 368.

that "arms and accoutrements should be provided at the public charge."[36]

These grievances amounted to little for a long while. They were sporadic and came from isolated battalions. Then starting February 1, 1776, James Cannon's Committee of Correspondence for the Committee of Privates began to send out bulletins to every battalion in the province. Soon several thousand volunteer soldiers scattered through the backcountry had been united by Cannon's letters from Philadelphia into an aggrieved group whose anger focused on the Assembly. Congress had provided that a brigadier general be chosen for the Pennsylvania militia; the Assembly, as in other colonies, set about choosing a man. Cannon's Committee of Correspondence told the soldiers that they and not the Assembly should choose the general. In every letter from Philadelphia the soldiers were given a new reason for distrusting the Assembly. The privations they endured, the paltry pay, the shoddy uniforms— all were blamed on the Assembly. A great many of the privates were apprentices and servants, some as young as fifteen years. Most, free for the first time from a master's discipline, were having the time of their lives. "The puritanical spirit was unknown among us," one soldier recalled. Every gathering of the battalion was a social occasion. For the weekly afternoon drill "capacious demijohns of Maderia were constantly set out in the yard where we formed, for our refreshment before marching out to exercise."[37] Cannon's committee refused to let the boys enjoy themselves. Its letters reminded the boys that many were, thanks to the Assembly, second-class citizens; they lacked the right to vote. Cannon noted "that it has been the Practice of all Countries, and is highly reasonable, that all Persons, (not being Mercenaries) who expose their Lives in Defence of a Country, should be admitted to the

---

[36] A Remonstrance from the Committee of Inspection and Observation of Chester County to the Assembly, signed by Anthony Wayne; in the *Pennsylvania Packet,* March 4, 1776.

[37] Graydon, *Memoirs,* 122–23, 108.

Enjoyment of all of the Rights and Privileges of a Citizen of that Country which they have defended and protected."[38]

By mid-May Cannon's Committee of Correspondence had developed contacts in every county and township in Pennsylvania. After the May 20 mass meeting and while the city Committee was sending delegations to the county Committees, Cannon saw to it that every backcountry battalion of Associators received an account of the meeting. He suggested that the Protest be read aloud to all battalions and that each of the resolves be put to the privates for a voice vote of approval. Soon miniature mass meetings were being held throughout the backcountry.[39] Most of these took place before the county committees had met to decide whether or not the county should send delegates to the Provincial Conference, as recommended by the protest meeting. James Smith had predicted that once the sense of the militia had been made known the decision of the committees could be depended upon to be favorable. He was right. Every county committee—even those in "Tory-ridden" Chester, Bucks, and Philadelphia counties—ended up sending a delegation to the Provincial Conference. Even Sam Adams must have admired the speed and skill with which the backcountry had been pressured into both supporting the drive for independence and acquiescing in the overthrow of Pennsylvania's government.

---

[38] The full petition, signed by Samuel Simpson and dated February 23, is in *Votes*, VIII, 7402–07. The quotation above appears on 7406.

[39] On May 27 the Second Battalion of Northampton County—nine hundred men—voted that the Assembly was "not competent to the exigencies of our affairs" (*Pennsylvania Evening Post*, June 1); the Fourth Battalion quickly followed suit (*ibid.*, June 6); on June 10 the First Battalion of Chester County approved the Protest, backed by a similar vote from the Elk Battalion (*Pennsylvania Gazette*, June 12); Colonel James Crawford's Battalion of Lancaster County voted its approval soon afterward (*ibid.*, June 19).

8 THE ASSEMBLY

For those refreshed by a good fight Pennsylvania politics in late May and early June in 1776 had its attractions. Among the several areas of combat scattered through the province the liveliest centered, after May 20, in a plainly furnished chamber on the second floor of the State House. Here the Assembly met and here for the next twenty-five days this body that had shaped and directed Pennsylvania affairs for nearly a century fought for its life.

The fight got underway the instant the multitude at the mass meeting dispersed through the rain, but the outcome was conditioned by forces long at work. Many things hindered the Assembly in its fight for survival. Among these was a myth, and there lies a story that requires a diversion.

The myth had it that the Society of Friends dominated and thus controlled the Pennsylvania Assembly in 1776. The myth flourished for obvious reasons. A visiting Englishman, for instance, noticed that "the Buildings are Brick, very plain, convenient and neat, no very grand edifices as the Quakers have the management of public affairs."[1] The Quakers set the tone for Philadelphia and so, presumably, they perpetuated that tone through control of Pennsylvania politics. John Adams had implicit faith in the myth. He knew for sure that Pennsylvania remained cool toward independence to a large extent because its politics was "encumbered with a large body of Quakers."[2]

---

[1] *Journal of Nicholas Cresswell,* 156.
[2] John Adams to Benjamin Hichborn, May 29, Adams, *Works,* IX, 379.

Strangely, those who knew the colony's politics from the inside helped the myth thrive. Edward Burd wrote: "The Quakers have too much Influence in the House for these times when a Defensive War is to be vigorously carried on."[3] Charles Thomson, recalling in late life some of Pennsylvania's troubles of 1776, placed the blame for many of them on the fact that "a majority of the Assembly were of the people called quakers."[4] The Committee of Privates complained in its many protests that it disliked the idea of being subservient to the Assembly because so many of its members were Quakers.[5]

As with all myths this one, too, was rooted once in truth. The Society of Friends maintained a tight grip on Pennsylvania politics up to 1756. When Indians began to raise havoc throughout the backcountry, the Assembly, after much temporizing, soon could not blink the fact that if Pennsylvania were to survive it must arm and fight back. The Quakers faced the choice of either abandoning politics or their pacific principles. They chose to leave politics.

This, perhaps, puts the matter too simply. The question of frontier defense raised more basic questions among Quakers. They began to re-examine their whole way of life to see how far they had drifted away from the simple existence their religion demanded of them. The departure from politics heralded only a phase of a quiet reformation among members of the Society of Friends. By 1776 the Society had retrieved much of the vigor and strength it had when Penn lived. Twenty years of discipline following the experience of 1756 had prepared the Quakers spiritually and mentally to resist the American Revolution. It was this that made possible the Quakers' remarkably complete resistance to the war.[6]

---

[3] Edward Burd to James Burd, March 15, Shippen Papers, vol. 7, HSP.
[4] Charles Thomson to W. H. Drayton, Stillé, *Life of Dickinson*, 348.
[5] See especially the petitions in *Votes*, VIII, 7402–07, 7546-48.
[6] An excellent account of the Quakers' retreat from politics appears in Tolles, *Meeting House and Counting House*, Chapter 10. The departure in 1756 does not seem to have been as lasting as Tolles suggests but it did open the reformation that prepared Friends for the Revolution.

This unity did not come all at once. The abandonment of political life in 1756 was neither complete nor permanent. Once the French and Indian War ended Quakers slowly drifted back in numbers to public life. They remained in political affairs in considerable numbers up through 1774. Only when America abandoned non-intercourse—a policy perfectly adapted to Quaker beliefs and thus one that had their full support—and traded passive resistance for a shooting war did the Quakers once again quietly depart from politics, so quietly that their withdrawal was little noticed by non-Quakers nor publicized by Friends. Of the forty-one members in the 1775-1776 Assembly only nine, or slightly more than one-fifth the membership, were or had been members of the Society of Friends.[7] Among the seventeen new members in the enlarged Assembly only Samuel Howell and James Rankin were of Quaker background. Of these eleven Quakers among the fifty-eight members of the Assembly, five had left or been asked to leave the Society of Friends.[8] They were all warm supporters of independence.[9] The remaining six seem to have held views similar to Jonathan Roberts, who classed himself as a "nonmilitant Whig."[10] They appear not to have opposed the idea of independence so much as the violence being used to achieve it.

The Society moved slowly but relentlessly to bring members into line. Joseph Pennock of Chester County was reproached for sitting on an Assembly committee "wherein he so far deviated from our

---

[7] The nine were: George Gray, Joseph Parker, Jonathan Roberts of Philadelphia County; Thomas Mifflin of the city; John Foulke, Thomas Jenks, and David Twining of Bucks; John Jacobs and Joseph Pennock of Chester. The job of determining Assemblymen's religion proved harder than expected. James Gibbons and Joseph Pyle of Chester may have been Quakers, but I could find no proof of it.

[8] They were: George Gray, who was turned "out of meeting for his part in warlike measures" (See sketch of Gray in *PMHB*, 11 (1887), 78-79); Joseph Parker, also disowned for being concerned in warlike measures (See Hinshaw and Marshall, *Encyclopedia of American Quaker Geneology*, II, 613); Thomas Mifflin; John Jacobs; and James Rankin.

[9] James Rankin must be noted as an exception.

[10] Klein, "Memoirs of Jonathan Roberts," *PMHB*, 61 (1937), 470.

peaceable principles as to hear evidence and subscribe his name in a report to that House respecting a matter pertaining to war." A contrite Pennock admitted his error; he left politics and was not disowned. John Jacobs, another Chester County Assemblyman, proved less amenable. A visiting committee from his local meeting reported "he did not appear to be convinced of the inconsistency of his Conduct . . . but endeavoured to justify Defensive War." Another committee tried in "a brotherly manner to endeavour to restore him to a sense of his Deviation." Jacobs refused to see the light and was disowned.[11] None of these committees relished the task of reprimanding their Friends. The son of Jonathan Roberts tells of the group that called on his father, "from a religious impulse." "He was not in," the son recalls, "& my mother was nursing sister Anna, her youngest daughter. The Senior Friend, after some civil conversation, remark'd that a young child always reminded him, of a flowery Garden. They arose to depart without having mentioned the object of their visit, when one of the company, Evan Lewis, whose religious merit consisted in a long face, & Buckram'd skirts to his coat; in a querelous tone said to the Elder, is this all thee had to say to Jonathan (meaning my father). . . ."[12] The committee left without speaking its piece but a few months later Assemblyman Roberts withdrew from politics.

The myth of Quaker domination in Pennsylvania politics thrived then and has persisted since for a simple reason: it offered, then and now, a handy way to explain why Pennsylvania lagged in enthusiasm for independence. Once facts replace the myth it becomes clear that instead of retarding the drift toward independence the Quakers' absence from public affairs helped hasten

---

[11] The material on Jacobs and Pennock comes from Gilbert Cope, " Chester County Quakers During the Revolution," *Bulletin of the West Chester Historical Society 1902–1903* (n.p., 1903). Quaker records are not as complete nor clear as one might wish. Jacobs, for example, was disowned on December 5, 1777, yet somewhere along the line he was reinstated apparently, for on December 7, 1780, he is again disowned for " holding in bondage a Negro Man of proper Age to be free."

[12] Klein, " Memoirs of Jonathan Roberts," *PMHB*, 61 (1937), 469–470.

THE ASSEMBLY

the decision. When the Friends departed from politics they left gaps to be filled, if not by Independents—it is doubtful that the Quaker population of the three eastern counties would send such men to the House—at least by moderate-minded men who were not opposed in principle to warlike measures. The strictest Friends, according to Charles Thomson, stayed away from all elections once the war began, thus weakening the Moderates' position at the polls.[13] None of the Friends who remained in politics through June of 1776 is known to have been a bitter opponent of independence and the majority of them were fervent supporters of the idea. On the city Committee the Independents drew strength from such ex-Friends as Matlack, Marshall, Isaac Coates, Nathan Brown, and Isaac Howell. In the Assembly Thomas Mifflin, John Jacobs, George Gray, and Joseph Parker advanced the cause.

The myth of Quaker domination of politics is not something historians dreamed up. The myth existed, as we have seen, in 1776. But to what extent did the myth influence people's opinions? Was there much bitterness against Quakers or was it only the ill-informed of the day who bore them a grudge? It is possible there was less anti-Quaker sentiment around than has been assumed. Friends, for example, made it clear they would not close their shops on the Fast Day that Congress had decreed; to do so would be to share in a warlike measure. The city Committee asked Philadelphians to "forbear from any kind of insult" to those who refused to keep the fast.[14] The request seems on the whole to have been respected.[15] The Independents' propaganda after May 20 does not make a single reference to "the people called Quakers." The broadsides and circular letters repeatedly censure "the proprietary dependents" which of course could include Quakers—though John Adams distinguishes between the two groups[16]—but shuns any

---
[13] Charles Thomson to W. H. Drayton, Stillé, *Life of Dickinson*, 351.
[14] Broadside Collection (1776), Item 56, HSP.
[15] Marshall, Diary, May 17.
[16] John Adams to Benjamin Hichborn, May 29, Adams, *Works*, IX, 379.

direct criticisms of the Society. The major share of what hostility existed came from the Associators, who resented the fact that conscientious objectors prospered while they served. Cannon played up this grievance for what it was worth in his bulletins from the Committee of Correspondence.

If only a myth had hampered the Assembly, its chance of survival would have improved considerably. It was also hindered by the continued cooperation between Independents in Congress and those in the city. Soon after the Assembly convened a member — one of the Allens, according to Benjamin Rush — suggested that Congress be asked to clarify the meaning of John Adams' measure.[17] If Congress agreed that the Assembly, after eliminating all vestiges of royal authority in Pennsylvania, was qualified to run the colony's affairs, the revolution would be stopped in its tracks. Rush got off a hasty note to Richard Henry Lee, warning him that the Assembly's seemingly innocent request "shows a design to enslave the people of Pennsylvania." He continued: "I conjure you . . . not to desert us in this trying exigency. 4/5 of the inhabitants of our colony will fly to the *ultima ratio* before they will submit to a new government formed by the present Assembly. Please to circulate the papers you will receive herewith among *all* the Southern delegates tomorrow morning."[18]

The "brace" of Adams took a hand in helping the city Independents block the Assembly request for clarification. On May 23 Marshall visited Sam and John Adams at their lodgings before breakfast. In the afternoon, after Congress adjourned, the two Adamses visited Marshall at his home. After they departed, Marshall, briefed by the experts, dropped over to James Cannon's place and there Rush, Matlack, and Paine joined the pair.[19] By the next day the Independents' answer — or Memorial, as it was called —

---
[17] *Votes,* VIII, 7516.
[18] Benjamin Rush to Richard Henry Lee, May 22, Butterfield, "Further Letters of Benjamin Rush," *PMHB,* 78 (1954), 14–15.
[19] Marshall, Diary, May 23.

THE ASSEMBLY 157

was completed. It was submitted to Congress on May 25.[20] It protested the Assembly's request for clarification by continuing its campaign to discredit that body: "The situation of our province," it said, "requires vigour and harmony in the direction of both civil and military affairs, but these can never be obtained when a people no longer confide in their rulers." It parried the Assembly maneuver by flattering Congress, a touch that perhaps one of the Adamses added: "The Committee have too much confidence in the wisdom of your body, to believe (when informed of the true situation of the province) that you meant to include the Assembly thereof in your recommendations to 'Assemblies' to form new governments."

Nothing came of the Assembly's request for amplification of the May 15 resolve. Once the city Independents had overcome their initial scare that the Moderates might outmaneuver them, they saw they had nothing to fear from the Assembly. They stumbled upon a weapon that condemned for certain the Assembly's lease on life and at the same time forced the legislature to jump at the Independents' slightest command. The Independents had failed to win direct control of the Assembly in May, but they had won sufficient power to bring legislative affairs to a standstill. A rule of the Assembly held that a quorum for conducting business required the presence of two-thirds of the members.[21] An almost plaintive notation in the Assembly record for May 24 indicates what the Independents were up to: "*Ordered*, That the Clerk write to absent Members, requesting their Attendance in Assembly as soon as possible."[22] Simply by boycotting the body the Independents could, whenever they wished, block all legislative affairs of the colony. The Moderates could either stand fast and thus reduce the government to impotence or compromise. They chose to compromise.

---

[20] Ford, *Journals of Congress*, IV, 390. See *Pennsylvania Gazette*, May 29, for full Memorial.
[21] Sister Joan de Lourdes Leonard, "The Organization and Procedure of the Pennsylvania Assembly, 1682–1776," *PMHB*, 72 (1948), 223.
[22] *Votes*, VIII, 7520.

John Dickinson, who was, so to speak, majority leader of the Assembly, persisted under the illusion that adequate concessions could preserve the government. For two weeks he used all his power and political skill to that end. The Independents had underscored that line in Adams' preamble which said all signs of the King's power in a colony should be totally suppressed. As a first step in compliance with that recommendation, Dickinson saw to it that the traditional oath of allegiance to the King, normally required of all new Assembly members before taking their seats, was abandoned. Some Moderates balked at this innovation. "We took our Seats without any qualification," James Allen reported, "whereupon Mr. [James] Webb of Lancaster left the house & Mr. [George] Ross declared he would have done the same, had all been qualified."[23]

This flurry only helped nourish a storm. Once seated, an Independent "then moved that the German inhabitants of this province be hereafter considered as legal voters without taking the oaths of allegiance."[24] James Allen, who, as an Independent noted, "had taken *his* seat *without* oaths," asked to have the question put off, "but finding that such a glaring partiality would not be supported by the House," the motion was withdrawn.[25] A committee was thereupon chosen, with Dickinson as chairman, "to prepare and draw up Resolutions for rendering Naturalization and the Oaths on Affirmations of Allegiance unnecessary in all Cases where they are required or have been usually taken within this Colony."[26]

Dickinson's handling of this question of oaths indicates that given an equal willingness to compromise among the Independents he would have led the Assembly step by step to a complete compliance with the resolve of Congress. The Independents—at least a hard core of them—would not compromise. Whatever Dickinson did failed to please them. In their eyes "he steered an indefinite

---

[23] Allen, Diary, *PMHB*, 9 (1885), 188.
[24] "To the People," *Pennsylvania Gazette*, June 26.
[25] *Ibid.*
[26] *Votes*, VIII, 7520–21.

course, sometimes agreeing with one side, sometimes with the other, sometimes with neither; seeming upon the whole to have no other fixed object in view than HIMSELF."[27]

Given sufficient time—say, two weeks—Dickinson might still have worked out something to save the Assembly. One of those unplanned events that so often shape history suddenly intruded itself into Pennsylvania affairs and hopes for a compromise promptly dissolved even for John Dickinson. On May 27 word arrived in Philadelphia that twelve days earlier—the same day Congress had passed John Adams' contentious preamble—the Virginia convention had passed a resolution asking Congress to declare the colonies free and independent states.

For three days the Independents watched to see how the Assembly would handle the challenge from Virginia. It procrastinated and so on June 1 the Independents proceeded to boycott the Assembly. They stayed away for four days, finally returning only when the Moderates agreed to debate a change of instructions for the Pennsylvania delegates in Congress. There was no chance for further stalling tactics on either side now, for below in the first-floor chamber of the State House the Virginia resolution had been presented to Congress.

When the Independents returned to the Assembly on June 5, their confidence received a temporary setback. The Moderates continued to show more grass-roots strength than expected. First, there had been the Remonstrance, which by the time it reached the Assembly, after circulating through the city and county of Philadelphia, had six thousand signatures. This had been followed up by an Address from the Committee of Philadelphia County which pleaded with the Assembly to oppose any change of instructions for the Pennsylvania delegates in Congress and to "oppose the changing or altering, in any the least Part, of our invaluable Constitution. . . ."[28] On June 5 came further cheering news for the

---
[27] "To the People," *Pennsylvania Gazette,* June 26.
[28] *Votes,* VIII, 7519.

Moderates: "A great Number of Petitions from divers Inhabitants of this Province, of the same Tenor with those presented . . . from the City and County of *Philadelphia,* were laid before the House and read."[29] Despite the well-organized tempest stirred up in the backcountry by the Independents, the Moderates' machine had not collapsed completely. Those in the Assembly who resisted both independence and all attempts to overturn the government clearly were not a tight little band of willful men who acted in self-interest and ignored the will of the people. They were, for the most part, men who had been in politics for many years. As long as they knew that they reflected the views of a sizeable number of their constituents they would continue to resist the Independents.

This new surge of support could not have been overwhelming, for on June 5 the Assembly appointed a committee, again headed by John Dickinson, to bring in a new set of instructions for Pennsylvania's delegates in Congress. There was need for haste. The debate on the Virginia resolution in Congress would begin Friday, June 7.

By Friday the Assembly had still not agreed on a new set of instructions. James Wilson used the delay to urge Congress to postpone a decision on independence a few weeks longer. Wilson, referring to himself in the third person, told Congress on June 7 that "he believed a Majority of the People of Pennsylvania were in Favour of Independence, but that the Sence of the Assembly (the only representative Body then existing in the Province) as delivered to him by their Instructions, was against the Proposition; that he wished the question to be postponed, because he had Reason to believe the People of Pennsylvania would soon have an Opportunity of expressing their Sentiments upon this point [through the Provincial Conference, which would meet June 18] and he thought the People ought to have an Opportunity given

---

[29] *Ibid.,* 7535. A search of the Public Archives in Harrisburg did not turn up any of these petitions supporting the Moderates.

them to Signify their opinion in a regular Way upon a Matter of such Importance."[30]

On June 8 the Assembly passed new instructions by a vote of thirty-one to twelve.[31] They authorized Pennsylvania delegates to "concur with the other Delegates in Congress, in forming such further compacts between the United Colonies, concluding such Treaties with foreign Kingdoms and States, and in adopting such other Measures as, upon a View of all circumstances, shall be judged necessary for promoting the Liberty, Safety and Interests of *America*."[32] There was no mention of independence. The Independents accepted these new instructions as "an artful and selfish compromise."[33] Artful they were meant to be. The aim was to temporize on the issue until the sense of the province could be determined from the Provincial Conference soon to meet.

When the word came down from above stairs that the new instructions had been passed, James Wilson rose from his seat in Congress and said that "being un-restrained, if the Question was put he would vote for it; but he still wished a Determination on it to be postponed for a short time until the Deputies of the People of Pennsylvania who were to meet should give their explicit Opinion upon this Point so important and interesting to themselves and to their Posterity. . . ."[34]

With the new instructions passed, attention in the Assembly now shifted to forestalling the revolution in government. Since May 20 the Independents had imperceptibly been drifting apart. Though all Independents shared in the campaign to discredit the Assembly, many now began to draw back from carrying their handiwork to

---

[30] Unpublished manuscript in Library of Congress, quoted by Hampton L. Carson, *American Law Register*, 55 (1907), 38. Also quoted in the two-volume biography " James Wilson " by Burton Alva Konkle, a typescript copy of which is on deposit in the Friends' Historical Library, Swarthmore College.
[31] Marshall, Diary, June 8, gives the vote as above. James Allen says in his Diary that the vote had thirteen nays, his among them, *PMHB*, 9 (1885), 188.
[32] *Votes*, VIII, 7542–43.
[33] " To the People," *Pennsylvania Gazette,* June 26.
[34] Carson, *American Law Register,* 55 (1907), 39.

its source of power. They neither wanted nor expected any radical changes in the form of government. Now it became clear that some among the Independents aimed at a revolution in government. They regarded the Assembly as the epitome of evil in Pennsylvania politics and wished it swiftly swept from existence.

Meanwhile, the Remonstrance, which seemed to accept independence as all but fact, had heralded a split among the Moderates. Many now reluctantly began to accept independence as inevitable, while a core of the Moderates still stubbornly balked at the idea. With both parties breaking apart the new alignments shaped up into three inchoate factions which, though nameless then, might have been labeled: Reactionaries — comprised of James Allen, John Dickinson, and all who refused to compromise their dream of reconciliation; Moderate Independents — which included men like Joseph Reed and John Morton, who had been brought around to favoring independence but hoped to preserve the old forms of government and keep the control of power in the hands of gentlemen; and Radical Independents — who aimed at a revolution in forms and ideas in Pennsylvania's government.

This new alignment of forces came out into the open on June 13. Matthias Slough of Lancaster tells what happened: "a Motion was this morning made by the Independants for the House to recommend the Choosing a Convention in Consequence of which the House will resolve itself into a Committee of the whole to consider the motion and I have no doubt it will be Carried."[35] The motion was a belated attempt by Moderate Independents to save the Assembly from extinction. If the Constitutional Convention, which was soon to meet with or without Assembly approval, did so on the invitation of the Assembly, there would be less likelihood of a revolution in government. This move was blocked by obdurate members who, according to a Radical Independent, "formed a scheme for carrying the matter respecting the Convention much farther than bare approbation; and were for entering upon the

---

[35] Matthias Slough to Jasper Yeates, June 13, Miscellaneous Collection, HSP.

business itself, by fixing the numbers the Convention should consist of, the proportion to each county, and other matters."[36]

The Radical Independents would have none of this. To justify their position they fell back on John Adams' handy preamble: "the House had never been requested, but on the contrary forbidden," they said, "to interfere in any part of the business of a new government." If that were not sufficient reason, there was a more practical one: "As nearly all the counties had at that time nominated their Deputies to the Conference, some of which were upon the road, for the express purpose of settling and adjusting the number, proportion, time, and place of the Convention, nothing but confusion could have been produced by the Assembly meddling therewith."[37]

To make certain that the Moderate Independents and Reactionaries did not unite to force through a plan that might preserve the Assembly, the Radicals revived the boycott. Now, the Moderates possessed the numerical strength and the Radicals perhaps had no more than the seven members who refused to sign the committee report exonerating the Committee of Safety from a "lax performance of duties."[38] But these seven men were enough to hamstring the Assembly. For a variety of reasons poor attendance had marked this session of the Assembly. Edward Biddle, for instance, was too ill to make the trip down from Reading; none of the deputies from Westmoreland or Bedford counties had bothered to travel to Philadelphia. On a question so crucial as new instructions for the delegation in Congress only forty-three members turned out to vote — a bare four over the quorum required for the Assembly to sit. Seven Radical Independents had no trouble in such a situation bringing Assembly business to a halt.

The hamstrung House met four days without a quorum. On June

---

[36] "To the People," *Pennsylvania Gazette,* June 26.
[37] *Ibid.*
[38] These seven were: Robert Whitehill (Cumberland), Henry Chreist and Henry Haller (Berks), Peter Kachlein (Northampton), John Brown (Bucks), Joseph Pyle (Chester), and Thomas Porter (Lancaster).

14, with a mass of routine business to be settled, it tried desperately to round up members. A messenger "was sent to summon four or five of the members supposed to be at their lodgings in the neighbourhood. He returned that they were not at home, and that they had paid off their lodgings. He was then sent to four or five others but he returned with the same account. Then the members found what conduct the absentees had pursued & with what design. Those who were present were not of a sufficient number to do any act but to adjourn. Their indignation was great. . . . And thus ended Legislation under the Proprietary Government in Pennsylvania."[39]

No one knew for certain when the Assembly adjourned on June 14 that its end had come. It set August 26 as the time for reconvening. Nothing in the future any longer seemed certain and even the ablest men in politics were confused what the course of events in Pennsylvania would be. "Our Affairs have been in such a fluctuating and disordered Situation," wrote James Wilson, "that it has been almost impossible to form any Accurate Judgment concerning the Transactions as they were passing, and still more nearly impossible to make any probable Conjectures concerning the Turn that Things would take." As Wilson wrote, the Provincial Conference was then sitting. The decisions of these men, he felt, would indicate the direction of Pennsylvania's affairs. "Matters are, however," he concluded, "now, in all Likelyhood approaching to a Crisis."[40]

---

[39] Charles Thomson, " Joseph Reed's Narrative," in " The Papers of Charles Thomson," *Collections of the New York Historical Society for 1878* (New York, 1879), 273.
[40] James Wilson to Horatio Gates, June, *PMHB,* 36 (1912), 474.

9 NEW MEN — NEW IDEAS

On May 10 John Dickinson left for a rest on his farm near Dover confident that the drive for independence had been slowed, perhaps, for the time being, even stopped. The Moderates would control the Assembly when it convened, and so long as the Pennsylvania legislature resisted independence, as it would under Dickinson's leadership, the other Middle Colonies would follow its lead. Dickinson could relax, too, with the knowledge that his old opponent John Adams was becoming disturbed that "the spirit of levelling, as well as that of innovation, is afloat."[1] This, alone, might be expected to slow up Adams' zeal for independence. Adams had even come round to agreeing that the colonies should confederate before breaking away from Great Britain. Dickinson, wiser if less bold than Adams, knew it would take time to devise a plan of confederation acceptable to all colonies; by the time differences had been eliminated Britain might have sent over acceptable peace proposals. The state of affairs was far from dismal from Dickinson's view as he set out for his farm in Delaware.

Ten days later Dickinson returned to Philadelphia to confront a changed world and within a few days he knew his fight to delay the break with Britain had ended in defeat. By early June Dickinson could see he was no longer a power in Pennsylvania politics. Men continued to listen but no longer to follow him.

June 8, the day the Assembly voted new instructions for its

---
[1] John Adams to John Lowell, June 12, Adams, *Works*, IX, 393.

delegates in Congress, marked the dismissal of Dickinson and his ideas from power. Sometime in the morning, apparently after the House had passed the new instructions but before they had been released to the public, Dickinson took time to attend a meeting of all battalion officers in the city.[2] He was there in his capacity of colonel of the First Battalion. The purpose of the gathering was to decide whether or not to let the Assembly appoint a brigadier general for the Pennsylvania militia. One officer, against the House having anything to do with the appointment, censured the Assembly's conduct unmercifully, particularly for its anti-independent instructions to the delegates in Congress. He said that "the authors and abettors of those instructions would find they had lost the Confidence & affections of the people."[3] He aimed this barb at Dickinson, who had written the old instructions. Dickinson rose to defend both himself and the Assembly.

"We are blamed," he said, "for appointing men who had not the confidence of the people & we are also blamed because we gave not those suspected men unlimited powers: You say the Assembly has no right to alter the constitution without the consent of the people, & you condemn the Assembly because they gave not their delegates powers to alter it."

"The loss of life," he went on, "or what is dearer than life itself, the Affection of my countrymen shall not deter me from acting as an honest man. These threats then that we just now heard might have been spared. I defy them, I regard them not — I stand as unmoved by them, as the rock among the waves that dash against it. — I can defy the *world;* Sir, but — I defy not

---

[2] Bradford, Register. The entry is undated but follows one for June 6. Internal evidence indicates the meeting occurred either on June 7 or 8, before the new instructions had been released to the public. On June 5 this notice appeared in the *Pennsylvania Gazette*: " The Officers of the four Philadelphia county battalions are requested to meet, on Saturday, the 8th inst. at 11 o'clock at Capt. Neff's, in Whitemarsh township, on business of immediate consequence." I have assumed that the meeting of the city battalions occurred on the same day at about the same time.

[3] *Ibid.*

heaven; nor will I ever barter my conscience for the esteem of mankind. So let my Country treat me as she pleases still I will act as my conscience directs."[4]

Men normally tend to suspect one who talks much of his integrity, of a conscience that defies compromise, and who uses heaven to justify his actions. They are doubly suspicious if that man be an experienced politician. John Dickinson somehow allayed such suspicions. His words, wrote William Bradford, Jr., "appeared to be the unpremeditated effusions of the heart. His graceful actions, the emotions of his countenance & a plaintive yet manly voice strongly imposed upon my judgment. He was clearly wrong yet I believed him right. Such were the effects of oratory."[5]

Politics only reflected deeper changes at work. The tempo of change picked up sharply after the river battle; it gathered more speed after May 20. The press by June had put aside its sense of fair play. Tolerance for the idea of reconciliation had died. Republicus, who seemed to voice the sentiments of the newspaper editors, wrote: "Reconciliation is thought of now by none but knaves, fools and madmen."[6] About the time the press lost its tolerance inflation began to be sharply felt. The value of the Continental dollar started to drop just as the price of goods, which had held steady through most of May, spurted ahead. By this time most merchants had cleaned out their stocks of West Indies goods and their advertisements began to disappear from the papers. Now at least half the advertisements offered a REWARD for a runaway servant or apprentice. The remaining ones showed the effects of war, too. The enterprising John McClur, out to solve the servant problem, announced he had opened "an INTELLIGENCE-OFFICE where any Gentleman or Lady, wanting servants, may hear of such as will suit them."[7] A druggist with a supply of "choice

---

[4] *Ibid.*
[5] *Ibid.*
[6] *Pennsylvania Evening Post,* June 29.
[7] *Ibid.,* June 20.

Jesuits Bark, Opium, and Spanish Flies" reminded buyers that these "excellent drugs are scarce at this time."[8] When the brig *Hawke* went up for sale her advertised virtues—"She sails remarkably flat, is just hove down, has a clean tallow bottom, is well calculated for a privateer or letter of marque, and is all ready to take her guns on board"[9]—aimed at a wartime buyer.

The pleasant, secure, and comfortable world Philadelphians had known on May 1 had all but vanished by June. The sudden and complete change left William Bradford, Jr., overwhelmed. "This day the amiable family of Shippens set of[f] for the Jerseys," he wrote in his diary on June 20. "Mournful was the hour of parting. I pursued the Coach with my eyes & then retired to the office disconsolate & forlorn. Every beauty had left the place: the usual scene that I had so often seen with pleasure charmed no more. A heavy heart finds comfort no where. I sought it in Company. I chatted & drank tea with Miss F[ishe]r and spent the Evening with Horton at Mr. Armitages [tavern]. I have hastened home & will retire to bed rather than to rest: Yet why this uneasiness: what concern have I with their going—None."[10] With these lines Bradford closed off the record he had begun with such enthusiasm less than two months earlier. It was as if he sensed that a way of life had ended and that a new one was about to begin.

With Dickinson's fall new men with new ideas, exploiting the confusion of the times to their advantage, rode unobtrusively into power. They rode in on the word "independence." But the new men in control were not merely Independents—that is, moderate-minded men open to compromise once independence had been achieved. If they had been, the Assembly could have adjusted to the changed times. The Radical Independents now ran Pennsylvania politics, and they were out to kill the Assembly and initiate

---

[8] *Pennsylvania Packet,* September 10.
[9] *Pennsylvania Evening Post,* June 20.
[10] Bradford, Register, June 20.

a revolution in government. They were few in numbers but they had the power to work their will on the province. They ran the "steering committee," which had been making the city Committee's decisions for weeks. The Committee of Privates answered to the bidding of James Cannon and his friends. Nearly all the Independents' propaganda in the press came from Radical pens. The two key men for the Independents in the backcountry— James Smith and Robert Whitehill—were Radicals.

The Radicals made effective use of the press to paint every act of the Assembly in dark colors. They twisted the seemingly non-political row-galley affair into a crusade in which the common people were pitted against the aristocratical Assembly. Shortly after the river battle gossip circulated through the city that several of the galley captains had acted in a cowardly fashion, lobbing in their shots at the warships from great distances rather than closing in, where the risk was greater but the chance of sending their cannon balls home greatly increased. The accused captains promptly printed up a broadside that turned the accusation on the Committee of Safety, which was responsible for all Pennsylvania's military affairs.[11] They stood off from the men-of-war, said the captains, because the Committee of Safety—that infamous body of moderate men appointed by the Assembly, not, mark it well, chosen by the people—had failed to supply sufficient ammunition for the galleys. The Assembly, as a court of last resort, stepped in to decide the issue. Midway in the Assembly's attempt at a fair investigation of the affair James Cannon saw to it that the following notice appeared in all Philadelphia papers:[12]

In COMMITTEE OF PRIVATES, June 3, 1776
Moved, That an address of thanks be presented to the officers and men belonging to the gallies for their spirited behaviour in the late engagement with the Roebuck and Liverpool men

---

[11] The galley commanders' defense appears in full in the *Pennsylvania Evening Post,* May 16.
[12] *Pennsylvania Evening Post,* June 4.

of war, and that the same be published in the several public papers of this city

Extract from the Minutes

JAMES CANNON, Clerk

N.B. The vote was delayed for some weeks to give the House of Assembly an opportunity of doing it first.

James Cannon's talent as a "hidden persuader" has been lost in the shadow of Tom Paine. He lacked Paine's knack for the incisive sentence, the colorful phrase. Yet, except for Sam Adams, possibly no one in colonial America was a more skilled publicist, more adept at using the press to shape men's minds, more brilliant in his timing of manipulated events. The Committee of Privates under his guidance abused the power and dignity of the Assembly at every turn. On June 5 a Memorial from the Committee appeared in the press. It circumvented both the Committee of Safety and the Assembly and turned directly to Congress for help.[13] On June 6 Cannon got another notice inserted in the papers:[14]

In COMMITTEE OF PRIVATES, June 6, 1776

Moved, and unanimously agreed to, That an application be made to the officers of the several battalions, to take the sense of each battalion whether they will support the Resolve of Congress of the 15th ult. and the proceedings of the public meeting held the 20th following, in consequence thereof.

JAMES CANNON, Clerk

The officers of the city troops, whether they liked it or not, were forced to accede to Cannon's pressure tactics. The troops were polled on June 10. In Colonel Dickinson's First Battalion, four officers and twenty-three enlisted men balked at supporting the May 20 resolves. In the Second Battalion all but two privates agreed to them. Lieutenant Colonel Lambert Cadwalader of the

---

[13] *Pennsylvania Gazette,* June 5, prints the full Memorial.
[14] *Pennsylvania Packet,* June 17.

Third or Silk Stocking Battalion, as it was nicknamed, refused to put the question to his men, thus strengthening the impression Cannon and his friends hoped to create in the public mind—that the artistocracy opposed independence. One of Cadwalader's privates, according to a newspaper report, shouted to his commander: "Take heed, Tories, you are at your last gasp!" The Fourth and Fifth Battalions, commanded by Colonels McKean and Matlack, supported the resolves unanimously. One observer said of the proceedings: "Any man who dared oppose their opinion was insulted and hushed by their interruptions, cheers, and hissings."[15]

Cannon had waited to force a public poll of the troops until the timing was right. On June 6 Sam Adams had written: "Tomorrow a Motion will be made, and a Question I hope decided, the most important that was ever agitated in America."[16] It was no doubt from Adams or another Independent delegate that Cannon and his friends had learned Congress would debate a declaration of independence on June 7. Public evidence that the troops supported such a declaration would create a favorable setting for the debate. The pressure tactic failed, in a sense, for by June 10 Congress had decided to postpone its decision on independence for three weeks. The effort was not altogether wasted. The soldiers' "enthusiasm" made an effective backdrop for the Provincial Conference, which was scheduled to hold its first meeting on June 18 in Carpenters' Hall.

On June 18 Christopher Marshall rose early. He was shaved and dressed before seven o'clock. After a hasty breakfast he hurried down to the Philosophical Hall, where the city Committee of Inspection and Observation, in its role as host to deputies from the backcountry committees, "agreed upon the mode to open the

---

[15] Accounts of the reading of the resolves to the troops are found in the Marshall Diary, June 10; in the *Pennsylvanid Packet,* June 17; and in " Extracts from the Diary of Dr. James Clitherall," *PMHB,* 22 (1898), 470.

[16] Sam Adams to James Warren, June 6, *Warren–Adams Letters,* I, 256.

conference at 10 this morning but to meet at 9 in order to introduce some of the Country members who are Strangers."[17] Thus obliquely did Marshall indicate that new men — like Benjamin Spyker and Nicholas Lutz of Berks; Andrew Graaf and Lodowick Lowman of Lancaster; John Harris and Dr. John Colhoon of Cumberland — had come to power in Pennsylvania. Of the one hundred and eight men chosen for the Provincial Conference only Benjamin Franklin — who did not show up for the sessions — and Thomas McKean had been prominent in politics.

This mediocre talent — perhaps inexperienced is a fairer way of putting it — was not the people's choice. The deputies had been selected by the county committees and generally from among their own ranks. Nearly all of Philadelphia's twenty-five deputies, for instance, came from the city Committee.[18] Men cool toward independence still remained on these committees but they had been easily circumvented. Edward Shippen, one of the most active members of the Lancaster County Committee, found that when the time came to choose deputies he was not "sent for nor do I expect it."[19]

Most of the deputies hoped that Benjamin Franklin, who had returned from his mission to Canada, would act as presiding officer of the Conference. But Franklin was laid up with an attack of gout, and too much in pain even to attend the sessions.[20] The post went to Thomas McKean, a lawyer and man of some ability, who had been in politics for twenty of his forty-two years. As the only veteran politician present he should have sensed the trend of affairs in Pennsylvania and attempted to head it back to more moderate channels. But though McKean was a man of talents he was also a man "of great Vanity, extremely fond of power and entirely governed by passions, ever pursuing the object present with warm

---

[17] Marshall, Diary, June 18.
[18] For a list of deputies see James E. Gibson, "The Pennsylvania Provincial Conference, 1776," *PMHB*, 58 (1935), 312–341.
[19] Edward Shippen to Joseph Shippen, Jr., June 8, Shippen Papers, APS.
[20] Boyd, *Jefferson Papers*, I, 405n.

enthusiastic zeal without much reflection or forecast."[21]

The main job of the Conference was relatively simple — to draw up rules for the Constitutional Convention soon to follow it.[22] The Conference sat for seven days straight without a break, meeting even on Sunday in order to rush through its business. A long delay might force the Convention to meet during the harvest season. There was also the chance that some "unhappy circumstance" might occur that would permit the Moderates to retrieve power. The Conference went about its business in "a Spirit of harmony," according to Christopher Marshall, who dismissed as trivial "some Small bickering between Col. [James] Smith of York County and the members of Chester County in which dispute Elisha Price of Chester got beside himself so farr that he run in the yard, jump'd over the fence so into the Street where he was pursued[,] took to his Lodgings & Continued so, as not to be Capable to attend again."[23]

Aside from this flurry the Conference went about its business quietly. The most important question to decide was who should vote for deputies to the Constitutional Convention. A group of German Associators — prompted no doubt by the Committee of Privates — submitted a petition asking that all who were taxable be entitled to vote. If a man — or boy — could fight for his country, so the reasoning went, he should be allowed to share in its political affairs. The Conference agreed. It did not go to the lengths that Elector had urged during the May election campaign, when he insisted that *all* associators, regardless of age, deserved the right to vote. It decided that any member of a military organization who was twenty-one or older, had lived in Pennsylvania one year, and

---

[21] Thomas Rodney, Diary, March 10, 1781, Burnett, *Letters of Congress,* VI, 20.

[22] The best summary of the Conference appears in Selsam, *Pennsylvania Constitution of 1776,* 136–145. The detailed record of the Conference is in *Pennsylvania Archives, Second Series* (19 vols., Harrisburg, 1847–1890), " Proceedings of the Provincial Conference," III, 635–65.

[23] Christopher Marshall to J. B. at New Jersey, June 30, Marshall Letterbook, HSP.

had paid either provincial or county taxes could vote in the election of Convention delegates. ("Depend upon it, Sir," John Adams had written a few days earlier, "it is dangerous to alter the qualification of voters; . . . every man who has not a farthing, will demand an equal voice with any other, in all acts of state. It tends to confound and destroy all distinctions, and prostrate all ranks to one common level.")[24]

The Conference widened the voting population to include those who favored independence, then narrowed it to exclude those who opposed it. Test oaths were required of all voters to prove that they would do their best to "establish and support a government in this province on the authority of the people only. . . .". Next, it was agreed that an oath of religious conformity should be required of all who would stand for election as deputies to the Constitutional Convention. Every elected deputy must "profess faith in God the Father and in Jesus Christ his eternal Son, the true God and in the Holy Spirit, one God blessed for evermore; and do acknowledge the holy scriptures of the old and new testament to be given by divine inspiration."[25]

The deputies seemed to feel a strong need for this oath, for even with some bitter opposition it passed almost unanimously. The Independents were convinced that America would win its struggle with Britain mainly because God was on their side. Of late the war had brought, along with other changes in society, signs of a growing dissoluteness in Pennsylvania. "The puritanical spirit was unknown among us," said an ex-soldier in later life.[26] This breakdown of virtue began to worry some. "But are we not a Sinful People?" asked one man. "Has not God a Controversy with us? Where is the Piety of our Military Men? I think the Swearing and all Manner of Profaneness, and Confidence in our own Strength, which are found among our undisciplined Soldiery,

---

[24] John Adams to James Sullivan, May 26, Adams, *Works*, IX, 378.
[25] *Pennsylvania Archives, Second Series*, "Proceedings," III, 642.
[26] Graydon, *Memoirs*, 122–123.

promise no very good Events."[27]

The religious test oath brought out a facet of Marshall's personality hitherto hidden from even close friends. Once the oath had been suggested Marshall "strenuously supported it." He was grieved to find himself "maltreated by sundry of my friends, as I thought & who, I believed was really religious persons & loved our Lord Jesus Christ, but now declare that no such Believe [Belief] or Confession is necessary in forming the N[ew] government."[28] Benjamin Rush had argued in the Conference that there were many good men — did he have in mind Paine and Young? — who did not believe in the Divinity of the Son of God. "I am not one of that Class," he hastened to add, but no man, he went on, "whose morals were good should be exempted because he would not take that declaration."[29] But it was James Cannon's reaction that especially grieved Marshall. Privately Cannon, who was not a member of the Conference, called those who supported the oath "fools, blockheads, Selfrighteous, and zealous bigots," and declared that it was passed with "a manifest view and tendency to keep Some of the most best and valuable men out of government...."[30]

How often a man's future decisions develop out of seemingly trivial events in his past. With the issue of the oath Christopher Marshall's friendship for James Cannon began to wane. Over this point alone he would within a few weeks detach himself from the Radical Independents and become a violent opponent of the Constitution of 1776.

The Cannon-Marshall friendship did not end instantly with the oath. On June 23 Cannon shortly past seven in the morning breakfasted with Marshall. Afterward they strolled over to see Sam Adams where they spent "some time in coversation."[31] Marshall

---

[27] James Read to Edward Shippen, May 29, Shippen Papers, vol. 7, HSP.
[28] Marshall, Diary, June 28.
[29] Christopher Marshall to J. B. at New Jersey, June 30, Marshall Letterbook, HSP.
[30] Christopher Marshall to James Cannon, July 1, Marshall Letterbook, HSP.
[31] Marshall, Diary, June 23.

then departed for the Conference. No doubt the discussion with Cannon and Sam Adams had something to do with the fact that in the Conference that morning it was recommended that the Constitutional Convention should choose new delegates to represent Pennsylvania in Congress and that the Committee of Safety should "exercise the whole of the executive powers of government, so far as relates to the military defence and safety of the province. . . ."[32] This move to usurp the powers of government came, it would seem, not so much from the innocent politicians in the Conference as from the Cannon–Adams combination.

On June 25 the Conference met till shortly past one o'clock, then adjourned to the Indian Queen for a final banquet and a round of toasts to the friends of independence in Pennsylvania. During the day the Conference's final declaration, written by Rush and James Smith, was presented to and read aloud in Congress. It stated that all members of the Conference "unanimously declare our willingness to concur in a vote of the congress, declaring the united colonies free and independent states."[33]

The day after the Conference broke up James Cannon had a broadside written and printed—no doubt in time for the backcountry delegates to carry it home with them—in which the Committee of Privates advised "the Several Battalions of Military Associators" about the proposed constitution for Pennsylvania. This new government, it made clear, should be more than one founded on the people's authority; it should be controlled by the people. "Would it not be prudent," it asked rhetorically, "to instruct your Deputies, when chosen, to reserve an Annual Return of all Power into your Hands." It took a strong view on the suffrage question: "Trust no Man but such who is determined to extend the Principle of a free Annual Election, by Ballot, to all possible Cases. . . . He who would incline to restrain it in any Case whatever, where it can be conveniently exercised, loves not liberty."

---

[32] *Pennsylvania Archives, Second Series,* "Proceedings," III, 652–653.
[33] *Ibid.,* III, 658.

NEW MEN—NEW IDEAS

What sort of men should be chosen to create this constitution? "A Government made for the Common Good should be framed by Men who can have no Interest besides the common Interest of Mankind . . . great and over-grown rich Men will be improper to be trusted." Clearly, if the electors do not take care they will, as before, "have an Aristocracy, or Government of the Great." Is training, intelligence, or learning needed for this job of making a constitution? Not at all. "Honesty, common Sense, and a plain Understanding, when unbiassed by sinister Motives, are fully equal to the task."[34] Cannon and his friends here gave fair warning the kind of government they planned for Pennsylvania, if they could keep control of affairs for only a few weeks longer.

On July 2 word swept through Philadelphia that Congress had passed the Declaration of Independence. John and Sam Adams had realized their cherished dream, but the revolution they had helped start in Pennsylvania to achieve it continued to roll on. The Moderate Independents who had also worked hard to get the revolution under way now sensed that affairs were out of control — or at least out of their control. Dissension would soon appear among the Radical Independents. Marshall would be the first to withdraw. Rush would belatedly realize that the government he had helped to demolish had been "one of the happiest governments in the world." When it was too late, he would see that "nothing was necessary to have made us a free and happy people than to abolish the royal and proprietary power of the state."[35] Although Paine and Cannon and their friends had made clear from the start exactly what sort of government they wanted to create after the old had been swept away, Rush, Marshall, McKean, and others who had been involved in destroying confidence in the Assembly piously disowned any responsibility for the final result of their efforts,

---

[34] "To the Several Battalions of Military Associators in the Province of Pennsylvania," dated June 26, Broadside Collection (1776), Item 19, HSP.

[35] Benjamin Rush to Anthony Wayne, May 19, 1777, Butterfield, *Rush Letters*, I, 148.

which materialized as the Pennsylvania Constitution of 1776. Cannon, Matlack, Young, and Paine were solely responsible for this *"mobocracy,"* as Rush called it.[36] John Adams also claimed innocence. "Good God!" he said on first reading the new constitution, "the people of Pennsylvania in two years will be glad to petition the crown of Britain for reconciliation in order to be delivered from the tyranny of their Constitution."[37]

John Dickinson, too, held himself completely guiltless of the debacle. He told his friend Charles Thomson he had "cheerfully & deliberately" sacrificed popularity "to Principles," and for his integrity had suffered "all the indignities that my Countrymen now bearing Rule are inclined if they could so plentifully to shower down upon my innocent Head. . . ."[38] Thomson blended affection with frankness in his reply:[39]

> I know the rectitude of your heart & the honesty & uprightness of your intentions; but still I cannot help regretting, that by a perseverance which you were fully convinced was fruitless, you have thrown the affairs of this state into the hands of men totally unequal to them. I fondly hope & trust however that divine providence, which has hitherto so signally appeared in favour of our cause, will preserve you from danger and restore you not to " your books & fields," but to your country, to correct the errors, which I fear those " now bearing rule " will through ignorance — not intention — commit, in settling the form of government.
>
> There are some expressions in your letter, which I am sorry for; because they seem to flow from a wounded spirit. Consider, I beseech you and do justice to your "unkind countrymen." They did not desert you. You left them. Possibly they were

---

[36] Benjamin Rush to John Adams, January 22, 1789, *ibid.*, I, 498.

[37] Benjamin Rush to John Adams, October 12, 1779, *ibid.*, I, 240. Rush's memory of Adams' remarks seems accurate. Almost the identical quotation, attributed only to " a member of Congress," appears in the *Pennsylvania Evening Post,* November 2, 1776. Perhaps Rush wrote it.

[38] John Dickinson to Charles Thomson, August 10, *New York Society Collections,* 31.

[39] Charles Thomson to John Dickinson, August 16, *PMHB,* 35 (1911), 500.

wrong, in quickening their march and advancing to the goal with such rapid speed. They thought they were right, and the only "fury" they show'd against you was to chuse other leaders to conduct them. I wish they had chosen better; & that you could have headed them, or they waited a little for you. But sure I am when their fervour is abated they will do justice to your merit. And I hope soon to see you restored to the confidence & honours of your country.

10 THE CONSTITUTION

Monday, July 8, dawned warm and sunny in Philadelphia. At eleven in the morning nearly all the hundred members of the city's Committee of Inspection and Observation gathered at the Philosophical Hall. After joining the Committee of Safety, the two groups walked to the State House yard. There, "in the presence of a great concourse of people, the Declaration of Independency was read by John Nixon." The crowd gave three huzzas, shouting with each, "God Bless the Free States of North America." Nine Associators chosen for the honor ripped down the King's arms over the entrance of the State House and carried them over to the London Coffee House.

After the multitude dispersed, several of the city Committee went over to Armitage's Tavern to celebrate the occasion with refreshment. In the afternoon the city's five battalions paraded on the city commons "and gave us," wrote John Adams, "the *feu de joie,* notwithstanding the scarcity of powder." In the cool and clear evening, the sound of clanging bells filled the air — "the bells rang all day and almost all night," reported John Adams — and bonfires flickered everywhere in the city. The high point of the celebration came in the evening at the Coffee House. There, as the great crowd cheered, the King's arms were tossed atop a huge mound of flaming wooden casks and within the flick of an eye the symbol of royal authority in Philadelphia had burned to an ash. With these and "other great Demonstrations of joy" Philadelphia celebrated the Declaration of Independence.[1]

In the midst of the festivities the election of city and county delegates for the Constitutional Convention passed almost unnoticed at the State House. Among those elected were James Cannon for the county and Timothy Matlack for the city of Philadelphia. As an old era ended two men who believed with fervor that "all men are created equal" prepared to usher in the new with a suitable constitution.

On July 9 the city turned back to the war. Philadelphia's battalions made ready to march for New York, where Washington was assembling all available troops to repel the British invasion. As the city troops marched out, Delaware troops were ordered up from Wilmington as a security for Philadelphia.[2] Meanwhile, Associators in the back counties had received their marching orders and all through July and August they continued to pour into the city, pause for a few days at the city barracks to rest and reorganize, pick up equipment and supplies, then move on.

By August talk of the Declaration had passed. An Englishman visiting the city found "Great preparations for War, and great numbers of ragged soldiers come into town." He saw a "Great many ships laid up and unrigged at the wharfs," and on the ways in the shipyards four Continental frigates which he supposed "will be ready for sea in a month, if they can get the hands to man them." The city impressed but did not fully please him. "Don't like my lodgings," he wrote; "full of Irish colnls., Captns., and Convention men, most of them profoundly ignorant and as impertinent as any Skipinnet. These are here for the purpose of making a new code of Laws for the Province. O, Happy people indeed that has such wise guides."[3]

---

[1] This description of events on July 8 in Philadelphia comes from Marshall's Diary of that date and July 5; John Adams to Samuel Chase, July 9, Burnett, *Letters of Congress*, II, 7–8; William Ellery to Benjamin Ellery, July 10, *PMHB*, 10 (1886), 320–21.

[2] Caesar Rodney to Thomas Rodney, July 10, Ryden, *Rodney Letters*, 98.

War and constitution-making do not mix well, especially with impertinent Irishmen involved in both. When additional ingredients include the ideas of Cannon, Matlack, Young, and Paine the final result is not likely to please moderate-minded gentlemen. It is not surprising, then, to find such gentlemen receiving Pennsylvania's Constitution of 1776 with howls of protest. But why such shocked greetings for this first child of the lamentable Age of Paine? The ideas of the parents were well known long before the birth. Paine had mapped out clearly in *Common Sense* his conception of the ideal government — one with a single legislature, an elected judiciary with limited terms, and a weak executive. Paine's views so disturbed John Adams that soon after the appearance of *Common Sense* he wrote a lengthy letter to George Wythe of Virginia stating his own ideas on government — one with two legislatures that could check one another's excesses, a reasonably strong executive that worked with the legislatures, a strong judiciary appointed for good behavior, and the usual property qualifications for voters. The letter was published anonymously as *Thoughts on Government* but the knowing were aware of the author. "Mr. Paine was so highly offended by it," Adams wrote long afterward, "that he came to visit me at my chambers at Mrs. Yard's to remonstrate and even scold me for it, which he did in very ungenteel terms."[4]

Paine's direct hand in the Pennsylvania Constitution amounted to nothing. He gave no vote for delegates to the Convention, "neither did I know the ticket for the city till it was public."[5] He was absent from Philadelphia when the Convention met. Shortly after the Declaration of Independence passed Congress "I went to camp, and continued there till a few days before Christmas. I held no correspondence with either party, for or against, the present

---
[3] *Journal of Nicholas Cresswell*, 153–54, 156, 153.
[4] Adams, *Works*, II, 507.
[5] " A Serious Address to the People of Pennsylvania on the Present Situation of Their Affairs," *Pennsylvania Packet*, December 1, 1778, in Foner, *Complete Writings of Paine*, II, 280.

constitution. I had no hand in forming any part of it, nor knew any thing of its contents till I saw it published."[6]

Paine departed in person but his spirit lingered in Philadelphia. That *Common Sense* was published in Philadelphia is of less importance than that its author lived there. For two years he roamed the streets and passed the hours in local taverns talking to the "common people," drank coffee with Christopher Marshall, visited with Benjamin Rush, talked away the night with Matlack, Young, and Cannon. Slowly his ideas began to appear in the press from a variety of pens. Elector, both before and after the May election, made it clear he wanted *"a radical reformation"* in Pennsylvania's government with, among other things, the vote extended to the common people.[7] A Watchman told "The Common People of Pennsylvania" that all their troubles stemmed from the "UNCOMMON PEOPLE."[8] The Committee of Privates in every communique dropped hints of the kind of government it planned.

These newspaper articles developed a line hitherto unknown in Pennsylvania politics — a class attack. The sporadic complaints that occasionally cropped up in the press in previous years had denounced specific ills — high taxes, bad roads, handling of Indian problems, the lack of tradesmen in the Assembly — but demanded no basic changes in the government. Paine's friends were the first to aim at a real revolution in Pennsylvania society. They were determined to shatter the shackles that bound the present to the past. Up to now the watchwords of the American Revolution had been "freedom" and "liberty." The Radical Independents adopted a new slogan — equality.

Moderate men knew from the start what the Radicals were up to. A few days before the mass meeting that touched off the revolu-

---

[6] "To the People," *Pennsylvania Packet*, March 18, 1777, *ibid.*, II, 270. Marshall verifies Paine's statement. He writes in his Diary for July 19: "John [*sic*] Payne call'd & took his leave of me being going to camp as Secretary to Gen'l Roberdeau."

[7] An Elector, *Pennsylvania Packet*, April 29; *Pennsylvania Gazeztte*, May 15.

[8] A Watchman, *Pennsylvania Packet*, June 10.

tion in Pennsylvania affairs John Adams wrote, not of himself, but of Paine: "It is the Fate of Men and Things which do great good that they always do great Evil too."[9] Within a few weeks Adams must have sensed that if to create a democratic government were evil, he shared in the sin. In deliberately setting out to wreck Pennsylvania's existing government to get one that voted "plump for independence" he — along with other Moderate Independents — opened the way for Paine and his friends to build exactly the sort of government they had said they would and which he considered "evil." The degree of Adams' and other Independents' "sin," if it can be called that, is unimportant. Only their sanctimonious protests of innocence make it worth mentioning.

After the mass meeting on May 20 the Moderate Independents narrowed their vision to the job of wrecking the old government without giving thought to what would replace it. Here they erred egregiously. "In truth," wrote Thomas Jefferson, a state constitution "is the whole object of the present controversy; for should a bad government be instituted for us in the future it had been well to have accepted at first the bad one offered to us from beyond the water without the risk and expence of the contest."[10] The Radicals saw things as Jefferson and while they ripped down the old government they worked on plans for the new one. Other Independents talked eloquently but vaguely about the magnificent opportunity they had now "of forming a plan of Government upon the most just rational & equal principles."[11] Or they held to the innocent belief that the new government would only be the old under a new name. When A Freeman tried to resolve the doubts of James Rankin of York about the Independents' plans, he promised that "a full and fair representation of this province, and the

---

[9] John Adams to James Warren, May 12, *Warren–Adams Letters,* I, 242–243.

[10] Thomas Jefferson to Thomas Nelson, May 16, Boyd, *Jefferson Papers,* I, 292.

[11] William Shippen to Edward Shippen, July 27, Shippen Papers, vol. 12, HSP.

suppression of all authority under the King of Great Britain, *are the only changes desired, and that the charter and laws of the province in every other respect will remain inviolate.*"[12] Such was the innocence of some Independents.

The Radicals knew what they wanted, they dominated the most powerful pressure group in the new state—the Committee of Privates—and they had James Cannon on their side. Cannon's career as a politician came to a climax with the Constitutional Convention. He stepped at last from behind the scenes, using the Committee of Privates' backing to obtain a seat in the Convention. On July 3 the Committee had met in Thorn's schoolroom and there, despite the recent assertion that men of "honesty, common Sense, and a plain Understanding . . . are fully equal to the task" of making a constitution, Cannon, Matlack, and Young "flourished away on the necessity of choosing 8 persons [for the city] . . . possessed of, viz., great learning, Knowledge in our history, Law, Mathematics, &c., and a perfect acquaintance with the laws, manners, trade, constitution & policy of all nations. . . ."[13] Only Young, of the three, failed to be elected to the Convention; Matlack was chosen by the city and Cannon by the county of Philadelphia.

Cannon, with his usual skill, managed to get appointed to the Convention committee that would draft the constitution.[14] He faced a problem more involved and subtle than simply framing a democratic constitution. Not long after the Convention convened a lengthy letter appeared in the press about constitution-making. Buried within it was a succinct statement of Cannon's problem:

[12] A Freeman, *Pennsylvania Evening Post,* June 11. Italics added.
[13] Marshall, Diary, July 3.
[14] Mystery has and apparently always will surround the making of the Constitution of 1776. It is not to my purpose here to debate the authorship, for Cannon's leading role is beyond question. I might say, though, that George Bryan's share in the authorship has probably been exaggerated. So far as I can find, the sole source for the importance of Bryan's role comes from Graydon and he only reports a rumor. Robert Whitehill's part, on the other hand, was much more, I think, than has been acknowledged. He and Cannon, to judge by Marshall's diary, were constant companions through July, August, and September. Wherever Cannon went Whitehill was not far behind.

Although it be granted on all hands, that all power originates from the people; yet it is plain that in those colonies where the government has, from the beginning, been in the hands of a very few rich men, the ideas of government both in the minds of those rich men, and of the common people, are rather aristocratical than popular. The rich, having been used to govern, seem to think it is their right; and the poorer commonalty, having hitherto had little or no hand in government, seem to think it does not belong to them to have any.[15]

Few, before or since, have stated better the political creed of, if not America, then the Middle States in 1776. No one of the day questioned the theory that political power originates with the people. Rich and poor alike accepted it. When the throng in the State House yard cheered the resolve that a new government must be established on the authority of the people, moderate-minded men could join in the shouting with an easy mind. The phrase aroused no suspicions, gave no hint that it might soon serve as a rallying call for a democratic revolution. For though government was founded on the authority of the people, tradition had it that the rich — that is, the elite, those with the training, intelligence, and background for public life — ran public affairs. Both the common and uncommon people accepted this as another of the facts of life. Cannon's problem, then, was to overcome in a few weeks' time the common people's aristocratical notions, their idea that the business of running the government did not belong to them. To do this he must create a constitution that made certain the people got control of politics in fact as well as theory. This meant, in turn, he must remove every obstacle that might hinder the people from getting control of the government and at the same time set up insurmountable obstacles to prevent the elite from retrieving control.

Cannon succeeded to an astonishing degree. Nearly every sug-

---

[15] The quotation comes from a letter from a citizen of New Jersey which appears in the *Pennsylvania Evening Post,* July 30.

gestion advanced in the Committee of Privates' broadside in June came to life in the Constitution.[16] The vote was extended to all men over twenty-one who had lived in the state one year and paid taxes. No special property qualifications hindered any voter from holding a public office. "Keep the Legislative and Executive Authority for ever separate," the broadside had advised. The Constitution acted on this advice by providing that both branches were chosen directly by the people. The single House was supreme in all legislation, and all members had to stand for re-election annually. If the aristocracy managed to capture control of the executive, it would do them little good. The twelve members of the Council, as the plural executive was called, had relatively little power and were required to leave office after their three-year term and could not stand for re-election for another four years. The broadside had recommended that "magistrates, though chosen annually by Ballot, should, like our Sheriffs, go out at a certain Time, at the End of five or six Years for Instance, to make Room for others." The Constitution accepted this suggestion fully, except to extend Justices of Peace's permissible years in office to seven. Judges no longer held office for good behavior. They were appointed by the Council for seven years and could be reappointed. As a final protection, the people each seven years would choose a Council of Censors, which would make sure the Constitution had not been violated by any branches of the government. Along with these protections there were provisions for a system of free schools, restrictions on high bails or immoderate fines, and abolition of imprisonment for debt.

After the Constitution had been accepted by the Convention, Cannon and his friends hedged their gamble on the people's natural wisdom with a couple of realistic decisions. The Constitution was not submitted to the people for approval, nor was the Convention willing to send out notices for the immediate election

---

[16] No attempt is made here to discuss the Constitution in full. For a detailed discussion see Selsam, *Pennsylvania Constitution of 1776*, 169–254. Douglass, *Rebels and Democrats*, 263–286, gives a briefer but reliable account.

THE CONSTITUTION

of a new Assembly. "They say," wrote a Philadelphian, "if you call an Assembly under a new Constitution to be elected in the Absence of the Militia, you will throw everything into the hands of the Disaffected, who perhaps are now a Majority."[17] As an added precaution to assure an Assembly sympathetic to the new Constitution the Convention produced an oath which would be required from all voters in any election. It read:

I ——————— ——————— do swear (or affirm) that I will be faithful and true to the commonwealth of Pennsylvania, and that I will not directly or indirectly do any act or thing prejudicial or injurious to the constitution or government thereof, as established by the convention.[18]

The Constitution of 1776 was not completely tailored to the desires of Cannon and his friends. The Committee of Privates' broadside in June said that "officers of the Militia should be chosen by the Militia." This referred indirectly to the Independents' stand against the Assembly selecting a brigadier general for the Associators. Yet the Constitution gave the militia the right to choose its officers only from the rank of colonel down.[19] The selection of generals remained with the Assembly. Cannon had objected to the oath the Provincial Conference had required of all deputies. His opposition could not prevent a similar oath being inserted in the Constitution. It read:

I do believe in one God the Creator and Governor of the Universe the Rewarder of the Good and Punisher of the Wicked. And I do acknowledge the Scriptures of the Old and New Testament to be given by Divine Inspiration.[20]

The best the Radicals could do was to have added to the oath

---

[17] J. Morris, Jr., to John Dickinson, August 8, Dickinson Papers, Ridgeway Branch of the Library Company.
[18] Quoted in Selsam, *Pennsylvania Constitution of 1776,* 164. Members of the Assembly were required to take a similar oath.
[19] Section Five of the Constitution. The most available copy of the Constitution of 1776 appears in Theodore Thayer, *Pennsylvania Politics and the Growth of Democracy 1740-1776* (Harrisburg, 1953), Appendix II,,211-227.
[20] Section Ten, Thayer, *Pennsylvania Politics,* 217.

this sentence: "And no further or other Religious Test shall ever hereafter be required of any Civil Officer or Magistrate in this State."[21]

Cannon's Bill of Rights failed to meet acceptance on an item he must have regarded with affection, since it was one of the few distinctive differences between his document and that passed by Virginia a few weeks earlier. The paragraph, as it appeared in the first printed draft of the Bill of Rights, read:

16. That, an enormous Proportion of Property vested in a few Individuals is dangerous to the Rights, and destructive of the Common Happiness, of mankind; and therefore every free State hath a Right by its Laws to discourage the possession of such Property.[22]

This section was eliminated by the Convention, partly no doubt because of its vagueness—when does the amount of property a man holds reach "an enormous proportion"?—and partly because most deputies, with a few notable exceptions like Cannon and Matlack, either had or still hoped to acquire an enormous proportion of property. After all, why had most of them gone to the backcountry?

Except for the religious oath these were minor defeats. The spirit behind the Constitution remained the radical spirit of Cannon, Matlack, Paine, and Young. "It is certain in theory," wrote John Adams, "that the only moral foundation of government is, the consent of the people. But to what an extent shall we carry this principle?"[23] Adams wanted to keep things as they were. Cannon and his friends were determined to translate theory into fact. They set out to make a sharp break with the past, with almost every tradition that had ruled Pennsylvania politics for nearly a century. "We are determined," wrote Thomas Smith with some bitterness, "not to pay the least regard to the former Constitution

---

[21] *Ibid.*, 217.
[22] Broadside Collection (1776), Item 10, HSP.
[23] John Adams to James Sullivan, May 26, Adams, *Works*, IX, 375.

of this Province, but to reject every thing therein that may be proposed, merely because it was part of the former Constitution. We are resolved to clear every part of the old rubbish out of the way and begin upon a clean foundation. You know that experimental philosophy was in great repute fifty years ago, and we have a mind to try how the same principle will succeed in politics! You learned fellows who have warped your understanding by poring over musty old books, will perhaps laugh at us; but, know ye, that we despise you."[24]

Smith implied what another writer said outright—"It all arose from so many plain country folks being in the Convention."[25] The country folks deserved hardly none of the blame. They had no deep, enduring complaints against the government. The suffrage qualifications did not prevent many of them from voting. Most of the backcountry deputies doubtless came to Philadelphia with no firm ideas about what the new government should be like. Men with open minds are impressionable and the Committee of Privates had made sure the right impressions were spread through the backcountry. Men innocent of government are easily led, especially when proposed innovations seem to fit perfectly with tradition, as the Radicals' plan for a single legislature. The debate on whether or not to have a unicameral legislature lasted only seven hours, and it lasted that long only because a few diehard moderates delayed the decision.[26] Just before the question came up for vote Benjamin Franklin, now recovered from his attack of gout and back in public life, was "requested by the Convention to give his opinion on the point. . . ." No record exists of his remarks to the Convention but certainly this would have been an apt time to retell his story of the two-headed snake confronted with a twig. ("One head

---

[24] Thomas Smith to Arthur St. Clair, August 22, Smith, *St. Clair Papers,* I, 374.
[25] "Orator PUFF and JOHN his friend . . . ," *Pennsylvania Evening Post,* October 19.
[26] J. Morris, Jr., to John Dickinson, August 8, Dickinson Papers, Ridgeway Branch of the Library Company.

chose to go on the right side of the twig, the other on the left, so that time was spent in the contest; and before the decision was completed the poor snake died with thirst.") The record is clear that he declared his opinion to be "clearly and fully in favour of a legislature to consist of a single branch, as being much the safest and best."[27] That settled the matter. The vote against a single House was only "a small minority."[28]

The backcountry delegates no doubt headed home pleased with a job well done. They had preserved the basic form of the old government. They had made certain that only God-fearing men would get elected to office. And their work had won the approval of the eminent Dr. Franklin. These men were probably as shocked and astonished as any when their handiwork met with instant and loud howls of protest.

In certain instances opposition to the Constitution had little to do with the merits or flaws in it. Some men opposed it for personal reasons that had nothing to do with its radical innovations. Christopher Marshall's deep feeling against the document emerged solely out of his religious quarrel with James Cannon. The ill feeling between the two men smoldered for several weeks. It broke into the open during a casual conversation when Cannon suddenly accused Marshall "of affronting him last night at my house & also now."[29] The burden of Convention duties, worries about the Constitution then in the making, his work as a newly elected member of the Committee of Safety, or Council of Safety, as it was now called, plus the teaching load at the College had probably put Cannon's nerves on edge. A sharp argument followed in which, said Marshall, "he rallyed me pritty severely & I think not friendly."[30]

---

[27] Timothy Matlack, *Pennsylvania Gazette,* March 31, 1779, quoted in Selsam, *Pennsylvania Constitution of 1776,* 185–186.
[28] Thomas Smith to Arthur St. Clair, August 3, Smith, *St. Clair Papers,* I, 371.
[29] Marshall, Diary, September 2.
[30] *Ibid.*

The altercation left its marks. Two days later Marshall had only sarcasm for "that wonderful performance called an Ordinance for the Appointment of Justices of Peace...." Marshall had been appointed, perhaps through Cannon's doing, to one of the offices but when two gentlemen came "to invite me to goe and be qualified," Marshall temporized. "I gave for answer it was to me to weighty affair & I must & would take time to consider maturely of it."[31]

On September 6 Marshall learned that it had been proposed in Convention that all officers of the new government "should qualify to their Christian belief as Established by the old & New Testament, which after a long debate was rejected by a majority of votes (in which number were Robert Whitehill & James Cannon) who asserted that a belief in one God Should be a Sufficient profession."[32] The religious oath as it passed ("I do believe in one God . . . and I do acknowledge the Scriptures of the Old and New Testament to be given by Divine Inspiration.") proved unacceptable to Marshall. The glorious future he had dreamed of when fighting with Cannon for independence horrified Marshall now — "farewell Christianity when Turks, Jews, infidels, & what is worse Deists & Atheists are to make laws for our State."[33] Marshall promptly took up the cause against the Constitution with all the fervency that he had once supported the drive for independence.

Benjamin Rush reacted against the Constitution, too, but for more complicated reasons. Cannon, Paine, Young, and Matlack were men of a reckless breed. They could afford to be. With little invested in the present, they had little to lose. Rush, discontented and convinced his professional colleagues in Philadelphia held him in contempt, joined up with this reckless crew. But all the while he steered a cautious course. He had a prosperous practice to

---

[31] *Ibid.*, September 4, 5.
[32] *Ibid.*, September 6, referring to a Convention decision made on the previous day.
[33] *Ibid.*, September 6.

protect. He had suggested that Paine rather than himself write a pamphlet promoting independence because "he had nothing to fear from the popular odium to which such a publication might expose him, for he could live anywhere."[34]

In August Rush was among the new delegation chosen by the Convention to represent Pennsylvania in Congress. Now, for the first time, he was accepted as an equal among some of the most eminent men in America. Rush's sense of discontent began to diminish. His break with old friends came more gradually than Marshall's. He was in Congress when he began to hear about the Constitution Cannon was devising. It was, he said, "thought by many people to be rather too much upon the democratical order."[35] Rush carefully avoided any personal commitment whether a democratical Constitution should be condemned or praised. John Adams soon told him what to think. "You were my first preceptor in the science of government," he later told Adams. "From you I learned to discover the danger of the Constitution of Pennsylvania. . . ."[36]

Marshall and Rush must have felt they were reliving an old dream when they joined in the organized campaign against the Constitution. The pattern of pressure tactics was identical to the one used only a few weeks earlier by the Independents. First, on October 21, came the mass meeting, held again in the State House yard. On the heels of this came a stream of letters, petitions, and delegations to backcountry committees advocating a new Constitutional Convention. Finally, in early November came the election for Assembly members. The day passed dully with a light turnout everywhere in the state. Neither side seemed able to work up either enthusiasm for or against the Constitution. The anti-Constitutionalists swept the city, where about one thousand voters turned out; the Constitutionalists took the backcountry, where their political machine, built around the Associators, was still working smoothly.

---

[34] Corner, *Rush Autobiography*, 114.
[35] Benjamin Rush to Anthony Wayne, September 24, Butterfield, *Rush Letters*, I, 114–115.
[36] Benjamin Rush to John Adams, February 12, 1790, *ibid.*, I, 530.

The anti-Constitutionalists had won enough seats to adopt a weapon the Independents had used so effectively a few weeks earlier—the boycott. Any distaste for the tactic John Dickinson had shown then he overlooked now. He had hardly accepted the Assembly seat won in the city election when he paralyzed the Assembly by putting it to use. The Constitutionalists saw instantly that within a few weeks they would have to grant Dickinson's demand for calling a new Convention. Word that General Howe planned to invade Philadelphia saved them from defeat. Opposition ceased till the crisis passed. It began again early in 1777, then in April Howe seemed ready again to invade Pennsylvania. "If a regular system was formed between General Howe and the friends of our Constitution," wrote James Wilson, "his motions could not have been better timed for them than they have in two different instances. When an opposition has been twice set on foot, and has twice proceeded so far as to become formidable, he has twice, by his marches toward Delaware, procured a cessation."[37]

By the time these crises ended the Constitutionalists were so well entrenched that thirteen years passed before moderate-minded men could force the kind of constitution on the people of Pennsylvania that appealed to them.

Was the Constitution of 1776 unworkable? No one will know for sure. Its opponents never gave it a chance to work. They adopted the tack the Independents had taken after the May election and refused to abide by the results, refused to join in a government they could not control. Dickinson, after his initial failure to unseat the Constitutionalists, would not serve in the government. After the Assembly removed Rush from Congress, he left politics and turned to scrap with Washington and his medical corps. John Cadwalader and Samuel Meredith refused to accept brigadier generalships voted by the Assembly because they were

---

[37] James Wilson to Arthur St. Clair, July 3, 1777, Smith, *St. Clair Papers*, I, 417.

determined not to help the new government survive. "Their enmity to it was so great, they intirely overlooked the fatal effects their opposition might produce in distroying the general Cause of Independence."[38] The lawyers of the province agreed among themselves "neither to practice or accept of any office under the constitution, which, in that case, they would be bound, by oath to support."[39]

Only one man—Thomas Wharton, who was elected the new state's first President—retained a semblance of tolerance, a sense of fair play. He liked the Constitution no more than most moderate-minded men. "True it is," he wrote, "there are many faults, which I hope one day to see removed; but it is true that, if the Government should at this time be overset, it would be attended with the worst consequences, not only to this State, but to the whole continent in the opposition we are making to Great Britain. If a better frame of government should be adopted, such a one as would please a much greater majority than the present one, I should be very happy in seeing it brought about; and any gentlemen that should be thought by the public qualified to take my seat, should have my hearty voice for it."[40]

None of the defenders—not even Cannon—argued the Convention had created a perfect government. The Constitution, they said, was an "experiment." The word crops up again and again in their arguments.[41] The word, and attitude that came with it, served as more than a handy tool to defend the Constitution's flaws. Most of those whose ideas were involved in the document—Cannon, Franklin, Rittenhouse, Paine, and Young—were scientists in the eighteenth-century sense of the term. They transferred intact the concept of experimentation from science to politics. Their Constitution was an applied experiment of the theory of popular sovereignty. Perhaps the experiment would fail but let us, they

---

[38] John Lacey, *PMHB,* 26 (1902), 104.
[39] Graydon, *Memoirs,* 307.
[40] Thomas Wharton to Arthur St. Clair, *PMHB,* 5 (1881), 436.
[41] Cannon, for instance, uses it in *Pennsylvania Evening Post,* September 26.

argued, give it a try. "To object against the present constitution because it is a *novelty*, is to give one of the best indirect reasons for trying it. . . ." wrote Paine. "We are a people upon experiments and though under one continental government, have the happy opportunity of trying variety in order to discover the best."[42]

The concept of experiment applied to politics had merits. It made clear that governments were not sacred and immune to change. It suggested to the perceptive that governments must be adapted to time and place. As with all transplanted concepts, this one proved unworkable when applied too literally. An experiment that breaks away completely from an old pattern may succeed brilliantly in science; it is certain to fail in politics. A scientist faced with an unsuccessful experiment can sweep the table clean and make a fresh start. Humans are less malleable. Traditions and habits hang on and won't be brushed aside with a single pass of the broom. An experiment that deprives men accustomed to rule of their power is sure to stir up a storm of opposition. Moderate-minded men's immoderate resistance to the Constitution stems largely from this fact. They "very rudely troubled the waters," as a man of the day put it, because "they aim to fish advantages to themselves out of the public disquiet."[43] They talked eloquently about the theory of popular sovereignty while discrediting the Assembly. When theory became fact they resisted.

The elite's opposition only helped, it did not ruin, all chance of success for the Radicals' experiment. The Constitution of 1776 eventually died because it lacked warm support from the people. Americans, it has been said, care more for equality than they do for liberty.[44] This may be true today. It was not true in 1776, at least in Pennsylvania. Cannon and his friends cared much for

---

[42] "A Serious Address to the People of Pennsylvania on the Present Situation of Their Affairs," *Pennsylvania Packet,* December 1, 1778, in Foner, *Complete Writings of Paine,* II, 281.
[43] Consideration, *Pennsylvania Gazette,* October 30.
[44] Lucien Price, *Dialogues of Alfred North Whitehead* (Mentor edition, New York, 1956), 167.

equality and they devised a government to put their ideas into practice. "There is no rank above freeman," Cannon insisted in one of his missives to the backcountry. No more than understanding, common sense, and natural wisdom is required to govern, he said. "Our principle," wrote the contemptuous Thomas Smith during the Constitutional Convention, "seems to be this: that any man, even the most illiterate is as capable of any office as a person who has had the benefit of education; that education perverts the understanding, eradicates common honesty, and has been productive of all the evils that have happened in the world."[45] Cannon and his friends brushed aside the tradition that only the elite should rule. They gave Pennsylvania a constitution that democratized government, that handed the people power in fact as well as theory. They failed when they thought they had succeeded. They gave the people democracy and the people spurned the gift. They still preferred the elite to run their affairs, and soon Dickinson was settled in the office of President of Pennsylvania. In Philadelphia in the early fall of 1776 the Age of Paine, the Age of Jackson—call it what you will—had, so to speak, a miscarriage.

Even a miscarriage is an accomplishment of some sort. How did the Radical Independents achieve this much? They slipped through their revolutionary ideas in 1776—about a half-century before America was ready for them—on the enthusiasm engendered by the idea of independence. It is wrong to assume only a minority in Pennsylvania favored independence in July. The mass of people were confused and noncommittal about the idea in May. After the May election came news that foreign troops were en route to America, followed closely by the river battle. About the same time prices began to spurt ahead, the intrinsic value of the Continental dollar started to slide, luxury goods disappeared from shops, and more and more servants and apprentices began to vanish into the army. By late May the discontent built up by these swift

---

[45] Thomas Smith to Arthur St. Clair, August 22, Smith, *St. Clair Papers*, I, 373.

changes helped the people look more tolerantly on the idea of independence. This discontent might have simmered for some time if the Radicals' political machine had not stood ready to exploit it. The presence of the Associators and cooperation from the Moderate Independents made the Radicals' work easy. The people agreeably backed the drive to overthrow the Assembly because they had been persuaded they must if they wanted independence, not because they expected or desired a radically new government. When a man sells a house in sound shape, he transfers the deed to the new owner; he may expect the buyer to make minor alterations but not to raze the house. Similarly, the people of Pennsylvania expected that to found a new government "on the authority of the people" would entail little more than a transfer of the "deed" from the Crown to the people. A Freeman had promised that aside from that change "the charter and laws of the province in every other respect will remain inviolate"; there was no reason to doubt him. The Radicals saw independence only as a means to an end. The people saw it as an end in itself which would preserve the comfortable, prosperous way of life they knew in Pennsylvania.

Tom Paine took the defeat philosophically. A lifetime of defeats and a resigned awareness of man's perverseness cushioned the shock. He had prophetically sensed the outcome of the revolution in Pennsylvania when it was no more than a dream in his mind's eye. He had protested in 1775, in an article titled "Useful and Entertaining Hints," "against that unkind, ungrateful, and impolitic custom of ridiculing unsuccessful experiments. . . . I am led to this reflection by the present domestic state of America, because it will unavoidably happen, that before we can arrive at that perfection of things which other nations have acquired, many hopes will fail, many whimsical attempts will become fortunate, and many reasonable ones end in air and expense."[46]

Cannon, more deeply involved in the Constitution than Paine

---
[46] " Useful and Entertaining Hints," *Pennsylvania Magazine*, February, 1775, in Foner, *Complete Writings of Paine*, II, 1022.

and unaccustomed to public abuse, took the defeat harder. It broke his spirit. Soon Rush and McKean and most of his old colleagues among the Independents were heaping vituperation upon him. On November 3 Cannon stopped round to visit Christopher Marshall, perhaps to repair the broken friendship. There was no conversation about politics, "tho' I waited & expected he would Introduce the Subject," Marshall said.⁴⁷ Cannon "seem'd to be poorly" to his old friend. He stayed about an hour, then departed. Within a few weeks his name vanished from the press. Six years later he was dead.

Paine stayed around trying to salvage some of his friend's handiwork, but he had little luck. Eventually he washed his hands of Pennsylvania's affairs and took off for Europe, still undaunted and still filled with high hopes for mankind's future. And why not? After all, he had his eye on another revolution.

---

⁴⁷ Marshall, Diary, November 3.

BIBLIOGRAPHICAL NOTE

Anyone who digs into the story of the American Revolution quickly learns that those directly involved in revolutionary activities knew the dangers they ran, knew clearly they were entangling themselves in treasonable acts. Much has been made of the vast amount of materials that survive the period without noting the equally vast amount "lost." Jacob Hiltzeimer's diary survives intact except for one year—1776. Riffle through the pages of Owen Biddle's letterbook at the Friends' Historical Library, Swarthmore College; the pages for 1776 have been ripped out. William Bradford, Jr., kept copies of his spirited series of letters to and from James Madison for 1774–75. He continued to correspond with Madison during the spring and summer of 1776; those letters failed to survive. The pages of journals for organizations like the American Philosophical Society and lodges of Free Masons are blank for 1776. The minutes for Philadelphia's Committee of Inspection and Observation, for the Patriotic Society, for the Committee of Privates—all have been "lost," that is, more likely burned, probably about the time the British marched into Philadelphia in 1777.

Pennsylvanians who worked hard to stir up the storm of revolt tried, quite sensibly, to cover up their tracks in case the British won. It was an empty gesture that hinders but fails to block the historian; indeed, only makes his search for the true story the more intriguing. He has, for instance, the newspapers to enlighten him. Five were published in Philadelphia in 1776. Their views on the idea of independence spread across the political spectrum. The pro-reconciliation *Pennsylvania Ledger* was counterbalanced by the independent-minded *Pennsylvania Evening Post*, while the *Pennsylvania Gazette*, *Pennsylvania Journal*, and the *Pennsylvania Packet* held to the middle of the road, at least until early June. None of these papers can be ignored by the historian, for the advertisements and notices that appear in one are often absent in another. And nothing in them can be ignored. A brief notice buried on a back page may give a hint of how the Committee of Privates manipulated public opinion. The advertisements indicate changing social conditions. Even the lack of advertisements provides the historian clues to the times; as sentiment for independence mounted, merchants began to pull their advertisements from the *Ledger* and place them in papers more acceptable to the public.

Much of the material in the newspapers is more available in that massive collection of documents known as the *Pennsylvania Archives. Selected and Arranged from Original Documents in the Office of the Secretary of the Commonwealth* (119 vols., Philadelphia and Harrisburg, 1852–1933). In the *First Series 1664–1790,* edited by Samuel Hazard (12 vols., Philadelphia, 1852–56), volume four gives the Committee of Safety's correspondence for 1776. The *Second Series* (19 vols., Harrisburg, 1874–1890) reprints the minutes of the Provincial Conference in volume three. The *Eighth Series* (8 vols., Harrisburg, 1931–35) otherwise known as *Votes and Proceedings of the House of Representatives of the Provinces of Pennsylvania,* provides in volume eight the minutes of the Assembly for 1776. Another collection of documents—*Minutes of the Provincial Council of Pennsylvania, Minutes and Proceedings of the Council of Safety, and Minutes and Proceedings of the Supreme Executive Council of Pennsylvania, 1683–1790* (16 vols., Philadelphia and Harrisburg, 1851–1853), known commonly as *Colonial Records*—gives in volume ten the Committee of Safety's minutes for 1776.

Several other massive collections were of use, though they dealt with the American Revolution as a whole. The Fourth Series of *The American Archives* (6 vols., Washington, 1837–46), edited by Peter Force, drew my attention to material missed on an early trip through the newspapers. The thirty-four volume collection of the *Journals of the Continental Congress* (Washington, 1904–37), edited by Worthington C. Ford and others, helped to point up the tie between Pennsylvania and continental affairs. Volume four deals with the months of 1776 relevant to my topic. More useful here than the *Journals* and a

BIBLIOGRAPHICAL NOTE

valuable complement to them is Edmund C. Burnett's *Letters of the Members of the Continental Congress* (8 vols., Washington, 1921-36). Burnett excised, apparently for reasons of space, considerable material from many letters but this defect is somewhat corrected by the full citations that note the locations of all letters.

None of these collections proved as valuable for me as the newspapers. That honor belongs solely to the collected volumes of the *Pennsylvania Magazine of History and Biography (PMHB)*, now in its eighty-fifth year. The superb cumulative index to the first seventy-five volumes makes the vast amount of material they contain incomparably accessible.

A virtue of the earlier volumes of the *Pennsylvania Magazine* is the extensive samplings from the Historical Society of Pennsylvania's huge collection of colonial manuscripts. A student who fails first to make a close check of the *Magazine's* contents invariably finds—as this one did—he has laboriously copied material from a manuscript already in print. Fortunately, the *Magazine* has only sampled the Society's collections. By far the most useful of these collections for my purposes was that of the Shippen family. I worked entirely from the manuscripts but it should be noted that a sampling of the best in this immense body of papers appears in Thomas Balch, editor, *Letters and Papers Relating Chiefly to the Provincial History of Pennsylvania* (Philadelphia, 1855). The Shippens and those who married into the family seemed to a man incapable of tossing away any scrap of paper with writing upon it. I doubt that any collection of colonial papers, excepting those of the Adams family, exceeds the Shippens' either in size or importance, especially when the allied Burd and Yeates Papers are included. The bulk of the Shippen Papers are at the Historical Society; a small body of them, of some use here, remain at the Philosophical Society, and a still smaller selection, which I did not use, at the Library of Congress.

The Shippen Papers, along with those of the Burd and Yeates families, give one side of the picture of Pennsylvania in 1776. Christopher Marshall gives another. Generally, William Duane, Jr.'s, edition of Marshall's diary, *Passages from the Remembrancer of Christopher Marshall* (Philadelphia, 1839) is satisfactory, but since the editor excised occasionally useful material I decided to rely completely on the manuscript of the diary in the Historical Society of Pennsylvania. Several of Marshall's letters in a letterbook hitherto apparently overlooked by historians helped to clarify the reasons for the old druggist's sudden disenchantment with Cannon and his friends and at the same time helped to clarify the violent opposition the Constitution of 1776 raised among some people.

Still another side of the revolution in Pennsylvania emerged out of William Bradford, Jr.'s "Memorandum and Register, for the months of May & June, 1776." Bradford's brief diary, plus his detailed, gossipy letters to James Madison in 1774–75, tell the story of Pennsylvania affairs through the eyes of an intelligent young man whose mind was often on other things than the struggle for independence. There are a few Bradford letters for 1776 in the Wallace Papers.

These were the main collections at the Historical Society found useful. Strangely, nearly all of perhaps a half-hundred diaries glanced at gave little direct help. Elizabeth Drinker, for instance, wrote in hers on July 2, the day word spread through Philadelphia that Congress had agreed to declare independence: "H. D. left home this Morng third day—with Joice Benezet, for By bary he returned in the Evening." The correspondence of Quakers and women showed almost complete absorption in private affairs and little concern for public events. The Pemberton Papers, for instance, dealt almost exclusively with religious affairs; Jasper Yeates's wife wrote mainly about such things as a son's bruised eye and the sleepless nights caused by a crying daughter.

There is other material at the Society that should be mentioned. Thomas Wharton's letterbook, 1773–84, refers to the Pennsylvania–Virginia boundary dispute; the Penn–Physick correspondence for 1776 reveals how hard up for cash the Penn family was and to what extent the payment of quit rents had fallen in abeyance; the York County Papers give some information about the operation of the Committee of Inspection and Observation there; and the Reynell–Coates Papers include several letters about economic affairs during this period. The Society's Broadside Collection contains in the 1776 drawer several items which, if published in the newspapers, slipped

BIBLIOGRAPHICAL NOTE

past me. Among them were "The Alarm" (or "Der Alarm" in the German version), a broadside distributed throughout Philadelphia on May 19; the Committee of Privates' broadside of June 26; and an early version of the Pennsylvania Constitution's Bill of Rights, containing a section later omitted by the Convention.

The Historical Society of Pennsylvania does not have *all* the manuscripts dealing with Pennsylvania in 1776. The Dickinson Papers at the Ridgeway Branch of the Library Company should not be overlooked. They contain several letters to Dickinson on events in the Constitutional Convention and some Benjamin Rush letters that do not appear in Butterfield's volumes. The American Philosophical Society's vast Franklin collection provided a few relevant letters. Charles Wilson Peale's brief diary for 1776, also in the Society, proved of some help.

The diary served in part as a sketch book for Peale, and anyone weary of the formal paintings that have made colonial Americans seem forbidding souls should glance at it, if only for the smudged sketch of a pretty girl sitting on the leg of an army officer, her arms looped about his neck as she plants a kiss on his cheek. (A second sketch, more typical of the period, shows the pair posed for posterity in a dignified position.)

Visits to or correspondence with several local historical societies in eastern Pennsylvania gave little aid in unraveling the story of the backcountry. Only the West Chester Historical Society provided information on local politicians I had been unable to find elsewhere. The Public Archives at Harrisburg produced nothing that is not already in print in either the *Archives* or *Colonial Records*.

The published source material for the months covered in this book probably exceeds that for any similar period in American colonial history. Burnett's *Letters* only taps the mass of material from the pens of Congressmen on Pennsylvania's affairs in 1776. John Adams is here by far the most important. Much more Adams material is available in print than is often realized. It is scattered in many books and the quality of editing varies from excellent to indifferent. The most important collection is, of course, *The Life and Works of John Adams* (10 vols., Boston, 1850–56), edited by Charles Francis Adams.

The grandson modernized and perhaps in spots polished Adams' letters; otherwise the editing seems to have omitted nothing that hinders a fair judgment of the man and his part in the events of his time. The *Works* is supplemented by several letters relevant to 1776 and Pennsylvania in "The Correspondence between John Adams and Professor John Winthrop," in the *Massachusetts Historical Society Collections,* fifth series, volume four (Boston, 1878). *The Warren-Adams Letters* (2 vols., Boston, 1917 and 1925), also published by the Massachusetts Historical Society, was the most valuable source for Adams' political views, his aims, and his activities during this period. A less intense, more amiable Adams appears in *The Familiar Letters of John Adams to His Wife Abigail Adams, During the Revolution* (New York, 1876), edited by Charles Francis Adams. Adams reminisced about the events of 1776 the rest of his life. Both *The Correspondence of John Adams and Thomas Jefferson 1812–1826* (Indianapolis, 1925), edited by Paul Wilstach, and Worthington C. Ford's edition of *Statesman and Friend—Correspondence with Benjamin Waterhouse 1784–1822* (Boston, 1927), show, among other things, the astonishing consistency of Adams's political views throughout his life. His later recollections with Benjamin Rush about these turbulent days in Philadelphia are found in *Old Family Letters: Copied from the Originals for Alexander Biddle, Series A* (Philadelphia, 1892).

Perhaps the most objective account of Pennsylvania affairs by a member of Congress is found in *Letters to and from Caesar Rodney 1756–1784,* edited by G. H. Ryden (Philadelphia, 1933). The papers of another Delawarian—William Thomson Read, editor, *The Life and Correspondence of George Read* (Philadelphia, 1870)—provided one or two useful letters. "The Diary of Richard Smith in the Continental Congress, 1775–1776," *American Historical Review* I (1896), 288–310, 493–516, gives a vivid picture of Congress's handling of Pennsylvania's boundary disputes. Thomas Jefferson remained aloof from Pennsylvania politics, or at least gives that impression in his letters. What views he expressed on events in mid-1776 appear in volumes one and fifteen of *The Jefferson Papers* (16 vols. to date, 1950–61), edited by Julian Boyd and others. Samuel Adams did not stand off from Philadelphia politics, as we know from Marshall's diary, but his *Writings of Samuel Adams* (4 vols., New York, 1904–08), edited by Harry A. Cushing, reveal no more than a hint of his involvement. *The Correspondence and Public Papers of John Jay* (2 vols., New York, 1890), H. P. Johnston, editor, contains several of James Duane's letters with material relevant to this period.

Aside from Marshall's diary, the published papers of no one Pennsylvanian dominate this period. Benjamin Rush's part in these events, as he saw it, is presented in his *Autobiography* (Princeton, 1948), edited by George W. Corner, and in Lyman Butterfield's excellent two-volume edition of Rush's *Letters* (Princeton, 1951), supplemented by Butterfield's "Further Letters of Benjamin Rush," in the *PMHB* 78 (1954), 3–44. Rush's views on the Provincial Conference's religious oath are found in Marshall's letterbook. Paine's views on government and the events of the day are found in newspaper articles written under the name of "The Forester," and, of course, in *Common Sense,* available in an admirable edition by Harry Hayden Clark, *Thomas Paine, Representative Selections* (New York, 1944). The most complete though not especially well-edited collection of his work is Philip S. Foner's *The Complete Writings of Thomas Paine* (2 vols., New York, 1945). Most of the little known about Paine's movements during this period stems from Marshall's diary and the correspondence of Rush and John Adams.

One man who could have told us what would have been close to a complete story of political events in Pennsylvania during 1776 was Charles Thomson. He refused to do so, carefully burning all his papers shortly before his death. What recollections he left behind are found in "The Papers of Charles Thomson," in the *Collections of the New York Historical Society for 1878,* 1–286, which includes "Joseph Reed's Narrative," 269–273; and in his letter to W. H. Drayton, which Stillé reprints in his *Life of Dickinson,* 340–351. Fortunately, few Pennsylvanians were afflicted with Thomson's respect for the reputations of the patriots; unfortunately, few others knew so much of the truth behind those reputations as Thomson. Joseph Reed gives some light on the public affairs of the day but little on the men in *Life and Correspondence of Joseph Reed* (2 vols., Philadelphia, 1847), edited by William B. Reed. Much more helpful, particularly for the comments on the British use of foreign troops, is William Henry Smith's, *St. Clair Papers: The Life and Public Services of Arthur St. Clair* (2 vols., Cincinnati, 1882). Volume one, 257–362, gives St. Clair's correspondence relevant to the Pennsylvania–Virginia boundary dispute.

Neither James Wilson's nor John Dickinson's papers reveals much about Pennsylvania politics in this period. Two items worth mentioning are Wilson's letter to Horatio Gates, June, 1776, in the *PMHB* 36 (1912), 473–75; and Dickinson's speech against independence, edited by J. H. Powell, also in the *Magazine* 65 (1941), 458–81.

Abundant published material exists on the Pennsylvania–Philadelphia social scene in 1776. The best single account is Alexander Graydon's *Memoirs of His Own Times with Reminiscences of the Men and Events* (Philadelphia, 1811). Graydon was reared in Philadelphia, lived in Reading, York, and later Harrisburg. A good deal of what we know about the people's attitude toward the Revolution and especially about men in the backcountry of this period we owe to Graydon. A minor flaw in the book is his exaggeration, to my way of thinking, of George Bryan's share in the Constitution of 1776.

Graydon's picture of the social setting is filled out by a variety of diaries by other contemporaries. *Jacob Hiltzheimer's Diary,* edited by J. C. Parsons (Philadelphia, 1893), was useful for facts about Timothy Matlack's escapades. "The Journal of Sally Eve," *PMHB* 5 (1881), 19–36, 191–205, gossips about Jacob Duché, Dr. Shippen, Rev. Coombes, and other worthies of the day with complete abandon. Duché's anonymously published *Observations on a Variety of Subjects* (Philadelphia, 1774) presents through a series of letters a lively picture of Philadelphia in 1771–72 by one who, at the time, had great affection for the city. An even livelier account is *Sally Wister's Journal—A True Narrative—Being a Quaker Maiden's Account of Her Experience with Officers of the Continental Army, 1777–1778* (Philadelphia, 1902), edited by Albert Cook Myers. The best report on Pennsylvanians' attitude toward New Englanders and of the capture of a runaway servant is in "Some Extracts from the Papers of General Persifor Frazer," *PMHB* 31 (1907), 129–34, 311–19, 447–51.

Native Pennsylvanians rarely bothered to discuss in detail their surroundings, for few waste time with the familiar. We must depend for such reports on tourists. Among the best accounts by travelers about Pennsylvania in general and Philadelphia in particular are: Jonathan Boucher, *Reminiscences of an American Loyalist* (Boston, 1925); Philip Padelford, editor, *Colonial Panorama—Dr. Robert Honyman's Journal for March and April, 1775* (San Marino, Calif., 1939); and Patrick M'Robert's "A Tour Through Part of the North Provinces of America—1774-5," edited by Carl Bridenbaugh, *PMHB* 59 (1935). Daniel Fisher, a visiting Englishman, in "Extracts from the Diary of Daniel Fisher, 1755," *PMHB* 17 (1893), 263-278, rambles interestingly about the Indian Queen Tavern, the city market, Pennsylvania farming, Chief Justice Allen, and Benjamin Franklin and his wife. Hector St. John de Crèvecoeur, *Letters from an American Farmer* (Everyman edition, London, 1912), lived in Carlisle, visited Philadelphia, and no doubt devised his definition of an American from his Pennsylvania experiences. Virginians' comments on Pennsylvania and its women are found in Hunter D. Farish, editor, *Journal and Letters of Philip Vickers Fithian 1773-1774* (Williamsburg, Va., 1943). Fithian's vivid descriptions of the Pennsylvania backcountry appear in Robert C. Albion and Leonidas Dodson, editors, *Philip Vickers Fithian: Journal, 1775-1776* (Princeton, 1932). A Tory's account of Philadelphia in 1775 is found in George A. Ward, editor, *Journal and Letters of Samuel Curwen* (New York, 1842). For a New England boy's reaction to the noise and bustle of the city see "Dr. Solomon Drowne," *PMHB* 48 (1924). "Extracts from the Diary of Dr. James Clitherall," *PMHB* 22 (1898), gives an aristocratic visitor's view of events in the city during the spring and summer of 1776. *The Journal of Nicholas Cresswell* (London, 1925) overlaps Clitherall's stay and describes the city at the time of the Constitutional Convention. *The Literary Diary of Ezra Stiles* (3 vols., New York, 1901), edited by Franklin Bowditch Dexter, offers two or three comments about Pennsylvania politicians during this period.

The source material on Quakers is voluminous in one sense, sparse in another. William Wade Hinshaw and Thomas Worth Marshall have relieved the historian of a lot of leg work with their *Encyclopedia of American Quaker Geneology* (6 vols., Ann Arbor, Mich., 1936–50). Volume two lists the records for Philadelphia Monthly Meeting and thus provides an easy way of checking whether a member of the Society of Friends was disowned or not, or whether a man was a member of the Society. The shortcut has a flaw; the Hinshaw–Marshall work includes only one of three meetings in the city. Another time-saver is Gilbert Cope's "Chester County Quakers During the Revolution," in the *Bulletins of the Chester County Historical Society 1902–03,* which reports on Chester County members of the Society disowned for participating in warlike measures. These records are not filled out with personal memoirs. The single personal account of a Quaker in the period covered here that I came across was the "Memoirs of a Senator from Pennsylvania: Jonathan Roberts, 1771–1854," in the *PMHB* 61 (1937), 446–74, edited by Philip S. Klein. Roberts' remarks about his father are the best we have on the dilemma of a Quaker in 1776 who sympathized with the Revolution.

If the Quakers' role in the Revolution has been misunderstood by historians, the fault stems mainly from the lack of attention given to them. Isaac Sharpless' *The Quakers in the Revolution* came out in 1899 and since then little of value has emerged to replace this work. Charles Wetherill's *History of the Religious Society of Friends Called by Some The Free Quakers in the City of Philadelphia* (privately printed, 1894), contains some useful facts about disowned Quakers but is all too brief, superficial, and pietistic. *Meeting House and Counting House: The Quaker Merchants of Colonial Philadelphia 1682–1761* (Chapel Hill, N.C., 1948), by Frederick B. Tolles, is excellent; the period covered limited its value here.

The Catholics have received even less attention than the Quakers. The single useful study turned up was Charles H. Metzger, "Catholics in the Period of the American Revolution," *American Catholic Historical Society of Philadelphia. Records* 59 (1948), 195–219, 294–317. The worth of Metzger's statistics is questionable, for he places the Catholics in Pennsylvania as high as seven thousand, a figure difficult to accept. His study should be balanced by John Tracy Ellis, "Catholics in Colonial America," *American Ecclesiastical Review* 136 (1957).

BIBLIOGRAPHICAL NOTE

No one who writes in the period of colonial Pennsylvania can ignore the work of Charles H. Lincoln. His *The Revolutionary Movement in Pennsylvania 1760–1776* (Philadelphia, 1901), is poorly organized and occasionally inaccurate, yet so great was Lincoln's knowledge of his period and so convincing his presentation that for half a century historians have used his work as a stepping stone for their own interpretations. J. Paul Selsam's *The Pennsylvania Constitution of 1776* (Philadelphia, 1936) lacks Lincoln's style and imaginative insights and only extends rather than re-examines Lincoln's interpretation of the period. Its merits are accuracy and thoroughness. The student who wades into Pennsylvania colonial history for the first time can only be grateful for a work like Selsam's. His full bibliography and detailed annotation serve as excellent guides to source material that might otherwise be missed.

All other accounts of Pennsylvania politics in 1776 lean heavily on Lincoln and Selsam. Elisha P. Douglass has in *Rebels and Democrats* (Chapel Hill, N.C., 1955) gone to the sources and returned with little new. He accepts the myth that a Quaker oligarchy dominated the colony's politics in 1776; he accepts the argument that the backcountry was estranged from the eastern counties; and he ignores the influence of Congress in Pennsylvania politics. Theodore Thayer's *Pennsylvania Politics and the Growth of Democracy 1740–1776* (Harrisburg, 1953) is marred by inaccuracy. The few relevant pages in Robert L. Brunhouse, *The Counter-Revolution in Pennsylvania* (Philadelphia, 1942) repeat the standard picture.

For details on government in colonial Pennsylvania I found Sister Joan de Lourdes Leonard, C.S.J., "The Organization and Procedure of the Pennsylvania Assembly, 1682–1776," *PMHB* 72 (1948), 215–39, 376–412, of great help. William H. Lloyd's *The Early Courts of Pennsylvania* (Boston, 1910) gave me insights into the organization of the colony's political machine. Of little use yet possibly worth a glance to other students is E. R. L. Gould's "Local Self-Government in Pennsylvania," *PMHB* 6 (1882), 156–73.

On the subject of Pennsylvania elections Cortland F. Bishop gives all the relevant statutes in "History of Elections in the American Colonies," *Columbia University Studies in History, Economics, and*

Public Law, volume three (New York, 1893), 1-297. The flaw in Bishop's thesis originates in his assumption that the statutes were obeyed to the letter. This same assumption mars the relevant chapters of Albert E. McKinley, *The Suffrage Franchise in the Thirteen English Colonies in America* (Philadelphia, 1905).

Of great help in placing Pennsylvania affairs in the continental setting was Burnett's *Continental Congress* (New York, 1941). Similarly useful was the first half of Allan Nevin's *The American States During and After the Revolution* (New York, 1924). Arthur M. Schlesinger's thorough *The Colonial Merchants and the American Revolution* (New York, 1924) offers the best account of Philadelphia merchants and the early years of the Revolution. Schlesinger's annotation guided me to several newspaper accounts in 1770-74 I might otherwise have missed. J. H. Hazleton's *The Declaration of Independence* (New York, 1906) gives a day-by-day account from early May through July 8 of events in Philadelphia leading up to the Declaration. Important as they are for other aspects of the Revolution, Merrill Jensen's *Articles of Confederation* (Madison, Wis., 1940) and Curtis Nettels's *George Washington and the American Revolution* (Boston, 1952) give only a condensed version of Lincoln's account of Pennsylvania affairs in 1776.

No one who touches on the economy of colonial Pennsylvania can fail to praise the work of Anne Bezanson. She covers thoroughly and expertly a vast amount of material in her *Prices and Inflation During the American Revolution in Pennsylvania 1770-1790* (Philadelphia, 1951) and in her excellent article "Inflation and Controls, Pennsylvania, 1774-1779," in the *Journal of Economic History,* Supplement for 1948. Crane Brinton's "The Manipulation of Economic Unrest," in the same Supplement, seems glib alongside Miss Bezanson's solid report.

The dominant historian of the social history of colonial Pennsylvania is Carl Bridenbaugh. Both *Rebels and Gentlemen—Philadelphia in the Age of Franklin* (New York, 1942), written with Jessica Bridenbaugh, and his *Cities in Revolt* (New York,. 1955) are marred for the student by their lack of annotation. On Freemasonry in colonial Philadelphia see volume one of Norris S. Barratt and Julius F. Sachse, editors, *Freemasonry in Pennsylvania 1727–1907* (2 vols., Philadelphia, 1908). Frank M. Etting's *The Old State House of Pennsylvania* (Philadelphia, 1891), though still useful, has been superseded by Harold Donaldson Eberlein and Cortlandt Van Dyke Hubbard, *Diary of Independence Hall* (Philadelphia, 1948). John F. Watson's *Annals of Philadelphia and Pennsylvania in the Olden Times* (3 vols., Philadelphia, 1884) must be used with caution. Much better is the reliable J. Thomas Scharf and Thompson Westcott, *History of Philadelphia 1609–1884* (3 vols., Philadelphia, 1884).

Two excellent articles dealing with Pennsylvania social history should be mentioned. Whitfield Bell, Jr.'s "Some Aspects of the Social History of Pennsylvania, 1760–1790," *PMHB* 62 (1938), 281–308, rounds up a mass of facts and is well annotated. It serves as an excellent starting point for anyone beginning to study the field. Frederick B. Tolles's "The Culture of Early Pennsylvania," *PMHB* 81 (1957), 117–135, discusses Pennsylvania's early eminence in American history and though it deals with the 1740's many of its insights are useful for the later period.

I found the following helpful in placing Pennsylvania's social history in a broader setting: Carl Bridenbaugh, *Myths and Realities* (Baton Rouge, La., 1952); Philip Davidson, *Propaganda and the American Revolution 1763–1783* (Chapel Hill, N. C., 1941); J. Franklin Jameson, *The American Revolution Considered as a Social Movement* (Princeton, 1926); Leonard Labaree, *Conservatism in Early American History* (New York, 1948); and Moses Coit Tyler, *The Literary History of the American Revolution* (2 vols., New York, 1897).

Information on the Pennsylvania backcountry is less abundant than an historian would prefer. Only three of the many available county histories proved of any help: George D. Albert, *History of the County of Westmoreland* (Philadelphia, 1882); J. Mombert, *Authentic History of Lancaster County in the State of Pennsylvania* (Lancaster, 1869); and M. L. Montgomery, *History of Berks County in the Revolution* (Reading, 1894). If Berks receives more space than it deserves in my chapter, it is due to some extent to the work of J. Bennett Nolan. His two slim volumes—*Neddie Burd's Reading Letters*

(Reading, 1927). and *The Founding of the Town of Reading in Pennsylvania* (Reading, 1929) — were more useful than their size would suggest.

The pietistic quality of Wayland Dunaway's *The Scotch–Irish of Colonial Pennsylvania* (Chapel Hill, N. C., 1944) made this work less useful than the early volume by Henry James Ford, *The Scotch–Irish in America* (Princeton, 1915). The backcountry Germans still await a scholarly study. Meanwhile, one can do little better than lean on the delightfully written but authoritative *Pennsylvania Dutch* (New York, 1950) by Frederic Klees, himself a Pennsylvania Dutchman, also useful is the collection of essays edited by Ralph Wood under the title *Pennsylvania Germans* (Princeton, 1942).

The expert on the Wyoming Valley dispute is Julian Boyd. His summary of the affair in volume six, 474–87, of the *Jefferson Papers* is the best available. Boyd details the story for the layman in his *The Susquehanna Company: Connecticut's Experiment in Expansion* (Tercentary Commission of the State of Connecticut, New Haven, 1933). The Indians' side of the story appears in Anthony F. C. Wallace, *King of the Delawares — Teedyuscung* (Philadelphia, 1949). Also worth a glance is *The Frontier Policy of Pennsylvania* (Pittsburgh, 1915) by George A. Cribbs.

Little attention is given to the transmontane region in this book. For fuller accounts see Solon J. and Elizabeth H. Buck, *The Planting of Civilization in Western Pennsylvania* (Pittsburgh, 1939), and the early chapters in Russell J. Ferguson, *Early Western Pennsylvania Politics* (Pittsburgh, 1938). One of the great books about colonial frontier life and deserving of much more attention is Joseph Doddridge's *Notes on the Settlement and Indian Wars* (Pittsburgh, 3rd printing, 1912).

Many of the men who helped shape the events covered in this book have been neglected so far as sound biographical studies go. Even national figures involved in Pennsylvania affairs lack the full treatment they deserve. There is still no distinguished biography of John Adams. Gilbert Chinard's *Honest John Adams* (Boston, 1933) says little more than Charles Francis Adams said with more style in the first volume of his grandfather's *Works.* Catherine Drinker Bowen's

John Adams and the American Revolution catches the atmosphere of the period wonderfully but the furniture of her story tends to obscure the characters. There are two excellent if brief studies of Adams' ideas—Zoltan Haraszti's *John Adams and the Prophets of Progress* (Cambridge, Mass., 1952) and Randolph Adams's *Political Ideas of the American Revolution* (Durham, N. C., 1922). Chapter III, "The Internal Revolution and Independence," in Jensen's *Articles* and Daniel J. Boorstin's *The Genius of American Politics* (Chicago, 1953), 66–98, give slightly different versions of the political ideas of the time.

Biographies of other national figures were also found wanting. Edward P. Alexander, *A Revolutionary Conservative—James Duane of New York* (New York, 1938) adds little to an understanding of Duane's ideas during the Revolutionary period. All biographers of Sam Adams face a lack of material that makes it difficult to assess his role in Pennsylvania affairs in 1776. The best brief study is Carl Becker's in the *Encyclopedia of Social Sciences.* James K. Hosmer's *Samuel Adams* (New York, 1885) was of little use; the best of the extended studies, despite its debunking tone, is John C. Miller's *Sam Adams* (Boston, 1935). Charles J. Stillé's *Life of John Dickinson* (Philadelphia, 1891) is marred by the author's attempt to justify rather than understand his subject. Dickinson's curious and still cloudy part in these events needs much more study. Another blind spot is James Wilson. Alva Burton Konkle's unpublished study on Wilson—on deposit at the Friends' Historical Library of Swarthmore College—is useless. Charles Page Smith's *James Wilson—Founding Father 1742-1798* (Chapel Hill, N. C., 1956) has misinterpreted his role during the Revolution in order to make him fit the picture of an early "liberal." Moncure Conway's exhaustive *Life of Thomas Paine* (2 vols., New York, 1892) has been superseded by Alfred Owen Aldridge's *Man of Reason* (Philadelphia, 1959). Neither provides great light on Paine's shadowy activities in Philadelphia during the spring and summer of 1776. Carl Van Doren's *Benjamin Franklin* (New York World reprint edition, 1948) helped in keeping track of the peripatetic Franklin. The *Dictionary of American Biography* has sketches on all these men that vary from brilliant to mediocre. Among the best are Becker's article on Franklin and Crane Brinton's on Tom Paine.

The student must scratch hard for material on the minor figures of this period. There is not a single article on James Cannon of any merit. The *DAB* overlooks him. For Matlack the best available is a pietistic pamphlet by A. M. Stackhouse, *Col. Timothy Matlack— Patriot and Soldier* (privately printed, 1910). The *DAB* write-up of Dr. Thomas Young remarks that Henry H. Edes, "Memoir of Dr. Thomas Young, 1731–1777," *Publications,* Colonial Society of Massachusetts, II (1910), 2–54, is spotted with inaccuracies. Several of Young's spirited letters can be found in Isaac Q. Leake's *Memoir of the Life and Times of General John Lamb* (Albany, 1850), 84–92. Irving Brant's *James Madison, The Virginia Revolutionist* (Indianapolis, 1941) gives the fullest account of William Bradford, Jr. On Bradford's father see John William Wallace, *Colonel William Bradford* (Philadelphia, 1884). An excellent essay on John Montgomery of Carlisle, by Whitfield Bell, Jr., appears in *John and Mary's College* (Carlisle, Pa., 1956). Konkle's *Life and Times of Thomas Smith* offers little. Kenneth R. Rossman's *Thomas Mifflin and the Politics of the American Revolution* (Chapel Hill, N. C., 1952) fails to live up to its title. On John Hughes, Franklin's friend who suffered from the Stamp Act, see Edmund S. and Helen M. Morgan, *The Stamp Act Crisis, Prologue to Revolution* (Chapel Hill, N.C., 1953).

No student of the American Revolution should miss Eric Hoffer's two thin but enlightening volumes—*The Passionate State of Mind* (New York, 1955) and *The True Believer* (New York, 1951).

Index

Abbotstown, 67
Accents: in Philadelphia, 43-44; Irish, 67; New England, 50 n.; Southern, 50 n.
Adams, John (1735-1826), 110, 177; admires Rev. Duffield, 39; and John Dickinson, 114-16; and May 10 resolve, 119; and May 15 resolve, 120; exploits river battle in Congress, 117, 119-20; helps Independents oppose Assembly, 156; ideas on government, 183; influences Rush's views on Constitution, 194; Nettels on source of militant views, 115 n.; on Age of Paine, 111-12; on celebration of Declaration, 181; on confederation, 165; on Dickinson, 115; on Dr. Young, 105; on Duane, 122; on innovation in government, 121; on Jefferson, 125; on May 20 meeting, 135; on May 15 resolve, 127; on Paine, 183, 185; on Paine's ideas, 111-12; on Pennsylvania's Constitution, 178; on Quakers in politics, 151; on theory of popular sovereignty, 190; on spirit of leveling, 165; on unity, 126; on virtue of free governments, 114; on voting qualifications, 174; on William Penn, 130; role in Philadelphia politics, 112-13, 114; share in Pennsylvania revolution, 185; three-step plan for independence, 113-14, 116
Adams, Sam (1722-1803), 110, 150, 177; and Cannon, 131, 175-76; and Dr. Young, 105, 113, 131; and Marshall, 112-13, 131, 156, 175-76; and May 15 resolve, 122-23, 125; and Provincial Conference, 175-76; compared to Cannon, 170; confers with "steering committee," 131; helps Independents oppose Assembly, 156; hints at Declaration, 171; on Catholics, 55; on foreign troops, 122-23; on influence of events on public opinion, 108; on Philadelphia reaction to *Common Sense*, 90; role in Philadelphia politics, 112-13, 114
Adcock, William, 102
Advertisements: by dentist, 96-97; by druggist, 167-68; for anti-scorbutic drops, 96-97; for brig *Hawke*, 168; for *Common Sense*, 91; for intelligence office, 167; for luxury goods, 47-48; for runaway servants, 97, 167; for sale of western lands, 52; for theater play, 96
Age of Jackson, 198
Age of Paine, 183, 198; John Adams on, 111-12
Age of Reason: John Adams on, 111-12
"Alarm, The," 134-35
Ale, Burton, 48
Alison, Francis (1705-1779): James Smith studies under, 107; on peace commissioners, 49

Allen, Andrew (1740–1825), 26, 60, 83; and Edward Burd, 80, 80 n., 81; call for Convention aimed at, 20; in Independents' campaign literature, 29; sketch of, 24–25; votes for in May election, 30

Allen, James (*d.* 1778): elected to Assembly, 60, 76; in reactionary faction, 162; on Assembly vote on new instructions, 161 n.; on first public reading of May 15 resolve, 127; on May 15 resolve vote, 124 n.; on omission of loyalty oath, 158; opposes giving vote to Germans, 158; sketch of, 60–61; votes to exonerate Committee of Safety, 62 n.

Allen, John, 19

Allen, William (*ca.* 1751–1838), 25; and Arthur St. Clair, 79; on foreign troops, 93

Allen family: and Arthur St. Clair, 79; Marshall on influence of in May election, 33; member of plans to ask Congress for clarification on May 15 resolve, 156

Alms House. *See* Bettering House

American Philosophical Society: ceases to meet, 95–96; city Committee meets at hall of, 106, 133, 146, 181

Amish, 41; in backcountry, 64–65

Armitage's Tavern, 168; scene of Declaration celebration, 181

Army. *See* Associators

Arndt, Jacob: votes to exonerate Committee of Safety, 62 n.

Assembly; and backcountry, 20–21, 68, 71, 151–64; and Charter of Privileges, 119–20; and Dickinson, 121; and row galley dispute, 61–62, 169–70; attacked in "The Alarm," 134–35; attempts to control creation of Convention, 162; boycotted by anti-Constitutionalists, 195–96; boycotted by Independents, 157, 159, 163–64; effect of February Convention call on, 19–20, 21–22; effect of May 10 resolve on, 119–20; effect of May 15 resolve on, 120–21, 132–33; fights for survival, 151–64; hindered by Independents in Congress, 157; hindered by Committee of Privates, 106–07, 149; hindered by myth of Quaker domination, 151–56; hindered by Radical Independents, 168–69; Independents campaign to discredit, 131–38, 147–48; oath to King abandoned, 158; Paine leads attack on, 131–32; petition to from Wayne, 148–49; powers assumed in 1775, 78; under new Constitution, 195; votes new instructions, 160–61; Wilson chosen by as delegate to Congress, 82; Yeates urged to run for, 76

Associators, 199; absence of and ratification of Constitution, 189; and Committee of Privates, 106–7; and Constitution, 194; and indentured servants, 98; and Provincial Conference, 173–74; and river battle, 117; attitude toward Quakers, 156; Cannon advises on proposed Constitution, 176–77; Cannon helps organize in city, 105; Civis on, 28; Committee of Safety alerts, 144–45; depart for New York, 182; Dickinson defends self before, 166–67; drill on city commons, 89; Elector on right of to vote, 28; formation of, 68, 84; grievances of, 148–49; lack of puritanical spirit, 174; May resolves read to, 145–46, 150, 150 n., 170–71; power under Constitution to elect officers, 189, rip down King's arms, 181. *See also* Committee of Privates

INDEX

Bache, Richard (1737–1811): on foreign troops, 116; on river battle, 117
Backcountry: after May 20 meeting, 140–42, 144–50; and Provincial Conference, 172; and Wyoming Valley, 85; attitude toward New England, 53–54; blamed for Constitution, 191–92; cultural barriers in, 66–68; economic pattern of, 70–75; effect of isolation on, 144; enthusiasm for war in 1775, 85; historical pattern of, 68–70; Moderates' success in, 59–62; pacifists in, 65; political pattern in, 75–86; population of, 64; propaganda aimed at, 147–48; religious-cultural pattern of, 64–68
Baltimore, 71
Barge, Jacob, 146
Barton, Reverend William: on clergy (1774), 143–44
Bayard, John, 100
Bayard, Phoebe. *See* St. Clair, Phoebe Bayard
Becker, Carl L.; and C. H. Lincoln's view of American Revolution, 63 n.
Bedford County, 83; and Arthur St. Clair, 78–79; cultural composition of, 64 n.; deputies absent from Assembly, 61 n., 163; sends Thomas Smith to Assembly, 60; settlers in, 66
Bell, Robert: publishes *Common Sense*, 90–91
Berks County, 163 n.; and Edward Biddle, 69; and Sheriff Nagle, 81; and Wyoming Valley, 85; delegates to Provincial Conference, 172; interference in politics of, 81; stronghold of "church people," 65; surplus of lawyers in, 83. *See also* Reading
Bethlehem: as Moravian center, 65
Bettering House, 37–38; visitor on, 38
Biddle, Edward (1738–1779), 84; absent from Assembly, 163; sketch of, 69
Biddle, James (1731–1797): issues writs in King's name, 143
Biddle, Owen (1737–1799), 27; chosen for Independent ticket, 26; votes for in May election, 30
Bird, Rachel. *See* Wilson, Rachel Bird
Blackstone, Sir William: Bradford reads, 15; volumes of in backcountry library, 60
Blockade of Delaware Bay: effect on advertisements, 97; effect on backcountry, 74; effect on Philadelphia, 45–46, 47–48; effect on river traffic, 95; Reed on, 109; warships leave stations, 116–17. *See also* River battle
Bond, Phineas (1749–1815): receives Remonstrance in Lancaster, 140
Boston, 48–49, 106, 113; as protection to Philadelphia, 49; Philadelphia shows sympathy for, 87; trade of compared with Philadelphia's, 73
Boston Tea Party: and Dr. Young, 105
Bradford, William, Sr. (1722–1791), 14; and London Coffee House, 126; publishes second edition of *Common Sense*, 91
Bradford, William, Jr. (1755–1795): and river battle, 117, 118; ends diary, 168; on Congress's use of philosophers, 88; on Dickinson's self-justification, 167; on Germans in May election, 16, 17; on May election, 14, 15, 16, 17; on May election results, 29–30, 130; on Philadelphia's location, 49; on rumors of Franklin as spy, 89; searches for seaman, 46; sketch of, 14; worries of, 94
Brand, William, 55

Braxton, Carter: and Pennsylvania-Virginia boundary dispute, 52; on May 15 resolve, 125; on vote for May 15 resolve, 124–25
Bridenbaugh, Carl, 50 n.
Brown, John: refuses to exonerate Committee of Safety, 163 n.
Brown, Nathan, 100, 155
Brown, Robert: on democracy in colonial America, 34 n.
Bryan, George (1731–1791): share in Constitution, 186 n.
Bucks County, 20, 64, 163 n.: and economic ties with Philadelphia, 70; former home of Jonathan Roberts, 80; Quakers from in Assembly, 153 n.; Sally Wister visits, 40; receives resolves of May 20 meeting, 146
Buffalo Valley, 53
Burlamagiu. *See* Burlamaqui, Jean Jacques
Burlamaqui, Jean Jacques: and Congress, 88
Burd, Edward (1751–1833): on influence of *Common Sense* among Germans, 91–92; on naturalization of Germans, 17 n.; on purpose of City Committee, 21; on Quakers in politics, 152; sketch of, 80–81
Burnsides's School, 131
Butte, Dr. L., 96

Cadwalader, John (1742–1786): orator at May 20 meeting, 135, 136; refuses to serve under Constitution, 195
Cadwalader, Lambert (1743–1823): refuses to read May resolves to battalion, 170–71
Cannon, James (1740–1782), 177, 183, 196; advises Associators on proposed constitution, 176–77; age of, 102; and anti-Quaker feeling, 156; and Associators' right to vote, 149; and Committee of Privates, 105, 106–7, 149–50, 169, 170; and Constitution, 186–92; and constitutional ideas, 176–77; and February election of city Committee, 101–2; and May election, 29; and May election post-mortem, 33; and Memorial, 156; and Protest, 132; and religious oath of Conference, 175; and religious oath of Convention, 193; and Sam Adams, 131, 170, 175–76; and Wilson, 82; as Cassandra, 24; broadside of June, 176–77, 188, 189; confers with McKean, 131; death of, 200; elected Convention deputy, 182; helps pick election candidates, 26; helps plan dissolution of Assembly, 133; Marshall friendship wanes, 175–76, 192–93; Marshall visited by, 200; on Committee of Safety, 192; on qualifications for Convention deputies, 176–77; philosophy of equality proves unacceptable, 198; political skill of, 169–71; political inexperience of, 106; Rush makes responsible for "mobocracy," 178; sketch of, 105, 170; visits Norrington, 146
Carlisle, 22, 64 n., 66, 72; and James Wilson, 83; and John Montgomery, 69; Thomas Smith leaves, 79
Cassandra. *See* Cannon, James
Catholics, 37, 41; and May election, 55–56; attitude toward New England, 55–56; in backcountry, 66; in Philadelphia, 44; influence of in May election, 33; New England delegates attend mass of, 56; number of in Pennsylvania, 55 n.–56 n.
Cato. *See* Smith, Dr. William
Centre Square: horse race at, 95

INDEX

221

Chaloner, John, 102
Chambers, Lieutenant, 146
Charter of Privileges, 119–20; Remonstrance on, 139
Chester County, 20, 64, 163 n.; and economic ties with Philadelphia, 70; Associators of favor Protest, 150 n.; delegates to Conference quarrel, 173; Quakers from in Assembly, 153 n., 154
Chreist, Henry: refuses to exonerate Committee of Safety, 163 n.
Christ Church, 43, 87, 123 n.; Joseph Swift vestryman of, 16 n.; visitor on, 38
Christianus: on New England tolerance, 56
Church of England, 37; in backcountry, 66; Marshall on role in May election, 33
"Church people": in backcountry, 65
Civis: critizes Elector, 28
Clitherall, Dr. James: on May 20 meeting, 135–36; on reading of May resolves before Associators, 171; on effect of river battle, 117
Clymer, George (1739–1813), 17; chosen for Independent ticket, 26, 27; votes for in May election, 30
Coates, Isaac, 155
Colhoon, Dr. John, 172
College of New Jersey, 117
College of Philadelphia: and Alison, 49; and Cannon, 24, 82, 192; and Dr. Smith, 22; and Wilson, 82
Committee of Correspondence. *See* Committee of Privates
Committee of Inspection and Observation: deputies for Conference chosen by, 172; in backcountry, 83–84; May resolves sent to, 145–46; shift of power within, 84. *Lancaster County*: receives orders from city Committee, 77; shuns Shippen, 172. *Philadelphia*: 84; and Cannon, 82; and May 20 meeting, 133; and May 20 meeting attendance figures, 140; as host to Conference, 171–72; as "sentinel" to backcountry, 144; attitude toward Quakers, 155; Burd on purpose of, 21; call for Convention (February), 19–20, 21, 22; call for Convention (May), 99; celebrates Declaration, 181; February election of members, 19; history of, 18–19; interferes in Lancaster affairs, 77; membership of, 99–102; Memorial issued by, 156–57; Protest heads drawn by "steering committee," 132; Quakers on, 155; rumors of John Adams's influence with, 112; Sam Adams's influence with, 112–13. *Philadelphia County*: address from, 159. *York*: backs May 20 meeting resolves, 145, 146; visited by Philadelphians, 146–47
Committee of Privates, 101, 173, 185, 186, 188, 189, 191; and backcountry opinion shaped by, 106–7; and Cannon, 82, 85, 105, 106–7; and Cannon's broadside to, 176–77, 188, 189; and ideas on government, 184; and May election, 25–26; and May resolves read to battalions, 170–71; and Quakers in politics, 152; and row galley affair, 169–70; Associators' grievances fomented by, 149–50; Associators' right to vote promoted by, 149; Committee of Correspondence formed by, 149
Committee of Safety (Council of Safety): and backcountry, 144–45; and row galley dispute, 61–62, 169–70; Cannon on, 192; celebrates Declaration, 181; Conference recommends increased power for, 176; created, 78;

Independents comment on, 61; report on exonerates, 163; Rush on new members, 102–3
Common Sense, 94; and Rush, 102; Cato attacks, 23–24, 99; ideas on government in, 183; influence of, 91–92; in theater, 96; John Adams on, 111–12; lack of answers to, 23 n.; publication and reception of, 90–91
Concord: effect of battle at on Philadelphia economy, 45, 46
Conewago, 66
Congress: adjourns for May election, 16; and city Independents, 156–57; and May 10 resolve, 119; and May 15 resolve, 120–26; and Pennsylvania-Virginia boundary dispute, 51, 122; and Pennsylvania-Connecticut boundary dispute, 53, 122; and Philadelphia social problems, 97–98; attitude of Independents in toward Pennsylvania, 130–31; attitude on rumored use of foreign troops, 92; authority of to interfere in colonies' affairs, 121–22; Philadelphia reception for New England delegates, 87; Provincial Conference communicates with, 176; refers to philosophers, 88; war contracts, 46–47; Wilson opposes independence, 92; Wilson asks postponement of independence, 160–61
Connecticut: boundary dispute with Pennsylvania, 52–54, 122; Remonstrance on, 139
Constitution (1776), 188–92; and experimental philosophy, 190, 196–97, 198; bill of right of, 190; opposition to, 192–96; religious oath, 189–90.
Constitutional Convention: argument for in "The Alarm," 134–35; Assembly moves to control, 162; city Committee votes to call, 133; Cresswell on delegates to, 182; delegates for elected, 182; empowered to choose new delegates to Congress, 176; religious oath debated, 193; religious oath required by Conference, 174; rules for electing deputies to, 173–74; test oath, 189
Council of Censors, 188
Council of Safety. *See* Committee of Safety.
Crawford, Colonel James, 150 n.
Cresswell, Nicholas: on American accents, 50 n.; on Philadelphia buildings, 151; on Philadelphia in August, 182; on delegates to the Convention, 182
Crèvecoeur, Hector St. John de, 44; definition of an American and relation of to Philadelphia, 42; guides Scotsman about city, 41
Cumberland County, 163 n.; and James Smith, 107; and James Wilson, 83; and John Montgomery, 69–70; cultural composition of, 54 n.; delegates to Conference, 172; settlers of, 66
Curwen, Samuel: on Philadelphia (1775), 87

Dana, Francis, 115 n.
Davidson, William, 102
Declaration of Independence: celebrated, 181–82; passed, 177
Deism: Marshall mentions, 193; Dr. Young accused of, 105
Delany (Delaney), Sharpe (*ca.* 1739–1799), 100
Delaware: troops of moved to Philadelphia, 182; vote on May 15 resolve, 124
Delaware Bay. *See* Blockade of Delaware Bay
Delaware River: Duché describes ships on, 95

INDEX

Dewees, Sheriff William: Paine on role in May election, 33; role in May election, 29, 30
"Dialogue on Civil Liberty, A" (Witherspoon), 117
Dickinson, John (1732–1808), 19, 84; absent from Congress, 121, 121 n., 165; and Arthur Lee's reports, 115 n.; and Assembly compromise to February Convention demand, 21; and Assembly's struggle for survival, 158–59, 160. 161, 162, 165–66; and call for Convention (1774), 99–100; and James Wilson, 82; and John Adams's drive for independence, 114–16; as campaigner, 27–28; as Pennsylvania president, 198; defends self, 166–67; draws up new instructions, 160–61; Independents on, 158–59; leads new boycott against Assembly, 195–96; on confederation, 165; on indignities suffered, 178; reaction to May 10 resolve, 119–20; refuses to abet new Constitution, 119–20; threatens secession, 115
District of West Augusta, 51
Dock Creek: stench of, 38–39
Down, Jacob: found by Persifor Frazer, 98
Duane, James: John Adams on, 122; letter to John Jay, 126; on May 15 resolve, 122; Sam Adams rebuts, 122–23
Duché, Jacob (1737–1798): and prayer to King, 123, 143, 144; description of Philadelphia, 95; hissed, 123 n., 143 n.; on State House, 15
Duffield, Reverend George (1732–1790), 39
Dunmore, Lord: and Pennsylvania, 51; and rumored use of Negroes in war, 90
Dunkards, 65
Dutch Presbyterian Church. *See* Reformed Church

Easton, 65, 66; economic ties with Philadelphia, 70
Economy: of backcountry, 70–75; of Philadelphia, 45–49
Eddy (Edie), Samuel: votes to exonerate Committee of Safety, 62 n.
Edinburgh, 104
Election: of 1764, 17–18; of February (1776), 19, 101–2; of November (1776), 194. *See also* May election
Elector, 173; ideas on government, 184; on anti-independent sentiment in Pennsylvania, 33; on voting qualifications, 28; tentative identification of, 28 n.
Elliott, John, 47
Epley, Andrew, 102
Ewing, Jesse: and Edward Burd, 81

Fall of Tyranny or American Liberty Proclaimed, 96
Falmouth, Maine, 49
Fast Day: and Quakers, 155; used by Independents, 133–34
Fellowship Fire Company, 117
Ferver, George; advertisement for, 97
Fielding, Henry, 40
Finns; in Pennsylvania, 66
Fisher, Miss: and Bradford, Jr., 117, 168
Fishing Creek, 69

Fithian, Philip Vickers: on backcountry, 72–73; on backcountry enthusiasm in 1775, 85; on James Potter, 59–60; on Scotch-Irish accent, 50 n.; on Wyoming Valley dispute, 53–54
Flax: in Reading–Easton economy, 70; price rise of, 60
Flour: price drop of, 74
Fodder: price rise of, 75
Forester, The. *See* Paine, Thomas
Foreign troops, 98; Congress's attitude on rumored use of, 92; news of, 116; news of, Duane on, 122; news of and influence in Pennsylvania, 129–30; rumors of, 49; rumors of and influence, 92–93; Sam Adams on, 123
Foulke, John, 153 n.
Fountain Tavern, 101
Franklin, Benjamin (1706–1790), 196; accused as spy, 89; and independence, 88–89; and Dr. Smith, 23; and John Hughes, 79; and proprietary party, 35; delegate to Provincial Conference, 172; favors single legislature at Constitutional Convention, 191–92; on Pennsylvania's population, 64 n.; receives news of foreign troops, 116; returns from England, 45, 87
Franklin, Mrs. Benjamin: and James Wilson, 82–83
Franklin, Governor William, 89
Frazer, Persifor: and search for servant, 98; on New Englanders, 54
Freeman, A, 140 n., 199; ideas on government, 185–86
Free Masons, 95
French and Indian War: and Edward Biddle, 69; and John Montgomery, 69; and Quakers in politics, 152, 153; atrocities of recalled, 70; German pacifists' reaction to, 65; in Independents' propaganda to backcountry, 147; supposed effect on backcountry attitudes, 62, 68–70

Galbreath, Bartram (1738–1804), 76 n.; votes to exonerate Committee of Safety, 62 n.
Galloway, Joseph: and Franklin, 89; and Pennsylvania–Virginia boundary dispute, 52
Galleys. *See* Row Galleys
Georgia: absence from Congress, 124
German Presbyterian Church. *See* Reformed Church
Germans: and May election in Philadelphia, 16–17; and naturalization of, 17 n.; and politics, 43; and Remonstrance, 141; as misleading term, 64–65; Assembly moves to give vote, 158; Associators petition Conference for right to vote, 173; candidate aimed at vote of in May election, 26; Catholics among, 66; *Common Sense* translated for, 91–92; diversity of crops, 60–61; in backcountry; in Philadelphia, 44–45; Paine on influence in May election, 33; "The Alarm" translated for, 134
Germantown: and election of 1764, 18
Gibbons, James, 153 n.
Goshenhoppen: and Catholics, 66
Graaf, Andrew: delegate to Provincial Conference, 172
Gray, Isaac: insulted at May 20 meeting, 136
Graydon, Alexander: on Bryan and Constitution, 186 n.
Great Wagon Road, 67; trade over, 70

INDEX 225

Grain: price slump, 75; trade in between city and backcountry, 73–74
Gray, George, 151; disowned, 153 n.
Gummere family, 44 n.
Gurney, Francis, 100

Hall, David: newspaper of presents answer to *Common Sense*, 23 n.
Haller, Henry: refuses to exonerate Committee of Safety, 62 n., 163 n.
Hamilton, Andrew: quoted on State House, 15
Hancock, John, 120
Hannach, James: advertisements for, 97
Harbison, Benjamin: at caucus, 131; visits Norrington, 146
Harris, John: deputy to Provincial Conference, 172
Harvey, ———: works of in James Potter's library, 60
Hastings, Sally: effect of frontier on writing of, 86 n.
Hawke: up for sale, 168
Hemp: price rise of, 75
Hoffer, Eric: quoted 103, 106, 108, 131, 148
Hoge, Jonathan: votes to exonerate Committee of Safety, 62 n.
Horton, Mr., 168
Howard, Leon: quoted, 86 n.
House of Employment. *See* Bettering House
Howe, General William: effect of invasion threats on Pennsylvania politics, 195
Howell, Isaac, 155
Howell, Samuel, 26, 36, 153; Paine on, 35; sketch of, 25; votes for in May election, 30
Hughes, John, 83; and Jonathan Roberts, 80; sketch of, 79–80

Immigrants: continue to arrive (1775), 89; stop arriving, 97
Indentured servants: advertisements for, 89 n., 167; effect of loss on small merchant, 100; runaways, 97–98
Independence: Assembly's new instructions avoid mention of, 161; declaration of, 177, 181–82; Edward Biddle on, 69; forces working against in backcountry, 59–62; forces working against in Philadelphia, 35–56; force promoting, 83–110; Franklin takes stand on, 88–89; in theater, 96; implied in May 15 resolve, 122; influence of *Common Sense* on, 91–92; influence of drive for on Pennsylvania–Virginia boundary dispute, 52; John Adams's plan to achieve, 113–14; Joseph Reed perplexed about, 109–10; Provincial Conference favors, 176; Remonstrance on, 143; Rush on key men in drive for, 129; Sam Adams on events' influence on, 108; social changes accompanying drive for, 94–99; Wilson asks Congress to declare against, 92; Wilson asks Congress to postpone, 160, 161
Independence Hall. *See* Pennsylvania State House
Indian Queen Tavern, 176
Indiana (western Pennsylvania): sale of lands in, 52
Inflation: effect in backcountry, 74, 75; effect in Philadelphia, 47–48; lack of in Philadelphia; value of dollar drops, 47, 167

Jacobs, John, 153 n.; disowned, 154
Jay, John: letter from Duane, 126
Jefferson, Thomas: on John Adams, 125; on need for May 15 resolve, 124; on Sam Adams, 125; on state constitutions, 185
Jenks, Thomas, 153 n.
Jensen, Merrill: and Lincoln-Becker view of Revolution, 63 n.
Johnson, Samuel: prothonotary of York, 140
Jonathan B. Smith, 100
Jones, Robert Strettel: visits Bucks County with May resolves, 146
Joseph Andrews, 40

Kachlein, Peter: refuses to exonerate Committee of Safety, 163 n.
Knox, John, 65
Kuhl, Frederick: called Mark by Read, 27; on independent ticket in May election, 26, 27; votes for in May election, 30

Lancaster, 22, 65; Catholics in, 66; economic ties with backcountry, 71; economic ties with Philadelphia, 70; politics in, 76–77; wagons of, 41; Young and Barge visit, 146
Lancaster County, 163 n.; and city Committee, 77; Associators favor Protest, 150 n.; Committee shuns Shippen as deputy for Conference, 172; deputies to Conference, 172; moderates in forced to disguise opinions, 141–42; "plain people" in, 65. *See also* Committee of Inspection and Observation
Langley, James, 102; visits Adamses, 131
Lawyers: refuse to accept Constitution, 196; surplus of in Berks County, 82–83
Lee, Arthur: reports of, 115 n.
Lee, Richard Henry: letter from Rush on Assembly, 156
Lesher, John: votes to exonerate Committee of Safety, 62 n.
Lewis, Evan, 154
Lexington, 45, 51, 115; effect of battle at on Philadelphia economy, 46
Library Company: and river battle, 118
Ligonier: and St. Clair, 78, 79
Lincoln, Charles H.: thesis of, 62 n.–63 n.
Little Britain, 50 n., 67
Liverpool: blockades Delaware Bay, 45; effect on backcountry, 74; leaves station, 116
Locke, John: and Congress, 88
London Coffee House: described, 126–27; King's arms burned at, 181; "steering committee" meets at, 131
"Looking-Glass" store, 71
Lowman, Lodowick: deputy to Provincial Conference, 172
Lukens, Charles: sheriff of York, 140
Lukens family, 44 n.
Lukins, Jesse, 54
Lutheran Church, 65; in Abbotstown, 67
Lutherans, 37; in backcountry, 65
Lutz, Nicholas: deputy to Provincial Conference, 172

INDEX 227

McClay, William: house of, 72; prothonotary of Northumberland, 140
McClea, William. *See* McClay, William
McClur, John, 167
McKean, Thomas (1734–1817), 177, 200; and Provincial Conference, 172; battalion of supports May resolves, 171; confers with "steering committee," 131; on enlistments, 98; orator at May 20 meeting, 135; Rush on part in independence drive, 129; sketch of, 172–73; visits Reading with May resolves, 146, 146 n.
Madison, James: fears slave revolt, 90; hears about Franklin and spy rumor, 89; letter from Bradford, 49
Manufacturing: in Philadelphia, 41–42
Marshall, Christopher (1708–1797), 155, 177; age, 102; and Protest, 132; and Sam Adams, 112–13, 131, 156, 175–76; confers with McKean, 131; helps pick election candidates, 26; helps plan dissolution of Assembly, 133; helps plan February election of city Committee, 101–2; on May election day, 29, 30; on May election day results, 33; on Paine's absence from Constitutional Convention, 184 n.; on Provincial Conference, 171–72, 173; on religious oaths, 175, 192–93; on Remonstrance, 140; political inexperience of, 106; sketch of, 103
Marshall, Mrs. Christopher: worries of, 94
Maryland: accent of man from, 50 n.; economic competitor of Pennsylvania backcountry, 71; delegates of leave Congress, 124, 125
Massachusetts, 49, 91; and Baptists, 68; and Quakers, 55; John Adams on innovations in, 121; John Adams warns on boldness, 126; writs issued in King's name
Massey, Charles, 100
Matlack, Timothy (1730–1829), 20, 155, 177, 183; age of, 102; and Committee Memorial, 156; battalion of supports May resolves, 171; elected delegate to Convention, 182; helps pick election candidates, 26; in on May election post-mortem, 33; on qualities required of Convention delegates, 186; orator at May 20 meeting, 135; political inexperience of, 106; Rush makes responsible for "mobocracy," 178; Rush on, 102–3; Shippen on role in call for Convention in February, 20; sketch of, 103–4; visits Adamses, 131; visits Norrington, 75
May 1 election, 13–31, 45, 84, 98, 108; and Germans in Philadelphia, 16–17; and Wyoming Valley dispute, 54; backcountry success of Moderates in, 59–62; background of, 18–29; campaign tactics of parties, 27–29; city candidates in, 24–27; democratic aspects of, 34, 34 n.; economic situation at time of, 45–49; Edward Shippen on need for good candidates in, 76; effect of results on John Adams's plans, 116; George Read on party tickets in, 26–27, 27 n.; in backcountry, 59–62, 76; influence of candidates' personalities on, 35; influence of *Common Sense* on, 92; influence of foreign troops rumors on, 94; results of, 30–31, 34, 59–62; results analyzed by Marshall and Paine, 33–34
May 10 resolve, 119–20
May 15 resolve: Assembly plans to ask Congress for clarification of, 156; Caesar Rodney on, 123, 125–26; Carter Braxton on vote, 124 n., 125; city Committee's reaction to, 133; debated in Congress, 120–26; effect in

Pennsylvania, 132–33; first reception of, 125–27; James Allen on vote, 124 n.; John Adams on, 127; read to Associators in city, 170–71; read to Associators in backcountry, 145–46, 150, 150 n.; Robert Livingston on city reaction to, 133; theoretical implications of, 122; used to rebuff Assembly move to control Convention, 162
May 20 meeting, 135–38; attendance figures, 135, 140, 147–48; effect on backcountry attitudes, 144–46; planned 134–35.
Meat: price rise of, 75
Memorial, The: of city Committee, submitted to Congress, 156–57; of Committee of Privates, 170
Mennonites: and Quakers, 67
Mercenaries. *See* Foreign troops
Meredith, Samuel: refuses to serve under Constitution, 195
Middleton, 73
Mifflin, Thomas (1744–1800), 153 n.; and river battle, 117; Quaker member of city Committee, 155; relies on Rush, 129
Miles, William, 146
Montesquieu, Baron de: and Congress, 88
Montgomery, John: sketch of, 69–70
Moravians, 65
Morris, Robert (1734–1806): on Pennsylvania's importance, 114; on Robert Whitehill, 107; leaves city Committee, 101
Morton, John (1724–1777): in Moderate Independent faction, 162

Nagle, Sheriff, 83; and Edward Shippen, 81
Neff, Captain Rudolph, 166 n.
Negroes: Catholics among, 66; in backcountry, 66; one said to insult Philadelphia woman, 90; Madison fears revolt of, 90
Nettels, Curtis, 115 n.
New England: attitude of backcountry toward, 85; attitude of Pennsylvania toward, 52–56; attitude toward Pennsylvania, 130; attitude toward Philadelphia homes, 38; delegates from attempt to pacify Philadelphia Catholics, 56; delegates' reception in Philadelphia (1775), 87; Jane Mecom thinks about returning to, 118; Remonstrance on, 139; Shippen on, 20, 76; vote on May 15 resolve, 124
New Jersey: vote on May 15 resolve, 124
New Oxford: Scotch–Irish settlement, 67
Newspapers: and newsprint shortage, 48; tolerance of, 109; tolerance of ends, 167
New York, 98; Dr. Honyman on, 17; expects invasion, 49; votes on May 15 resolve, 124
Nixon, John (1733–1808): reads Declaration, 181
Norfolk: razed, 39, 108
Norrington, 146
Norris, Deborah, 40
North Carolina: Sam Adams on hostilities in, 108; votes on May 15 resolve, 124, 124 n.
Northampton County, 163 n.; Associators of favor Protest, 150 n.; sends James Allen to Assembly, 60

INDEX 229

Norton, Mr.: surgeon, 96–97
Northumberland, 72
Northumberland County: and Edward Burd, 80; and Wyoming Valley dispute, 85; sends James Potter to Assembly, 59
Oliver, Samuel: and his lost cow, 36, 38
Oxford township: and Remonstrance, 141
Paine, Thomas (1737–1809), 36, 63 n., 177, 183; age of, 102; absence from Constitutional Convention, 183, 184 n.; and Cannon, 82, 170; and Cato, 24; and Constitution, 183–84; and Memorial, 156; and Protest, 132; and reaction to publication of *Common Sense,* 90–91; and Rush, 102, 184, 193, 194; arrives in Philadelphia, 104; at caucus, 131; compared to Cannon as publicist, 170; departs America, 200; helps pick election candidates, 26; ideas on government, 183; John Adams on, 111–12; leads attack on Assembly, 131–32; on Catholics in election, 56; on experiments, 196, 197, 199, 200; on ineffectiveness of property qualifications, 34; on May election day, 29; on May election day results, 33, 34; on Samuel Howell, 35; political inexperience of, 106; suspected author of "The Alarm," 135; suspected author of campaign piece, 27–28. See also *Common Sense*
Parker, Joseph, 154; disowned, 153 n.
Parkes, Henry Bamford: quoted, 143 n.
Patriotic Society: consulted on Independent ticket in May election, 26
Peace commissioners, 99; Caesar Rodney on, 116; effect of rumors on Dickinson, 115; Francis Alison on, 49; James Duane on, 122; James Read on type enroute, 143; Richard Bache on, 116; rumors of continue, 85
Peale, Charles Wilson; attends Catholic mass with New Englanders, 56; on Duché, 123 n., 143 n.
Pemberton, Joseph: puts house up for sale, 118
Penn Square: *See* Centre Square
Penn Valley: home of James Potter, 60
Penn, Governor John, 78
Penn, William, 66, 77; and Philadelphia, 36, 37, 42; John Adams on, 130
Penn, Lady Juliana, 51
Penn family, 35, 36; and sale of western lands, 51–52; and Thomas Willing, 25; appointive power in Pennsylvania, 78
Pennock, Joseph, 153 n.; pressured to withdraw from Assembly, 153–54
Pennsylvania: application of May 10 resolve to, 119–20; application of May 15 resolve to, 120–21; boundary disputes and Congress, 51, 53, 122; boundary dispute with Connecticut, 52–54; boundary dispute with Virginia, 50–52; Braxton forecasts effect of May 15 resolve on, 124–25; economy of backcountry, 70–75; economy of Philadelphia, 45–49; effects of May 15 resolve in, 120–21; government of, 77–78; influence of *Common Sense* in, 91–92; John Adams's contempt for, 114; social changes in, 94–99, 167–68; vote for May 15 resolve, 124, 124 n. *See also* Philadelphia and Backcountry
Pennsylvania Constitution. *See* Constitution (1776)
Pennsylvania Gazette: article on New England tolerance, 56; on troops enroute to America, 123–24

Pennsylvania Hospital: Joseph Swift on board of manager, 16; visitor on, 38
Pennsylvania Journal, 14
Pennsylvania Land Office, 51–52
Pennsylvania Packet: cuts back size, 48
Pennsylvania State House, 151; and King's arms, 123, 181; Convention delegates elected at, 181; description of, 15–16; visitor on, 38; Declaration read in yard of, 181; May 20 meeting held in yard of, 135–37; October meeting held in yard of, 194
Peters, Richard: on Associators, 148
Philadelphia: and Germans in, 44–45; and Quakers, 42–44; and William Penn, 36–37, 38, 42; attitude toward elections, 17–18; attitude toward New England, 52–56; churches in, 37 n.; Cresswell on, 182; cultural interaction in, 43–44; democracy in, 34, 34 n.; descriptions of, 36, 44; descriptions of inhabitants, 41–45; Duché on, 95; economic prosperity of, 45–49; economic ties with backcountry, 70, 71; families depart, 109, 167; Free Masons in, 95; German influence on accent, 43–44; influence of location on attitude toward war, 49–50; manufacturing in, 41–42; May election in, 13–31; merchants and blockade, 46–47, 47–48; political importance of, 22; population of, 36; Quakers from in Assembly, 153 n.; reception of *Common Sense* in, 91–92; religious freedom in, 42–43; religious sects in, 37; Samuel Curwen on, 87; shipbuilding in, 41; sin in, 42; social changes in, 94–99, 167–68
Philadelphia County, 19, 64; economic ties with city, 70; and Jonathan Roberts, 80, 83; Quakers in Assembly, 153 n.
Physick, Edmund: and sale of western lands, 51
"Plain people": in backcountry, 64–65
Plain Truth, 24 n.
Pope, Alexander: works of in James Potter's library, 60
Population: of backcountry, 64; of Pennsylvania (1775), 64 n.; of Philadelphia, 36
Porter, Thomas, 76 n.; refuses to exonerate Committee of Safety, 62 n., 163 n.
Potter, James: elected to Assembly, 59; sketch of, 59–60; votes to exonerate Committee of Safety, 62 n.
Price, Elisha: quarrels with James Smith, 175
Printers: scarcity of work for, 48
Proctor, John: absent from Assembly, 61
Progressive Era: and effect on colonial historiography, 63 n.
Proprietary party: and Franklin, 35; and Remonstrance, 141; in Independents' propaganda, 147, 155; influence of in May election, 33; role in politics, 35–36
Protest, The: Cannon urges reading of to Associators, 150; carried to Bucks County, 146; heads of drawn up, 132; read at May 20 meeting, 137; read to Associators, 150 n.
Provincial Conference, 171–76; and Assembly, 163; city Committee calls for (February), 19–20; Cato on needlessness of, 23; city Committee calls for in May, 99–100; county Committees choose deputies for, 150; in propaganda to backcountry, 148; religious oath of, 174–75; test oath of, 174;

INDEX

voted for by May 20 meeting, 136; Wilson expects to end confusion, 160–61; York votes to send delegates to, 146
Pusey, Mrs.: brewhouse of, 36
Pyle, Joseph, 153 n.; refuses to exonerate Committee of Safety, 163 n.

Quakers: absence in Independence propaganda, 155; and Fast Day, 155; and French and Indian War, 152, 153; and Mennonites, 67; and politics, 43; attitude toward New England, 54–55; disowned members, 25, 26, 103, 104, 153–54; in backcountry, 64, 66; intermarriage with Germans, 44–45; influence in May election, 33; myth of domination of Assembly, 151–56; on Franklin, 88; set tone of Philadelphia, 15, 37, 42–43, 151–52
Quebec: Paine on importance of in May election, 33; St. Clair at, 78
Quebec Act (1774), 55

Randolph, Edmund: on *Common Sense*, 91
Rankin, James, 153, 185; arrested, 145; elected to Assembly, 59; send Remonstrance to York, 140; votes to exonerate Committee of Safety, 62 n.
Raynal, Abbé G. T. F.: pamphlet of considered answer to *Common Sense*, 23 n.–24 n.
Read, George: on influence of river battle, 129; on party tickets in May election, 26–27, 27 n.
Read, James: on hopes for reconciliation, 142; on sin among soldiers, 174–75
Reading, 163; and Edward Biddle, 69, 80; and James Wilson, 82–83; burns Remonstrance, 141; Catholics in, 66; economy of, 71; economic ties with Philadelphia, 70; gambling in, 80–81
Reasonable Whiggess, A: letter to Benjamin Towne, 109
Reed, Joseph (1741–1785), 19: in Moderate Independent faction, 162; on river blockade, 45; perplexed on independence, 109–10; shares in Assembly compromise on February Convention threat, 21; signs Remonstrance, 140
Reformed Church, 65
Religious freedom: effect on Philadelphia's character, 42–43
Religious oath: in Constitution, 189–90; of Provincial Conference, 174–75
Remonstrance, The, 159, 162; circulated, 140–41; contents of, 139, 142–44; on independence, 143
Republicus: on reconciliation, 167
Reynell, Abbe. *See* Raynal, Abbé G. T. F.
Rhode Island: Remonstrance on, 139; vote on May 15 resolve, 124
Rittenhouse, David, 196
River battle, 116–17; influence of in drive for independence, 129–30; debris of at Coffee House, 126; social changes that follow, 167
River Brethren, 65
Roberdeau, Daniel (1727–1795), 139; moderator at May 20 meeting, 135, 136; exemplifies split in Independent ranks, 137–38; on Independent ticket, 26; Paine as secretary of, 184 n.; votes for in May election, 30
Roberts, Jonathan (1731–1812), 83, 153 n.; calls self "non-militant Whig," 153; on Assembly and treasonable acts, 143; on county Committee's powers, 19; pressured to withdraw from Assembly, 154; sketch of, 80
Rodney, Caesar (1728–1784): forecast of on May election, 18; on May 15

resolve, 123, 125–26; on misuse of May resolve, 135, 136–37; on news of foreign troops, 116
Rodney, Thomas (1744–1811): on Thomas McKean, 172–73
Roebuck: blockades Delaware, 45; effect on backcountry, 74; forced aground, 117–18; leaves station, 116
Ross, George, 158
Row galleys: Assembly enters dispute over, 61–62; in river battle, 116–17; Radicals exploit dispute, 169–70
Rudolph, John Tobias, 141 n.
Rush, Dr. Benjamin (1745–1813), 24, 200; age of, 102; and Memorial, 156; and Paine, 102, 193, 194; assigns responsibility for "mobocracy," 178; at caucus, 131; co-author of Conference's final paper, 176; joins city Committee, 101; letter to Lee on Assembly, 156; leaves politics, 196; on *Common Sense*, 91; on Constitution, 193–94; on Dr. William Smith, 22, 23; on Cannon, 102–3; on key men in drive for independence, 129; on Matlack, 102–3; on old Pennsylvania government, 177; on reception of Remonstrance, 141; on religious oath of Conference, 175; on the future, 106; opposes Constitution, 193–94; political inexperience of, 106; sketch of, 104
Rye: as coffee substitute, 75; in Reading–Easton economy, 70; increased planting of, 73; traffic in on Susquehanna, 73

Sailors: lack of in city, 46
St. Clair, Arthur (1736–1818), 83, 84; and Bedford County, 78–79; and Westmoreland County, 51; on use of foreign troops, 93–94; sketch of, 78–79
St. Clair, Phoebe Bayard, 78
Salt: and backcountry, 74
Schwenkfelders, 65
Scotch–Irish, 69; and "church people," 65; and politics, 43; Cresswell on, 182; diversity of crops, 75; in backcountry, 67, 68; influence on Philadelphia character, 43–44; locations of, 66
Scotland: visitor from to city, 41
Sectionalism: effect on Pennsylvania attitudes, 50–56
Selsam, J. Paul: view of revolutionary Pennsylvania, 63 n.
Sentiments of a Foreigner, The (Raynal), 23 n.–24 n.
Shaffer, Christian, 141 n.
Shee, Colonel John: James Allen joins battalion of, 60
Shippen, Edward (1703–1781) (Lancaster): reproves Edward Burd, 81; requests Burton ale, 48; shunned by local Committee, 172
Shippen, Edward, Jr., (1728/29–1806) (Philadelphia): and Edward Burd, 80–81; leaves politics, 84; on effect of river battle, 118; on foreign troops, 92–93; on need for good candidates in May election, 76; on state of backcountry affairs, 141–42
Shippen, Joseph (1732–1810): leaves politics, 84; on lack of answers to *Common Sense*, 23 n.; on foreign troops, 93; on Matlack's part in call for Convention, 20
Shippen, William: ideas on government, 185

INDEX

Shippen family: departs Philadelphia, 168
Shipbuilding: and labor problem, 98; Cresswell on, 182; in Philadelphia, 46
Shipping: Duché describes amount on Delaware, 95; insurance rates on rise, 45; tonnage owned by Philadelphia merchants, 45-46
Ships: merits of Philadelphia-built, 41
Shoemaker family, 44 n.
Simes's Military Guide, 95
Simpson, Samuel, 101, 102
Slough, Matthias: on Assembly, 162
Smith, James (*ca.* 1737–*ca.* 1814): co-author of Conference's final paper, 176; enters politics, 84; on power of Associators' opinions, 150; quarrels with Elisha Price, 173; works for Radical Independents, 169; shapes York County opinion, 145; sketch of, 107
Smith, Thomas (1745-1809): absent from Assembly, 61; and Bedford County political posts, 79; on Constitution, 190-91; on influence of experimental philosophy in Constitution, 198; sketch of, 60
Smith, Dr. William (1727-1803), 24, 60; as Cato, 19 n., 23-24; Rush on, 141; sends Remonstrance to backcountry, 140; sketch of, 22-23
Society of Friends. *See* Quakers
South Carolina: vote on May 15 resolve, 124
Southwark Theater, 96
Spyker, Benjamin: deputy to Provincial Conference, 172
Stamp Act: and John Hughes, 79
Standley, Miss, 117
Stedman, Charles: arrives in York, 147; carries Remonstrance to York, 140; reception in York, 145
"Steering Committee": activity after May election, 130-33
Stiles, Ezra: on Dickinson, 115
Stiles, Joseph, 101, 102
Stonehouse, George, 113
Sunbury, 69; and Edward Burd, 80; and invaders from Connecticut, 53-54; house of McClay in, 72
Susquehanna Company of Connecticut, 53
Swedes: in Pennsylvania, 66
Swift, Joseph, 29; on Germans in May election, 16-17

Test oath: of Provincial Conference, 174; of Constitutional Convention, 189
Thomson, Charles (1729-1824), 104; leaves city Committee, 101; on end of Assembly, 164; on Quakers in politics, 152; on Quaker voting, 155; on self-government in Pennsylvania, 77; replies to Dickinson letter, 178-79
Thorne, William, 102
Thorne's (Thorn's) school, 29, 186
Thoughts on Government (John Adams), 183
Ticonderoga, 98
Tolles, Frederick B.: quoted, 43 n.
Towne, Benjamin: letter from "A Reasonable Whiggess," 109
Treason: Moderates' awareness of, 143-44
Twining, David, 153 n.

United Company of Philadelphia for Promoting American Manufactures, 82, 105
Universal Restitution (Stonehouse), 113
Universal Restitution Further Defended (Stonehouse), 113
Upland, 77
"Useful and Entertaining Hints" (Paine), 199

Vattel, Emmerich von: and Congress, 88
Virginia, 49; accents of inhabitants, 50, 50 n.; as protection to Philadelphia, 49; boundary dispute, 50–52, 79, 122; citizens dislike of Philadelphia, 39; influence of *Common Sense* in, 91; Madison on fear of Negro revolt in, 90; resolution of Convention reaches Assembly, 159; vote on May 15 resolve, 124

Walnut Grove: home of Hughes, 79
Walnut Street Prison: visitor on, 38
Washington, George: and Philadelphia races, 95; and Rush, 195; Edward Biddle on, 69; in New York, 182; letters from go unread in Congress, 120
Washington, Martha: ball planned for, 113
Water pumps: number in Philadelphia, 37
Watchman, A, 184
Watkins, Joseph: visits Bucks County with May resolves, 146
Wayne, Anthony: petition to Assembly, 148–49
Webb, James: leaves Assembly, 158
Welsh Baptists: in backcountry, 66
West, Mr.: moves family from city, 118
West Augusta, District of, 51
West Indies, 95; absence of goods from felt, 167; Catholic slaves from in backcountry, 66; effect of blockade on goods from, 48, 100; trade with Philadelphia, 73
Westmoreland County: and Arthur St. Clair, 79; created, 51; cultural composition of, 64 n.; deputies absent from Assembly, 61 n., 163; settlers in, 66
Wharton, Thomas, Jr. (1735–1778): and Pennsylvania–Virginia boundary dispute, 52; leaves city Committee, 101; on Constitution, 196
Wheat: in Reading–Easton economy, 70; increased planting of, 73; traffic in on Susquehanna, 73
Whitehill, Robert (1738–1813): at Constitutional Convention, 193; enters politics, 84; refuses to exonerate Committee of Safety, 62, 163 n.; share in Constitution, 186 n.; sketch of, 107; works for Radical Independents, 169
Whitemarsh Township, 166 n.
Wilcox (Wilcocks), Alexander (1742–1801): on ticket in May election, 25, 26; votes for in May election, 30
Wilcox, John, 19
Wilkins, John, 102
Willing, Thomas (1731–1821), 26; and Pennsylvania–Virginia boundary dispute, 51; Bradford on defeat of, 30–31; in campaign literature, 29; sketch of, 25; votes for in May election, 30

INDEX

Wilmington, 70
Wilson, James (1742–1798), 84; and Cannon, 82, 105; argues against May 15 resolve, 121; asks Congress to declare against independence, 92; asks Congress to postpone independence, 160, 161; on confusion of the times, 164; on Constitutionalists' luck, 195; sketch of, 82–84
Wilson, Rachel Bird, 83
Wistar family, 44 n.
Wister, Sally, 40, 44; on Southern accents, 50 n.
Wister family 44 n.
Witherspoon, Dr. John: essay by, 117
Wolfe, Henry, 141
Wolfe, General James: St. Clair with at Quebec, 78
Women: Amish, 64–65; help ease labor shortage, 47; of Philadelphia, 39–40
Wyoming Valley: and backcountry, 85; and boundary dispute, 53–54; Elector on, 28 n.
Wythe, George, 183

Yard, Mrs., 183
Yeates, Jasper (1745–1817): and backcountry affairs, 141–42; and Edward Burd, 80, 81; on city interference in Lancaster affairs, 77; travels to Pittsburgh for Congress, 76 n.; urged to run for Assembly, 76
Yeates, Mrs. Jasper: worries of, 94
Yerkes family, 44 n.
York, 22; and Germans, 66, 67; Anglican church in, 66; Committee creates support for May resolves, 145–46; Fithian describes, 71; Philadelphians visit, 146–47
York County: Committee of and May resolves, 145–46; sends Rankin to Assembly, 59
Young, Dr. Thomas (1731/32–1777), 82, 102, 175; and May election postmortem, 33; and Sam Adams, 105, 113, 131; Edward Shippen on, 146; fails to get elected to Convention, 186; on qualities needed for Convention delegates, 186; political inexperience of, 105; Rush makes responsible for "mobocracy," 178; sketch of, 104–5; suspected author of Elector articles, 28 n.